Be Still

....and know that I am God

To Margaret
Be blessed!
Be well!
Charles Mashburn

Charles L Mashburn

Copyright © 2010 Charles L Mashburn

All rights reserved. No part of this book may be used or reproduced by any means, graphic, electronic, or mechanical, including photocopying, recording, taping or by any information storage retrieval system without the written permission of the publisher except in the case of brief quotations embodied in critical articles and reviews.

Unless otherwise noted, Scripture quotations are from the HOLY BIBLE, NEW INTERNATIONAL VERSION ®. Copyright © 1973, 1978, 1984 by International Bible Society. Used by permission of Zondervan. All rights reserved. Scripture quotations marked NASB are from the NEW AMERICAN STANDARD BIBLE ®, Copyright © 1960, 1962, 1963, 1968, 1971, 1972, 1973, 1975, 1977, 1995 by the Lockman Foundation. Used by permission.

WestBow Press books may be ordered through booksellers or by contacting:

WestBow Press
A Division of Thomas Nelson
1663 Liberty Drive
Bloomington, IN 47403
www.westbowpress.com
1-(866) 928-1240

Because of the dynamic nature of the Internet, any Web addresses or links contained in this book may have changed since publication and may no longer be valid. The views expressed in this work are solely those of the author and do not necessarily reflect the views of the publisher, and the publisher hereby disclaims any responsibility for them.

Any people depicted in stock imagery provided by Thinkstock are models, and such images are being used for illustrative purposes only.

Certain stock imagery © Thinkstock.

ISBN: 978-1-4497-0792-7 (sc)
ISBN: 978-1-4497-0793-4 (dj)
ISBN: 978-1-4497-0791-0 (e)

Library of Congress Control Number: 2010941168

Printed in the United States of America

WestBow Press rev. date: 11/16/2010

For Mom

INTRODUCTION

Just before Christmas in 2008, I bought a small book by Rick Warren, entitled *The Purpose Of Christmas*. So many things Rick said in the book spoke to me in profound and awesome ways. You know how sometimes something you've read or heard a hundred times suddenly goes, "ding", and you understand? This happened several times while I read Rick's book about Christmas.

One such instance came when I read a paragraph where he talked about how we can't go through life on our own power. He compared trying to live on our own power to living a life where God wants us to trust Him and depend on Him. He also discussed how God allows problems to come into our lives that we have no chance of solving on our own. Rick explained that in these times of trial, God is waiting for us to stop trying to solve the problem and start trusting Him to solve it.

Ding!

A voice in my head, or perhaps it was in my heart, said, "Be still, and know that I am God."

How simple is that?

Let go, and let God!

Although I'd heard it so many times before, in so many different ways, I really didn't get it until that moment.

I had already had a revelation of sorts at an earlier point in the book. It came when I read a sentence Rick had written, saying there are 365 places in the Bible where God says, "Don't be afraid!"

Upon reading that, I told my wife, Sherry, it would be a good premise for a book of daily devotionals. She must have told me, "You should write it!" five times in the few minutes following my statement.

So I decided to write a book of devotionals using each of the three-hundred-sixty-five verses that say something to the effect of "do not fear."

But then as I was writing the devotionals and approaching the end of the month of January, I looked at the list of 365 verses I'd printed and thought it didn't appear there weren't enough left to add up to 365. It was only then that I read the note at the top of the page I'd printed which said there are actually only a hundred or so verses that say, "Do not be afraid," or some equivalent thereof. I was extremely disappointed at first. But I considered how much I was enjoying writing these daily encouragements, and decided I would search for another phrase or word I could use as a theme to continue once the "Do not be afraid," verses were exhausted. I decided on "Love," because after all, love is what I believe God and life to be about.

According to at least one of the sources I found on the Internet, the word love appears 319 times in the Old Testament and 232 times in the New Testament. My plan is to use the ones that speak strongest to me. I trust God will guide me in my choices, and they will speak to others who read this book of devotionals, too.

Before you read even the first day's encouragement, you need to know who I am.

I'm just another guy—a redneck kind of guy. I play golf, fish and drink a beer now and then. I am so far from perfect, that some may say, "What does he know about God?"

My answer would be, "Not enough."

I *do* know enough to know that God works in strange and wondrous ways, and if He chooses to reach a segment of the population through this simple man, then that He will do. If you choose to read these devotionals/encouragements, please remember I am not the author of the words that follow, I am merely the pencil.

January 1

After this, the word of the Lord came to Abram in a vision: "Do not be afraid, Abram. I am your shield, your very great reward." Genesis 15:1

At first, just like you or I would, Abram questioned the words of the Lord. After all, he probably thought this was a little far out, don't you think? But Abram, not having the miracle of TV, radio, the Internet, and print media to constantly remind him that his vision was surely some sort of hoax or wild imagining, was quickly convinced that the Lord *could* do what He said He *would* do. And basically, all it took to convince Abram was a trip outside and a look at the stars in the night sky.

What I'd like to say to you on this first day of the New Year is it *is* that simple!

Fear is a choice you make. Trusting God is a choice you make.

By choosing to be afraid, you are denying God's power.

Start this New Year by taking a look around you at what God has done. Throw your shoulders back, hold your head high and go boldly into the new day and the New Year.

All things are possible!

January 2

God heard the boy crying, and the angel of God called to Hagar from heaven and said to her, "What is the matter, Hagar? Do not be afraid; God has heard the boy crying as he lies there." Genesis 21:17

I need to point out that I am not a theologian. I am not a preacher, or in any way a learned man of God. I don't even attend church. I say all this merely so you will understand that I will not be able to take each and every verse about fear and expound on it in some sort of ingenious way. But then, maybe God will. After all, I'm just the pencil.

This verse seems rather simple though. The boy and his mother had been sent away with a skin full of water, and when the water ran out they were afraid, and they began to cry. You can't blame them for that! But then God, speaking through an angel, told them, "Do not be afraid." He provided water, and they went on to do what God had planned for them to do with their lives.

My take on this is that sometimes we see only that we are out of water—or whatever we may be in need of. At those times we despair and think we can't possibly go on. That is just simply not true.

What? That's it? It's over? We're done?

What kind of sense does that make?

Whatever your needs might be today, crying and being afraid will do nothing to fill them. Go into this day knowing God will supply all your needs. He always has, whether you realize it or not!

January 3

That night the Lord appeared to him and said, "I am the God of your father Abraham. Do not be afraid, for I am with you; I will bless you and will increase the number of your descendants for the sake of my servant Abraham." Genesis 26:24

This verse intrigues me. What it says to me at first, of course, is the Lord tells Isaac to not be afraid because He is with him. *That* is pretty simple, wouldn't you say? And wouldn't you also agree that we, too, should not be afraid today, because God is with us? He's always with us! Every day! Everywhere we go! How awesome is that? What do we have to fear?

What it also says to me, though, is that it's not all necessarily all about me!

God is telling Isaac there is no reason to be afraid because He is with him, but then He says He's taking care of business for the sake of Abraham.

Excuse me? What's up with that?

Well, it's *not* always about me—or you. Sometimes we are the vessel God uses to get someone else where He needs them.

Hey! I'm cool with that!

January 4

And as she was having great difficulty in childbirth, the midwife said to her, "Don't be afraid, for you have another son." Genesis 35:17

This is a big one. You see, right after the midwife spoke those soothing words, Rachel, wife of Jacob, gave birth to Jacob's twelfth son. She named him, and then she died.

In my limited understanding of these things, I think this all had something to do with the future and Jesus. I know many of the Old Testament events were foretelling of the days when Jesus would inhabit the earth, but again, I am no scholar and cannot say with any surety this was the case.

What I can say is that because of Jesus, I have no fear of death. I don't challenge it, mind you, but I have no fear of what lies beyond this earthly world and this body I inhabit with my soul. I will spend eternity with my God and Savior. End of discussion. And so, why would I fear death?

I believe Rachel believed as I do, and knowing she had completed her duties to God, was able to go peacefully to Him after the birth of her second son (Jacob's twelfth).

Death is a confusing thing to some. I believe it is not the end but the beginning. If I can go into my day knowing when my work here is done, I will spend eternity with God that makes me smile, and I can forge ahead knowing nothing can keep me from completing my appointed tasks!

Go confidently into this day. Do your best. Fear nothing. No one can ask for more from you than that.

January 5

"It's alright," he said. "Don't be afraid. Your God, the God of your father has given you treasure in your sacks; I received your silver." Then he brought Simeon out to them. Genesis 43:23

This is a story I am somewhat familiar with. It is the story of Joseph and his reuniting with his brothers who had sold him into slavery. They told Jacob—their father—Joseph had been killed. Eventually, Joseph became ruler of all Egypt, and his brothers unknowingly were seeking his help. Joseph tricked them—in a nice sort of way—and they were fearful they would be thought thieves by this mighty ruler. Joseph meant them no harm and eventually made himself known to them. At this point, the brothers were doubly terrified. But Joseph held no ill will and even told them it was not they who had sent him here, but rather God had used them to accomplish His plan.

There it is again. It wasn't about them; it was about God's plan. They had nothing to fear because, unwittingly, they were doing God's work.

How many times have you wondered why you are doing what you do? Maybe you feel like your job is meaningless. Maybe sometimes you feel like you're just spinning your wheels in a world gone mad. I know I do!

Think about this; how do you know you are not doing God's will, even in the smallest thing you do during the day? What a wonderful thought, that in some strange and wonderful way, you are part of the *big* plan!

Awesome!

January 6

"I am God, the God of your father," he said. "Do not be afraid to go down to Egypt, for I will make you into a great nation there."
Genesis 46:3

Israel, as Jacob was renamed by God, had it made in my book. Can you imagine if God spoke directly to us like He did to those guys back then? Wow!

Yet they still had fears. It's like when we know what's right, and we know what we should do, but we procrastinate and try to think of all the reasons it won't work. Why? Fear of failure.

We all suffer from this kind of fear. Failure is one of the worst things we face in our daily lives. We fear failure because of how we will look to our family, friends and co-workers. But the worst fear is how we might look to God.

He doesn't care. I mean sure, He cares, but He knows you are going to fail sometimes. He knows before you even begin the task. But He doesn't care how you look when it's over and you've failed. God loves you no matter what! I think that is the best news I've ever heard, because I have to tell you, I mess up on a pretty regular basis.

The hardest thing for me to get a hold of is the fact that Jesus took all that away when He died on the cross and rose again on the third day. Like Rick Warren said in *The Purpose of Christmas*, "It's not about what we do. It's already done. What needed to be done for us was done two thousand years ago by Jesus."

Don't start your day thinking what you are going to do for God. Start your day thanking God for what *He* has done for you!

January 7

But Joseph said to them, "Don't be afraid. Am I in the place of God?"
Genesis 50:19

Good one, Joseph!

How cool is it that? After all he'd been through, seen and accomplished, Joseph could still be humble and show such love and compassion to the brothers who had mistreated him. Man, would I give anything to have that kind of forgiveness in me!

Then I think, *Hey, wait a minute. After all the rotten things I've done, God still loves me unconditionally? Who am I to hold a grudge or un-forgiveness?*

I'm not going to start lying to you now. I am nowhere close to being where Joseph was. Shoot, I'm still mad because they didn't have any shrimp at the Chinese buffet this afternoon! (Not really, but not long ago I would have been.)

As you start this day, start it with the spirit of forgiveness in your heart. Know you are forgiven, too. The peace that comes with forgiveness is like sunshine on your face through the windshield of your pickup on a cold, clear day.

Bask in it!

January 8

*"So then, don't be afraid. I will provide for you and your children."
And he reassured them and spoke kindly to them.* Genesis 50:21

Why did Joseph have to keep reassuring his brothers and keep telling them to not be afraid?

Because they felt guilty!

Guilt is an awful thing and in my mind is synonymous with fear. If you feel guilty about something you've said or done, it's because you fear the consequences.

I had a man tell me one time that his wife made him feel guilty. I remember looking the man in the eyes and telling him, "No, your wife can't make you feel guilty." He stared back at me with a questioning look, and I said, "You *choose* to feel guilty."

I was in my late twenties when I made that statement, and it probably made more of an impact on me than it did him. I pondered the statement considerably and came to the conclusion it was true of almost every emotion. Guilt, anger, sadness, happiness—they don't just come upon us; we invite them in. We choose to have the feelings we have.

We will talk more about this as the year goes on, but for now, let's go into this day choosing to be happy. Let's choose faith, not fear.

I'm in!

January 9

> *Moses answered the people, "Do not be afraid. Stand firm and you will see the deliverance the Lord will bring you today. The Egyptians you see today you will never see again."* Exodus 14:13

Moses was another of the Old Testament men who rose to greatness in spite of adversity. His mother, fearing for his life, put him in a basket in the Nile. The Pharaoh's daughter found him, and the rest, as they say, is history.

How lucky can you get?

I don't think luck had anything to do with it. God had a plan. Moses was a big part of the plan.

There we go again. All those people involved in the life of Moses—his mother, Pharaoh's daughter, the Hebrew woman who nursed Moses—they were all a part of the plan.

You and I are a part of God's plan. To some of us it may seem obvious what role we play, but to others—most of us I'd say—we may never know what part we play. Wouldn't it be great though, if when we see the Lord at the end of our days on earth, He says to us, "Come here, I want to show you how you helped me with My plan."

Do your part today. Live your life without fear or reservation, knowing you are a part of God's wonderful plan. You or I may not be the star of the play, but our name will be on the credits when they roll.

January 10

Moses said to the people, "Do not be afraid. God has come to test you, so that the fear of God will be with you to keep you from sinning."
Exodus 20:20

We don't have to be in fear of the Lord anymore. God kind of gave up on our being able to do it on our own, so He sent Jesus to die on the cross for our sins. I know that's a pretty simple explanation, but I believe God's love for us is just that; plain and simple.

Even back then, I don't think God wanted His people to fear Him in the same way they would fear dangerous animals or their enemy. I think He wanted them to fear the fact that they had disappointed Him when they sinned.

The great thing about Jesus and the grace he bought for us, is that fear of God was wiped out. Jesus took it away.

That doesn't mean we can just go on our merry way, sinning like crazy, but I think it does mean God knows we are weak and sometimes not very bright, so He worked out a way to forgive us and give us another chance.

Love God, and He will fill you with His Spirit and love, enabling you to live your life in a way that will please Him. But if you slip or make a mistake, don't beat yourself up over it. Tell God you're sorry, ask His forgiveness and get on with your day! You're part of the plan!

January 11

Only do not rebel against the Lord. And do not be afraid of the people of the land, because we will swallow them up. Their protection is gone, but the Lord is with us. Do not be afraid of them. Numbers 14:9

What was up with those Israelites? They were shown so many signs and wonders by God, and yet they never seemed to trust Him. The search party Moses had sent to check things out in the Promised Land returned with fabulous reports about a land flowing with milk and honey and samples of the fruit of the land. But then they grumbled and spread discord throughout the Israelites, saying the people of the land were large and there was no way the Israelites could take the land from them.

Two of the scouts, Caleb and Joshua, told a different story when it came to taking the land. They were convinced God would give them victory, and they were not afraid. They told the Israelites, "Do not be afraid!"

Do you know that all the other scouts died of a plague and only Caleb and Joshua survived? They had faith and were not afraid!

Whatever challenges await you today, take them on knowing the Lord is with you. Have faith! Do not be afraid!

January 12

> *The Lord said to Moses, Do not be afraid of him for I have handed him over to you, with his whole army and his land. Do to him what you did to Sihon king of the Amorites, who reigned in Heshbon.*
> Numbers 21:34

I sometimes think the book of Numbers should be called the book of Wars! Moses and the Israelites seemed to finally get the message, and they went into the Promised Land, kicking butts and taking names.

Yet it seems like God still had to keep telling them not to be afraid. You would think at some point, they would have said, "Hey, we're undefeated, and nothing can keep us from winning the whole shebang!" But they never seemed to grasp the fact that if the Lord was with them they could beat anybody.

I kind of feel like an armchair quarterback talking about Moses and the Israelites. It's easy to read the stories and say how the Israelites should have had more faith in God. But how many times do you and I fret and fear what lies ahead? And let me ask you this: how many times have you gotten to the other side of a situation and said, "Whew! That wasn't so bad."

In Romans 8:31, Paul says, *"If God is for us*, who can be against us?"

I say, "Amen to that, brother!"

Start this day knowing God loves you, and He is with you.

You can accomplish anything!

January 13

"See, the Lord your God has given you the land. Go up and take possession of it as the Lord, the God of your fathers, told you. Do not be afraid; do not be discouraged." Deuteronomy 1:21

In this part of the book of Deuteronomy it appears Moses is reminding the Israelites of all the times they had not trusted the Lord and had been afraid. The Israelites—like you and I—seemed to need to be constantly reminded that God was on their side.

I can relate to that. I don't know how many times in my life I have caught myself grumbling and worrying about a situation I'm up against, when all I had to do was say, "God, I got this thing I need to do, and it's going to take both of us to get it done. You busy?"

I have to tell you; sometimes it seems so simple it's downright funny!

But really, sometimes—maybe all the time—we have to let God do the heavy work.

He will, you know.

January 14

Then I said to you, "Do not be terrified; do not be afraid of them."
Deuteronomy 1:29

Moses must have been one patient dude. I wonder how many times he had to tell his people to not be afraid. Probably a lot more than what is written in the Bible!

Maybe we have to give those folks a break, too. I remember playing high school football, and sometimes the guys on the other team were a lot bigger than the guys on our team. I vividly remember one game we played against a team that had a defensive end on it that was 6'-8" tall and weighed about 220. I was a wide receiver and was 6' tall and weighed 145. If I told you I wasn't scared, would you believe me?

I made it through the game with only a few bumps and bruises, and I think we even won the game.

Can you imagine, though, if I had gone into that game knowing God was with me, and He would help me defeat that giant lining up across from me? I'm grinning ear to ear just thinking about it.

There are no problems bigger than God. And like it says in the song, "It is no secret what God can do."

All we have to do is all we can do. God will do the rest.

January 15

The Lord said to me, "Do not be afraid of him for I have handed him over to you, with his whole army and his land. Do to him what you did to Sihon king of the Amorites, who reigned in Heshbon."
Deuteronomy 3:2

In the book of Deuteronomy Moses is telling a new generation about the mistakes made by the former generation. It has been said it is a book of the Bible that would not have been needed if the first generation Israelites had gotten things right. And even though the Israelites finally made it into the Promised Land, they still had problems with disbelief, idols and things of the world. Sound familiar?

It sure sounds familiar to me. I battle daily to stay focused on what I know is right and what I believe God wants me to do and be. But in this chaotic world we live in, it is so easy to get distracted and find yourself smack dab in the middle of something you had no intention of getting involved in.

The good news is that you don't have to stay in the middle of it. My philosophy is that you can start over at any time. Not only is each day a fresh new day, but if need be, the very next minute can be a new beginning. Grace is a wonderful thing!

To quote the oh-so-quotable Yogi Berra, "It ain't over 'til it's over."

If you stumble and find yourself where you—and God—don't want you to be, shake the dust from your feet, walk away and get back on the right path.

January 16

"Do not be afraid of them; the Lord your God will fight for you."
Deuteronomy 3:22

This was what Moses told Joshua when he was about to send him across the Jordan. If you recall, Joshua was one of the spies that went out to see the Promised Land. He and Caleb were convinced they could defeat the giants that inhabited the land. God rewarded his faith!

I believe God rewards our faith, too! It seems to me the more I love and trust Him, and the more I seek Him and His will for my life, the easier my life becomes. And I'm not talking about material things, although I can tell you they certainly appear to be a part of the reward.

The biggest thing I've noticed though is the peace and the joy. And it makes sense if you think about it.

Look at it this way; if you go through the day worried and fearful about the myriad of things life throws at you all day every day, how much peace and joy can there be in that? But on the other hand, if you go through your day knowing no matter what comes your way, God will be there to assist you, and you will be at peace with whatever happens. It's a no-brainer if you ask me.

I'm not saying everything will go exactly the way you want it to. But I am saying you will be at peace with whatever way it goes, and you can be joyful, knowing it went the way God wanted it to go.

Be still! Be patient! Be faithful! God knows what He's doing!

January 17

When you go to war against your enemies and see horses and chariots and an army greater than yours, do not be afraid of them, because the Lord your God, who brought you out of Egypt, will be with you.
Deuteronomy 20:1

War seemed to be a way of life in Old Testament times. And unfortunately, at times it seems it is a way of life in our current time, too. War is divisive, holds no value, and there is no joy in it. Even victory is joyless when the costs are counted.

As I write these pages, attempting to encourage others like myself, I realize not everyone who reads these words will be sitting comfortably in their home like I am. How do I encourage those folks? How can I speak to one of our soldiers, not knowing what his or her life is like, not knowing the challenges they face each day.

I think all I can do is take a hint from Moses and tell them to not be afraid, because God is with them in everything they do and anywhere they might be.

It saddens me to know that some of these soldiers will not come back from the wars they are fighting. All I can say is if they don't come home to their earthly families, they will go home to the Lord and the members of their families that have preceded them.

Pray for our men and women fighting on faraway battlefields today. Pray they know God is there with them. Pray for our leaders, that they will know what God would have them do, and that they have the faith and courage to do it.

January 18

He shall say: "Hear, O Israel, today you are going into battle against your enemies. Do not be faint hearted or afraid; do not be terrified or give way to panic before them." Deuteronomy 20:3

Unfortunately, there will probably always be wars on earth. I sincerely wish it wasn't so, but the very thing we are talking about in this book of devotionals—fear—is one of the biggest reasons there is and always will be wars.

The fear I'm talking about is the fear of not being right. Sadly, the thing that seems to be most often fought about is religion, and it always seems to be based on the fact that one religion thinks their way is the right way and another religion thinks their way is the right way. I know many religious wars are fought over land ownership, but even then, if you get to the core of it, it is about who is right in their beliefs and who is wrong.

I have always wanted to believe that all of them are right to the degree God will understand and forgive them for the parts they got wrong. Religion, in my opinion, is not about God, but about man. Man, in his attempt to follow and worship God, has gone in so many directions and interpreted God's commands and desires in so many ways that even *God's* head is probably spinning!

I believe God is an individual thing. Yes, I believe some need fellowship, but I believe at the center of it all, it is a personal, one-on-one relationship with God.

It's between *me* and God. It's between *you* and God

January 19

> *Be strong and courageous. Do not be afraid or terrified because of them, for the Lord your God goes with you; He will never leave you nor forsake you."* Deuteronomy 31:6

The words of encouragement Moses spoke to the Israelites were full of faith and power. He had seen the works of the Lord and was certain in his thoughts and plans for his people. So certain he could tell them God would never leave them nor forsake them.

I believe the key word in that statement is *never*!

Think about it for a moment.

God *never* leaves us! He is *always* with us!

Do I need to say more?

Is this going to be a great day, or what?

January 20

> *The Lord Himself goes before you and will be with you; He will never leave you nor forsake you. Do not be afraid; do not be discouraged.*
> Deuteronomy 31:8

Moses told Joshua—the man God had chosen to lead the Israelites to the Promised Land—the same thing he told the people. The big difference I see in what Moses told Joshua, though, is he told him the Lord would go before him.

I have this vision of God sitting across the Jordan on a big rock, waiting for Joshua and the Israelites. He had such big plans for them and was probably anxious for them to arrive. God must have been excited and happy, even after all the times they had disappointed Him. They were finally coming!

I think that's how God sees each one of us. He knows we're coming to Him, because He chose us. He knew before we knew that we would come to Him, and He has been waiting patiently with open arms for us to join Him and live the life He has planned for us.

Man! Just picturing Him sitting on that rock, leaning forward excitedly, smiling and watching us come to Him… it gives me goose bumps!

I'm going!

January 21

Then the Lord said to Joshua, "Do not be afraid; do not be discouraged. Take the whole army with you, and go up and attack Ai. For I have delivered into your hands the king of Ai, his people, his city and his land. Joshua 8:1

Joshua took over where Moses left off, fought many battles and won many victories. He led the people into the Promised Land, conquered the inhabitants and occupied the territory. He was able to succeed in doing all this because he was a man of extreme courage and faith. Even then, he still needed to be constantly encouraged by God.

We all need encouragement. We need it every day and sometimes all through the day. I know I could not keep writing these daily messages if it were not for the constant encouragement of my wife. But too, the writing of them actually encourages *me*. I feel as though I am doing what needs to be done—helping others—and yet I feel as if I am doing it for myself at the same time.

I guess it goes along with the idea of it being more blessed to give than to receive. But it is even more than that. By writing these things, I am, in a strange sort of way, talking to myself, teaching myself and encouraging myself.

Encourage someone today. I'm going to bet that in doing so, you, too, will be encouraged.

January 22

The Lord said to Joshua, "Do not be afraid of them. I have given them into your hand. Not one of them will be able to withstand you."
Joshua 10:8

Again and again God said these same words to Joshua. Yet it seems each time a new enemy was approached, Joshua sought the Lord's help. I wonder sometimes if he really needed the assistance, or just needed to hear the words and be reminded that God was there with him.

I can't count the times my wife has told me how much she has enjoyed something I've written, and I have asked her, "Are you sure it's okay, are you sure it's good?"

I think I just need to hear her say it again. I need her support and assurance.

Asking her is such an easy thing for me to do, because I know she loves me and will do all she can to make sure I am confident and sure of myself.

We need to be that sure of God. We need to know He loves us more than we can even imagine and He will be there when the battles of life are raging. And even more than that, we need to get hold of the idea that He goes before us and prepares our way. He gives our enemies into our hands before the battle even begins.

Be encouraged today, knowing God has gone before you and nothing or no one can keep you from the blessings He has for you. Know, too, He might use you to bless and encourage someone else.

January 23

Joshua said to them, "Do not be afraid; do not be discouraged. Be strong and courageous. This is what the Lord will do to all the enemies you are going to fight." Joshua 10:25

You da man, Joshua!

In this scene, it appears Joshua has gotten the Lord's message and is now encouraging his men. His confidence and faith has grown and now he wants to teach his troops to not fear, just as Moses and God have taught him.

Moses spent years mentoring Joshua. Sometimes it was with words and sometimes it was by example. In any case, what Moses knew, and what God had shown him, he passed on to Joshua so the people could confidently follow him and finally make it to the Promised Land.

You and I are mentors. We may not even know sometimes who we are mentoring, but someone is watching us, following us and wanting to be like us. That's a powerful responsibility, my friends. People are constantly watching us; watching how we live, how we react to things, watching every move we make.

Our lives are on display each and every day. Live like everything you do and say is going to be on the ten o'clock news.

January 24

The Lord said to Joshua, "Do not be afraid of them, because by this time tomorrow I will hand all of them over to Israel, slain. You are to hamstring their horses and burn their chariots." Joshua 11:6

Joshua died at the age of a hundred and ten, and I would have to surmise that he was a mentor to thousands of people. He must have died a very satisfied man. I mean, can you imagine coming to the end of your life and being able to look back and know you had mentored and encouraged so many people and helped lead them to their God-ordained destination? And not only led them to the Promised Land, but led them to trust the Lord and live happy and purposeful lives. I can't even imagine that!

I wrote a poem in 1998 called "Pennies From Heaven". It was based on a short story I'd written a few months earlier with the same title, about a grandfather who told his grandson how found-pennies came from heaven. The grandfather explained that when you find a penny, it has been tossed down from heaven by a departed loved one—an angel—to tell you they are thinking of you.

That poem has been around the world via the Internet, and every now and then it comes back to me. Sometimes by way of someone wanting to use it for an organization for the bereaved or something like that, and sometimes just because someone found it, sent it to someone else, and eventually a person I know sends it to me. Sometimes the person sending it to me doesn't even know I'm the author of it.

It sometimes awes me to think how many hearts that one poem has touched. I tell my wife if that poem was all I ever did to help and encourage people it would be enough for me. She scoffs at the idea. I think she is expecting more from me than just one little poem.

We all need encouragement. I encourage you to encourage someone today.

January 25

Jael went out to meet Sisera and said to him, "Come, my lord, come right in. Don't be afraid." So he entered her tent, and she put a covering over him. Judges 4:18

The book of Judges is one of the more tragic books of the Bible. After the great leaders, Moses and Joshua, were gone, the Israelites returned to sinful practices and greatly displeased the Lord. They had not learned the lessons from the teachings and examples of their leaders. In those days—the days before Jesus died on the cross for us—God did not take sinful acts lightly. I believe the acts of the Israelites during this time could have been part of the reason God had to send Jesus to us. He knew we couldn't do it on our own, so He gave us another way.

Grace.

In Old Testament times, disobedience brought judgment. In a way, I think it still does, because even though we are saved by grace, we still suffer when we stray from God's will for us.

We suffer because when we don't love God and seek God, we are not able to rest in His peace and experience His joy. I realize that explanation is a bit on the simplistic side, but if I haven't said it already, I am a simple kind of guy. And I believe God is a lot less complicated than some might think.

Keep it simple. Love God, seek God and trust God.

Try it. It works.

January 26

And I said unto you, "I am the Lord your God; you shall not fear the gods of the Amorites in whose land you live. But you have not obeyed me." Judges 6:10 NASB

You just have to shake your head in wonder when you read some of these stories. It's hard to imagine that with God right there with them, the Israelites would just go on their merry, sinning way. The thing that really makes you shake your head, though, is how many times God gave them another chance.

He does the same for you and me, though, and I guess if you get right down to it, we have the same advantage the Israelites had. He may not be right here in front of us, talking to us, but He's here. As long as we allow Him to be here, that is. That's the way I see it anyway. It's a choice we make every day. Either we let God be a part of our lives, or we don't.

You remember how I said a few days back that I could just see God sitting across the Jordan River waiting excitedly for the Israelites to come across? Well, imagine just the opposite; God standing on the other side of the river, watching sadly as you go on your merry way without Him, not even giving Him a second thought. He walks along, paralleling us, anxiously hoping we will look His way. When we finally round the bend and our backs are to Him, He sighs and follows at a distance, ever hopeful we will turn back to Him.

I don't want to be the one to make God sad. Although, I'm sorry to say, I have so many times.

But you know what's really cool? He's always glad to see me when I turn around and come back.

January 27

But the Lord said to him, "Peace! Do not be afraid. You are not going to die." Judges 6:23

Gideon was told by the Lord that he would be made strong and he would save Israel from the oppressive Midianites. He raised a massive army of 32,000, but after several tests by the Lord, the army was whittled down to a mere three hundred. God did this so the people of Israel would know they had not saved themselves by their own strength, but by His.

I can think back on things that have happened in my life—both large and small—where I know the hand of God was in them. I hesitate to think how many times I took the credit and boasted about my accomplishments. All I can say in answer to that is it's a good thing God is a forgiving God.

In Philippians 4:13, Paul says, *"I can do all things through Him who strengthens me."*

I tend to think that, likewise, we can do *nothing* without Him to strengthen us.

I think I'll take Him along with me today. I can't bear the sad look He gives me when I leave Him behind.

January 28

And now, my daughter, don't be afraid. I will do for you all you ask. All my fellow townsmen note that you are a woman of noble character.
Ruth 3:11

Ruth was a virtuous woman, devoted to her family and faithfully dependent upon God. In her the sovereignty of God is clearly seen as He guides her through life preparing her to fulfill His plan. His plan was for her to become an ancestor of Jesus Christ. The story of Ruth should assure each of us that we, too, are a part of God's plan. Naomi and Ruth trusted God to provide for them, and He did. We should trust Him, too.

On my wife Sherry's wedding band there is an inscription that comes from verse 1:16 of the book of Ruth that says, "*Where you go, I will go…*"

Sherry sought out that band and that inscription, and being the typical man I am, I did not make a big deal out of it at the time nor have I expressed my feelings about it since. The fact is, though, I knew what she was saying by putting that band and that inscription on her finger, and I was humbled and honored by it. I knew then, and she has proven many times over since, it was more than a symbolic gesture. The words on the ring were and still are true. She loves me unconditionally, and I am overwhelmed at times by the depth of her patience and confidence in me.

She is my "Ruth", and I am so very fortunate and proud to be her partner in this life.

God has blessed me richly.

January 29

> *And about the time of her death the women who stood by her said to her, "Do not be afraid, for you have given birth to a son." But she did not answer or pay attention.* 1Samuel 4:10 NASB

From my limited knowledge and point of view, this passage has no bearing on the plight of the Israelites. Except, perhaps, to show that as they began to fall away from God and lose battles, they were becoming despondent, much like the woman who was giving birth. She had lost her husband and father-in-law in a recent battle and evidently saw no reason her life should go on.

I believe also that giving birth to a son was an honorable thing for a woman to do in those days, and that is why the women attending her during her labor encouraged her by saying she should not fear because she had given birth to a son; an heir.

There have been too many times in my life when I became despondent and discouraged. It can happen in the blink of an eye. I can be on top of the world, and then a series of disappointments comes along, and boom, I drop into a funk deeper than Lake Tahoe.

I've often said it is sometimes okay to let yourself feel disappointed and sad, but only if you do it knowing it is only for a brief time, and after you have allowed yourself the period of sadness, mourning or whatever, you shrug it off and get on with life. Too often, though, I wallow in the depths of my disappointment, sorrow or grief for too long, and it becomes difficult to pull myself out of it.

I'm lucky God gave me Sherry to throw me a rope when I get too far down in the dumps.

As a matter of fact I'm holding onto that rope right now, and my dear, faithful wife is pulling with all she has. Thank you, God, for her. And thank you, God, for loving me.

January 30

> *"Do not be afraid," Samuel replied. "You have done all this evil; yet do not turn away from the Lord, but serve the Lord with all your heart.* 1 Samuel 12:20

The Lord had told Samuel He was unhappy with the Israelites because they had asked for a king. God wanted them to recognize that He was king. When Samuel told the people this, they asked him to pray to the Lord and ask Him to spare them. They knew they had done wrong so many times, and now, they had sinned again!

Samuel encouraged them and told them not to be afraid, but rather to serve the Lord faithfully, so they and their new king would not be swept away by the Lord.

Sometimes when I do something I know I shouldn't have done, I can relate to the Israelites. I don't know how many times I have sat and wondered at my foolishness and thought how disappointed God must be. And after all is said and done, I am amazed to realize and know He forgives me and continues to love me.

Do you realize that God's love is constant? It's the same right this moment as it was at any given time in your past, and it will be the same every moment you live on.

Never more, never less, and always there; God's love never wavers.

That, my friends, is incredibly awesome!

January 31

"Stay with me; don't be afraid; the man who is seeking your life is seeking mine also. You will be safe with me." 1 Samuel 22:23

Saul wanted David dead more than anything, and David knew it. That was why David could be sure Abiathar would be safe with him. Saul would be so tuned in to killing David he would not even notice anyone else.

Sometimes when I read these stories I don't understand what is going on. I get so lost in all the wars and the fighting, I can't figure out who the bad guys are and who the good guys are. But the way it usually works out in the Old Testament, the good guys are the last ones standing.

I sure hope that's how it works out in our time, because it's really hard sometimes to not look at all that's going on in the world today and say, "Hey! The bad guys are winning big time!"

I think that is one of the hardest things we have to do these days. We have to know God is in control when sometimes it looks like evil has taken over and God has gone on vacation. Those are the times when we have to "Be still."

We have to take a deep breath, relax, and know God is in control.

February 1

"Don't be afraid," he said."My father Saul will not lay a hand on you. You will be king over Israel and I will be second to you. Even my father Saul knows this." 1 Samuel 23:17

David seemed like an ordinary guy in the beginning, but as his popularity grew, Saul became jealous of him and tried to do away with him. But David had not only gained favor in the eyes of the people, he had gained favor with the Lord. His humility and integrity, combined with his love for and faithfulness to the Lord, would take him far in life.

Several years ago it became popular to shout out to a golfer who'd just made a great shot, "You da man!" I use the accolade quite often, and more often than not, it is in a humorous/sarcastic manner—all in the spirit of fun.

Some friends of mine have a young son, and when he was just learning to converse well—he is amazingly articulate for his age—and I would see him with his parents down by the lake. I would yell at him, "You da man, Cooper!" After several weeks of this, I yelled at him one afternoon, "You da man, Cooper!" He yelled back, "No, Charlie. You da man! I'm just a boy!" That has become our game. I yell, "You da man, Cooper!" He yells, "No! You da man!"

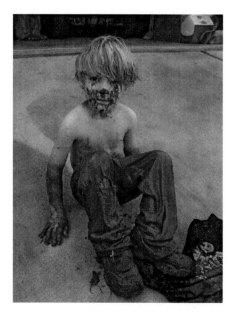

I was dumbfounded when Cooper first refuted my playful accolade. I decided it was because he literally knew in his young mind that, no, he wasn't the man—a man—Charlie was. To Cooper it was merely simple childlike logic.

I think as David's popularity and status grew, he knew it was not by his might that he succeeded, but by the Lord's. He gave credit where it was due and stayed humble.

February 2

The king said to her, "Don't be afraid. What do you see?"
1 Samuel 28:13

Saul had prohibited mediums, but he disguised himself and went to one so she could call up Samuel and ask for his advice. When Samuel appeared, the woman realized she'd been tricked and that it was for Saul she was calling the spirit of Samuel.

It seems Saul thought he was above the rules, and eventually his low opinion of God and high opinion of himself was his undoing. He took his own life in battle by falling on his sword.

I've seen guys like Saul. They start having some success and getting some breaks, and somewhere along the line they start thinking they arrived at their lofty station of their own volition. They begin to believe they gained success because of *their* brain, or *their* brawn. They forget that if God had not prepared the way for them, they would not have gotten where they are.

Yes, I've done it, too. There probably isn't one among us that can say they haven't.

Many times, I have seen athletes being interviewed after a big game, and some of them are quick to say if it had not been for God, they couldn't have accomplished what they had. That takes guts, because if you say it on television or radio and millions of people hear it, you best not mess up later on. Folks are mighty quick to throw you under the bus these days!

We can climb any mountain with God as our guide. But when we reach lofty goals, we need to remember that without Him we would still be in the valley looking up.

February 3

"Don't be afraid," David said to him, "for I will surely show you kindness for the sake of your father, Jonathan. I will restore to you all the land that belonged to your grandfather Saul and you will always eat at my table." 2 Samuel 9:7

Kings were the highest human authority. Their subjects feared even to come before them, and so when David sought out the only living relative of Saul in order to restore to Saul's family what was rightfully theirs, Mephibosheth—grandson of Saul—came before him and fearfully bowed to pay David honor. David told him not to be afraid and restored the lands of Saul to him.

I believe God wants us to honor Him much the way people in days past honored kings. Remember in 1st Samuel, when the Lord was unhappy with the people because they had asked for a king. The Lord wanted to be recognized as king!

I believe that more than anything, kings want to be loved. God wants to be loved. Everyone wants to be loved. When you get right down to it, what is life if you are not loved?

It is possible, I suppose, to be afraid of someone and love them at the same time. But then again, does that make any sense? I have a hard time believing God wants us to wallow in the fear and failure of our misdeeds and His retribution. I believe God wants us to rest in Him, without fear, and to love Him. God wants us to experience His love, His peace, and His joy.

The funny thing is, the more you love God, the less failure and misdeeds there will be, and the more peace and joy there will be. What a great system!

February 4

Absalom ordered his men, "Listen! When Amnon is in high spirits from drinking wine and I say to you, 'strike Amnon down,' then kill him. Don't be afraid. Have I not given you this order? Be strong and brave." 2 Samuel 13:28

The last part of King David's reign did not go so well. He fell from grace, and his family was in a shambles. This part of David's life is an example to us that no matter who we are, or how great our faith and love for God, we can still fall prey to the temptations of this earthly life. Not exactly news, is it? It certainly isn't news to me.

Back in the early 1980's, I attended a small Baptist church in Enumclaw, Washington for a while. One summer the church formed a softball team and joined a local league. We bought T-shirts and put numbers on the back of them, but unfortunately, the pastor of the church and I chose the same number—three. I immediately told him to keep the number, and I would change mine. That was a bit of a problem as I did not want to buy a new shirt, so I thought on it for awhile and arrived at a solution.

I decided to add a colon and the number thirteen to the three—3:13—and then place Philippians above the number. I came to those numbers and that book of the Bible after much searching for a verse I thought said something about me and my relationship with God.

The verse applies to what I'm talking about today, and has become "my" verse and is always in my mind. In the verse, Philippians 3:13, Paul says, *"Brothers, I do not consider myself to have taken hold of it. But one thing I do: Forgetting what is behind and straining toward what is ahead."*

If we stumble or fail, we must not continue to look back at our mistakes. Look up to God, and press forward. We aren't perfect—we will make mistakes—but we *are* forgiven.

February 5

Elijah said to her, "Don't be afraid. Go home and do as you have said. But first make a small cake of bread for me from what you have and bring it to me, and then make something for yourself and your son." 1 Kings 17:13

God allowed the prophet Elijah to do wonders in His name, much as Jesus and His apostles would later do, in order to prove he was truly a man of God. Elijah also had an experience much like what we go through today. He experienced a tremendous victory over 450 prophets of Baal on Mount Carmel, then his joy over the victory turned to sorrow when he was pursued by Jezebel and had to flee for his life.

I have had many times in my life when I thought I had finally "got it". Times where everything made sense and the way appeared clearly before me, only to suffer tremendous discouragement and disappointment that knocked me back to earth. More and more though, I am learning to not let the disappointments and defeats destroy the victories. I mean, after all, no matter what might come to try and make you think your victories are meaningless, can it really do so without your permission?

I don't think so! Those victories are your victories, and no one can diminish them unless you allow it. They will always be victories, no matter what might follow. When a football team wins a game and then loses the next one, do they erase that first game from the win column? I don't think so!

Every win is a win! Cherish each one, and if disappointment follows, shrug it off and go for the next victory!

February 6

The angel of the Lord said to Elijah, "Go down with him; do not be afraid of him." So Elijah went down with him to the king.
2 Kings 1:15

2nd Kings tells of the downfall of the divided kingdom (Israel and Judah). Israel was ruled by wicked kings, and though a few of Judah's kings were good, Elijah and the other prophets could not stop Israel's decline.

I sometimes look at the troubles our nation is experiencing these days and wonder if it can survive. Americans are a proud and fearless people, but have we become "too big for our britches," as my grandpa used to say? Has the entitlement generation taken over?

Have believers allowed non-believers to take control to the extent that the believers—God's people—no longer have a say in what they can or cannot do? Sometimes it seems that is exactly what we have done. It seems to me our nation is divided—the God-fearing on one side and the Godless on the other—and we could easily compare that division to Israel and Judah.

Even if those things are true, it is not too late to turn back, and it's not too late to step forward. Step forward, and look upward to God. He will show us the way to regain control of our lives and our country.

Will we stand up for what we believe in, or be forced to live in a nation where God is not politically correct?

February 7

"Don't be afraid," the prophet answered. "Those who are with us are more than those who are with them." 2 Kings 6:16

The story of Elisha capturing the army from Aram by having God blind them, then sending them back home, is one of those biblical stories that seems to be of great meaning. And yet, it is another of the stories that seem to hover just out of my grasp and understanding. Elisha was a great prophet, and in this story, chose to spare the army from Aram. But not long after that, the king of Aram set out to kill Elisha.

This story seems to again parallel today's attitudes. The United States has always been first to come to the aid of other nations in distress, whether it is from hurricanes, tsunamis, wars, disease, or just plain poverty. Yet those very countries we have aided are quick to criticize and turn on us. That baffles me.

The same thing happens to us quite often in our personal lives. It has always been a mystery to me that we can do good things over and over again, and we are considered good and a friend. But even after we have done so much good, it seems if we do one bad thing, it erases all the good. Why is that? Why does one bad outweigh a multitude of good?

I'm going to keep pondering those questions, and I'm sure they will pop up again in the days to come. But one thing is for sure; I'm going to keep trying to do the good and right thing in the meantime.

February 8

> *35: With whom the Lord made a covenant and commanded them, saying, "You shall not fear other gods, nor bow down yourselves to them nor serve them nor sacrifice to them." 37: "The statutes and the ordinances and the law and the commandment which He wrote for you, you shall observe to do forever; and you shall not fear other Gods. 38: "The covenant that I have made with you, you shall not forget, nor shall you fear other Gods.* 2 Kings 17:35, 37, 38 **NASB**

God told the Israelites all that, and still they chose to disobey and persisted in their former practices. It's easy to look at a passage such as the one above, read on to discover that the Israelites did not obey, and then wonder how they could possibly do that. History had proven to them if they obeyed the Lord good things happened, and if they disobeyed Him, bad things usually beset them. But can we be so hasty as to wonder at and judge their actions?

I don't know about you, but I do the same thing they did—know what God wants, and not do it—on a fairly regular basis, and when I do, the words of Paul from Romans 7:15 ring loud and clear in my mind: *I do not understand what I do. For what I want to do I do not do, but what I hate I do.*

It seems to me Paul is talking about the war between the mind and the flesh—good and evil, if you will—and explaining to the Romans how difficult it is to overcome sin. This section of scripture is somewhat hard to understand, and I am sure it has and will continue to be heavily discussed and debated. As for me, for now, I must lean on the concept that it all comes down to grace. We all sin, but by the grace of God we have been forgiven. Jesus took our sins with Him to the cross.

I don't mean we can just go around sinning at will. What I believe is if we love God and focus on Him, He will fill us with His love and Spirit, and we will be more likely not to sin. We are sinners—it is our nature—but God created us in His image, and if we sincerely love Him, I believe we will become more like Him.

February 9

> *Isaiah said to them, "Tell your master, this is what the Lord says: Do not be afraid of what you have heard—those words with which the underlings of the king of Assyria have blasphemed me."* 2 Kings 19:6

How many times do we get bad news about something and allow worry to immediately set in? Almost every time!

The natural reaction to bad news of any kind is to start conjuring up all the "what ifs." You know, like: What if gas prices keep going up? What if I lose my job in this struggling economy? What if I can't make my mortgage payments?

The answer to all of those questions is: That is not what God says! He says He will provide for our every need. It says so in many places in the Bible. Over the years I have come to believe that He will provide whatever we need when we need it. The key word there is "need."

I have come to the conclusion that the key to true happiness is to not want anything. That's another way of saying what Paul told the Philippians in chapter four, verse eleven of his epistle to them: *"I am not saying this because I am in need, for I have learned to be content whatever the circumstances."*

Be happy where you are, with what you have. Love God. He will supply your every need and bless you abundantly.

February 10

Gedahlia took an oath to reassure them and their men. "Do not be afraid of the Babylonians officials," he said. "Settle down in the land and serve the king of Babylon, and it will go well with you." 2 Kings 25:24

Unfortunately, this turned out to be bad advice.

It illustrates to me, though, that the people of Israel were out of the loop, so to speak, and rather than trust in and look to God for guidance, they chose instead to look to men for their direction.

I find this to be true of most of us today. We look to men—some who say they represent God—and trust them explicitly to guide us. I think we have to be careful not to let the men we trust replace God. It's easy to do and sometimes can sneak up on us without our even knowing we've started doing it.

Some of the saddest times in my life were when religious leaders I respected and listened to fell. I won't name them—you probably know who they are—but it was a blow to me to find out they too, were susceptible to the same temptations and failures the rest of us are subject to.

I still learned from those men, and I have a difficult time condemning them for the evils they succumbed to. I believe if they have repented and asked God to forgive them, He has.

I believe we each have to love God and stay in tune with Him, so He will help us discern who and what He wants us to hear. We have to be careful to not let a man or doctrine become our God. Always remember: God is infallible, man and man's doctrines are not.

February 11

"Then you will have success if you are careful to observe the decrees and laws that the Lord gave Moses for Israel. Be strong and courageous. Do not be afraid or discouraged. 1 Chronicles 22:13

Something has occurred to me while doing these first forty-some devotionals; often when a verse says not to be afraid, it also says not to be discouraged. And I have to admit grudgingly that I get discouraged quite often, and so even though I claim not to be afraid of anything, I guess I am. For it seems to me when we are discouraged, it is usually because we are fearful we cannot complete the task we have before us, or we feel we have failed. I have to confess, that was one of my first thoughts when I realized there were not 365 places in the Bible that said not to be afraid.

I did not allow that line of thought to prevail. I quickly decided I would write this devotional book anyway and set out to find a theme to carry it on after the one hundred or so verses of "do not be afraid" were exhausted.

My goal here is to encourage those who read this book, so how could I allow myself to be discouraged before it was even finished?

When we become discouraged we should not remain that way. We need to look to the Lord and say, "No big deal. Where do we go from here, Lord?" After all it's *His* plan, not ours.

February 12

He said, "Listen, King Jehoshaphat and all who live in Judah and Jerusalem! This is what the Lord says to you: 'Do not be afraid or discouraged because of this vast army. For the battle is not yours, but God's.'" 2 Chronicles 20:15

If we seek to follow God's plan for our lives, the battle will not be ours, but His. This alone encourages me to seek God and His plan for my life. Unfortunately, it's much harder to do than it is to say. For some reason we always tend to think we are in charge and can decide what is best for us. Only after we have managed to get ourselves trapped in the maze of life, do we look upward and say, "I need a little help here!"

You, like me, probably wonder how we know what God wants us to do. It was easy for the Israelites (although they didn't take advantage of it most times) because as in this verse, God spoke directly to them through someone—Jahaziel. He spoke to the Israelites throughout the Old Testament, either through men or angels.

I believe God speaks to us, too, but usually not in a voice we can hear with our ears. His words come in the form of knowing in our conscience and heart what is right and what is wrong. If we seek Him through His word in the Bible, love Him and do what we know is right, then I believe we are following His plan for our lives. I believe when we do so the plan He has for us that fits in with His greater plan for mankind will be easy to discern and follow.

In Luke 12:31, Jesus says, *"But seek His kingdom and these things will be given to you as well."*

I believe that means *all* things, including understanding what His will for our lives is!

February 13

"You will not have to fight this battle. Take up your positions; stand firm and see the deliverance the Lord will give you, oh Judah and Jerusalem. Do not be afraid; do not be discouraged. Go out to face them tomorrow, and the Lord will be with you." 2 Chronicles 20:17

This is more of the same speech the Lord was giving to King Jehoshaphat and the Israelites through Jahaziel in yesterday's encouragement. It seems God needed to re-emphasize the fact they should not be afraid or discouraged. Only this time God added He would be there with them.

God also admonished them to take up their positions and stand firm. I think this is important in our lives, too. We should not only seek the Lord and do our best to follow His plan for our lives, but stand firm when we know in our hearts what we are doing is His will.

It is so easy to veer from the path He lays before us. I know in my own life, I can be going along believing in God, being contented and happy, then suddenly… I look around at where I am and what I'm doing and say, "What am I doing *here*?"

The world is full of distractions. We have to stay focused. It's like when you are trying to hit a baseball that is coming at you eighty miles an hour. The only way you can connect solidly with it is to keep your eyes on it and swing at the right time. You have to stay focused!

Focus on God today. He is with you! He loves you! You're part of His plan!

February 14

> *"Be strong and courageous. Do not be afraid or discouraged because of the king of Assyria and the vast army with him, for there is greater power with us than with him."* 2 Chronicles 32:7

As I have regretfully admitted before, I sometimes—too often—get discouraged. Sometimes it seems no matter how hard we try, things just don't work out the way we expect them to. I often start to think the other side—whatever the situation might be—just has too much going for them, and there is no way I can overcome the odds. Wouldn't it be great, if at times like those, God would send an angel to us and tell us not to be afraid of the odds against us?

Wow! That would be awesome!

But check this out; maybe He does.

Maybe, if instead of being discouraged, we go to and read passages in the Bible where He says He will be with us, fight our battles for us, provide for our every need; that is His way of speaking to us.

I know some of you will say that is simply another way of saying we should think positively and things will work out. Well… you are saying the same thing I am, only in a different way.

Thinking positively is always a good thing, but standing shoulder to shoulder with God and saying it is much more effective, don't you agree?

Be strong and courageous! Don't be afraid or discouraged! The *greatest* power is with us!

February 15

After I looked things over, I stood up and said to the nobles, the officials and the rest of the people, "Don't be afraid of them. Remember the Lord, who is great and awesome, and fight for your brothers, your sons and your daughters, your wives and your homes." Nehemiah 4:14

Nehemiah was rebuilding the wall around Jerusalem, and the enemies of Israel wanted to stop him so they could more easily attack them. Jeremiah encouraged the people and told them they must fight for their families and homes.

Sometimes enemies come against us and our families. The enemy may not be an army of men, but rather an army in the disguise of drugs, alcohol or some other habit. These things can destroy families and homes as well as any terrorist, tornado or hurricane.

I have a friend whose younger brother has fought the demon alcohol for most of his adult life. He is a binge drinker, and when he drinks he cannot stop. It has destroyed his life, and he now lives on the streets and begs for money to live. My friend is most unhappy about her brother's plight and has tried in vain to help him. But through it all, she remains unafraid of the enemy and continues to trust God to bring her brother out of the wilderness he is wandering in. She is faithful and believes God can save him. I know she gets discouraged at times, but I know, too, she will never give up.

When we face the enemies that come against us in our lives, we must face them unafraid and know God is more powerful than anything that can come against us. And most of all, we must know He is with us, and He will never leave us.

February 16

Do not be afraid when a man becomes rich, when the glory of his house is increased. Psalm 49:16 NASB

This Psalm speaks on the matter of trusting in your earthly riches rather than your heavenly God—a problem that is typical to almost all of us. It is so easy to get caught up in the "things" of this world and forget they are not ours, but God's, and He is merely allowing us to use them while we are here. I believe God wants us to have and enjoy things while we are here on this earth, but I believe, too, He wants us to know it is only through Him we can experience and enjoy these good things.

I'm sure though, many of you look around and see people who are rich and seem to have so much more than you do. Like me, you may often wonder, how can this be? They don't know or trust in God, and yet they have everything this world has to offer. That, I believe, is the key. They have *only* the things this world can offer.

I believe the key to our happiness is not in the things of this world, but in knowing we will spend eternity with God in heaven. We cannot take these earthly possessions with us, and even though we may enjoy them while we are here, the happiness they may bring us is small compared to the things God has in store for us when we go to be with Him in heaven. And even while we are here, the joy and peace God provides those that love Him are more valuable than any earthly thing we might own.

I am not rich, by any means, nor am I poor, but I have everything I need.

February 17

They shoot from ambush at the innocent man; they shoot at him suddenly without fear. Psalm 64:4

In Psalm 64 David talks about evildoers who speak evil words like arrows at innocent men. He tells how these evil men plot and think they can devise perfect plans of wrongdoings. But then he tells how God will strike them down, and the righteous will rejoice.

There are times in my life where I am concerned with what people are saying about me. But most of the time I know it is not people's opinions of me that matters, it is God's opinion that is important.

I have to admit sometimes that is not as comforting as it should be. Sometimes when I know I am not doing what God would want me to do, I feel like a kid with his hand in the cookie jar. That cookie is going to taste mighty good, but Mom won't be too happy with me if she catches me. And the thing is, God can see me all the time!

All I can say is, "It's a good thing God is a forgiving God." Because as much as I want to do what is right, I know I'm not perfect—never will be—and I will make mistakes. I praise God that He knows this and it is why He sent Jesus to us.

Don't allow the opinions of others to sway your good judgment. God's opinion is the only one that really matters.

February 18

Have no fear of sudden disaster or of the ruin that overtakes the wicked. Proverbs 3:25

The previous verse in this book three of Proverbs says when you lie down, your sleep will be sweet. I don't know if this is where I got the idea, but for most of my life I have been able to sleep well even when my mind was awhirl with worry or fret. I knew it was time to rest and whatever was going on could be dealt with the next day.

Today's verse takes it to the next level and to me says not to worry or fret. Period!

As I said previously, worry is a form of fear, and looking at it another way, it is a lack of faith in God. For if we truly trust God to take care of us and provide our every need, there is no need to be afraid or to worry.

Simple, simple, simple!

Then there's the latter part of today's verse about the ruin that overtakes the wicked, and I immediately think, "But what about when bad things happen to good people?"

I've already told you I'm no learned man when it comes to God and the Bible, so I can't explain some of these things. All I can do is tell you how I deal with them, and basically, all I figure we can do is continue to trust that all things God allows to happen will be used for His good. Because, just like worrying, what good can come from not trusting God?

No matter what happens, our happiness—our joy—depends on our ability to go with whatever circumstance comes our way—good or bad—with our head up, shoulders back and a smile on our face.

February 19

Say to him, 'Be careful, keep calm and don't be afraid. Do not lose heart because of these two smoldering stubs of firewood—because of the fierce anger of Rezin and Aram and the son of Remaliah.' Isaiah 7:4

King Ahaz and the city of Judah were about to be attacked. The Lord sent King Ahaz a message and told him not to be afraid. God went on to tell Ahaz that the plot of his enemies to invade and take over Judah would not happen, and Ahaz must stand firm in his faith. This book in Isaiah is extremely interesting because it goes on to foretell of the birth of Christ.

I used to wonder why the Old Testament was relevant after the coming of Christ. It seemed to me to be boring historical stuff, and it seemed like we didn't need it anymore. But then I discover things like the foretelling of the coming of Christ in this chapter, and I begin to understand the relevance of the Old Testament. It seems to me it is proof that God had a plan all along.

I get a kick out of today's verse, because it appears God is scoffing at Rezin and Aram and their anger. He calls them two smoldering stubs of firewood! Ha!

If we stand firm in our faith, trusting God to be with us through all our battles and trials, we can look at our enemies and opponents in the same way, knowing that in spite of their anger and posturing, their fire does not have any heat to harm us. It is only smoke and ashes.

No matter what challenge you might be facing today, do not lose heart and do not be afraid.

God is with you!

February 20

> *Therefore this is what the Lord, the Lord Almighty says: "O my people who live in Zion, do not be afraid of the Assyrians, who beat you with a rod and lift up a club against you, as Egypt did.* Isaiah 10:24

I sometimes wonder what purpose there is in this life on earth. Many times in my life I have looked around at the people rushing here and there and wondered what it was they were rushing to.

You get up each morning, rush to get ready for work, and rush to work. Then you hurry all day to get as much done as you can, so you can rush home and do your chores—fix dinner, mow the lawn, pay the bills—then eat dinner, watch TV and go to bed. Then you do it all again the next day, and the next, and the next. We all seem to be rushing to the next thing, only to realize there is another thing to rush to immediately after we finish that one. Man! This is starting to sound like a "Who's on first?" gag!

I have to laugh when I'm on the highway and look in the mirror to see someone right on my tail that eventually races past me, scowling as they go by. Then a few miles down the road at the next light I pull up next to them. I know my grin must really tick them off.

I believe it is fear causing us to run from place to place—fear we will miss something or not get everything done. I think we're chasing our tails, and we need to stop letting life and our fear of missing something beat us up. We need to slow down and realize most of the hurrying and scurrying we do is only to get to the next hurry, scurry activity. If you don't get it done today, it will be there tomorrow. Slow down and enjoy life. Relax and savor each thing you do. The next thing will be there when you get to it. Our purpose is to love God and do our part in His plan. What if, in all our racing about, we rush right past Him and miss what He has in store for us?

February 21

Say to those with fearful hearts, "Be strong, do not fear; your God will come, He will come with vengeance; with divine retribution He will come to save you." Isaiah 35:4

No matter what we might face each day, we should face it knowing God is with us, and we can do all things with His help. But, more than knowing this, we need to *share* this. We need to say to those around us that are struggling, that not only will God come, but He is already there if they—we—will just turn to Him and follow Him.

If you're like me, sometimes you think you can't tell someone about God. You might think, as I often do, I'm not a preacher, and I don't know the right thing to say. I think the best we can do sometimes is to show them by the way we live and the way we deal with things.

Then again, if you look to God, He will show you how to handle any situation, including how to share His love and goodness. I feel like God has blessed me with the ability to say and share through writing. I believe, also, He has a niche for each of you, and if you seek Him, He will show you what it is.

Love God and trust Him to guide you. You're part of His plan!

February 22

You who bring good tidings to Zion, go up on a high mountain. You who bring good tidings to Jerusalem, lift up your voice with a shout, lift it up, do not be afraid; say to the towns of Judah, "Here is your God!" Isaiah 40:9

I have been told that each and every writer has a style, and that style is called his or her "voice". As I am not a preacher or pastor of any sort and do not consider myself one to go out and spread the word of God, this passage from Isaiah encourages me. I believe by providing me the talent and a "voice", God has given me a way to bring good tidings about Him to people. With these simple daily encouragements, I am able to lift up my voice and shout to those who will read them, "Here is your God! Love Him and do not be afraid!"

The words I would shout to you today are found at the end of this fortieth book of Isaiah and are among some of my favorite words in the Bible; *but those who hope in the Lord will renew their strength. They will soar on wings like eagles; they will run and not grow weary, they will walk and not be faint.* Isaiah 40:31.

I know many times when I am tired and feel like I can't go another step, this verse comes to my mind, and I am able to reach down deep and come up with the energy to push on with whatever I might be doing. My high school football coach always admonished us to dig deep and get our second wind. I wonder if he knew his encouragements were Biblical. It is amazing to me that most of the time when I encourage myself to keep going (I often send a quick prayer to God when I do) I am not only able to go on, but I am full of energy—sometimes more energy than I started the task with!

When your strength, or your hope, begins to wane, get your second wind; hope in the Lord, and let Him renew your strength. Soar like eagles!

February 23

So do not fear, for I am with you; do not be dismayed, for I am your God. I will strengthen you and help you; I will uphold you with my righteous hand. Isaiah 41:10

I know sometimes it is hard to get hold of the idea that God is with us. Sometimes when life seems so mundane or when things aren't going well, we tend to wonder, "Okay, God, where are you? Why am I feeling so down today? Why am I dismayed?"

I wonder those things myself many times, but I have found that is when I need to just be still. And by being still, I don't mean I need to sit, lay or stand motionless, I mean I need to keep doing the best I can at life in general and know God is working out the details.

One of the things that always disturbs me is when I have gone through a period of depression or aggravation, and at the end of it—the other side, I like to call it—I realize how much time, sometimes days, I have spent in an unhappy state of mind. I am dismayed! Dismayed at the moments, hours or days I cannot get back. We don't get a mulligan or do-over in life. When the time or day has passed, it is done.

One of these days, I'm going to get to the point where, when every time something comes against me, I can forge onward, telling myself as I go, God is with me, and He will strengthen me and help me out.

I'm not there yet, but I'm headed that way!

Anybody want to come along?

February 24

For I am the Lord, your God, who takes hold of your right hand and says to you, "Do not fear, I will help you." Isaiah 41:13

The image of God reaching down to take hold of my hand is startling and awesome to me! I can imagine Him gently squeezing my hand in the reassuring way a parent squeezes the hand of their child.

Imagine yourself preparing for a day that promises challenges you are not sure you can overcome or conquer. You can do like most of us do and worry yourself sick over the fact you won't be able to accomplish the things you need to accomplish, or you can reach your hand out to God in the form of a quick, "Thank you, God, for being with me to help me today," and tackle the situation. Maybe as you walk out the door in the morning, you raise your hand and say, "High five, God!"

I'm not going to promise you everything will go exactly like you want it to in those circumstances, but I will promise you that you will spend less time worrying about it beforehand. And I will encourage you to be confident and satisfied at the conclusion of that day or period of time, knowing you did your best.

That is all we can do each day, you know? Our very best.

And hey! As you are walking to your front door when you return home from your day, raise your hand and yell, "High five, God!"

February 25

> "Do n*ot be afraid, O worm Jacob, O little Israel, for I myself will help you,*" declares the Lord, your redeemer, the Holy One of Israel.
> Isaiah 41:14

Hey! Did God refer to Jacob as a worm in this passage of scripture? That seems odd. But then, maybe it was an expression meant to illustrate to Jacob and "little" Israel that they were small compared to God and His overall plan. Just like us.

Sometimes I look around at this world, which itself is small when you realize how vast the universe is, and I feel so tiny. I even look at something that we think of as very large, like a huge cruise ship, and compared to the ocean, it is just a speck. Yet when we are on the ship it seems enormous, and we think what a marvel it is that man could construct such a wonder.

The feat of constructing that marvelous ship is child's-play to God, and the men scurrying about building it must appear to Him as no more than a colony of ants constructing a home. What feels to us like a gargantuan accomplishment is to Him no more impressive than one of His smallest creations.

The miracle in it all is even as small and insignificant as we might be, we are His and He has a plan for our life. The plans God has put in place are vast and wonderful, and each of us He has chosen has an important part to play in those plans.

No matter what you do today, love and seek God *before* you do it and continue to love and seek Him *as* you do it.

February 26

> *But now this is what the Lord says—He who created you, O Jacob, He who formed you, O Israel; "Fear not, for I have redeemed you; I have summoned you by name; you are mine."* Isaiah 43:1

Sometimes as I write these encouragements, I am amazed at what the verse for a particular day says. It often speaks about something going on in my life at that very moment. As big a surprise as it is to me, God must chuckle at my amazement, because he put it there, knowing it was what I would need to read or hear at that very moment.

It was that way this morning as I read Isaiah 43:1. I had just written an email attempting to comfort a friend whose brother had died a few days earlier. I mentioned this woman and her brother earlier this year. He was the man that was living on the street and battling a severe, lifelong drinking problem.

What I her was though her brother was with the Lord now, his work on this earth might go on. I told her that things her brother had said to someone, his paintings (he was a very talented painter) or perhaps even the story of his life, would help someone even after he was no longer with us.

I also reminded her that each of us God calls to Him has a purpose in His overall plan. Her brother had a part in God's plan, too, and I told her I hoped she could find comfort in that fact. She told me that her biggest comfort was in knowing her brother had accepted Jesus as his Savior.

Whether you realize it yet, or not, you have a part in God's plan. We may never know what our part was, but it will be played. Wouldn't it be great if, at the end of our earthly days when we see God, He beamed a big smile at us, raised His hand and said, "High five! Good job!"

Fear not, for God has redeemed you, summoned you by name and you are His.

February 27

Do not be afraid, for I am with you; I will bring your children from the east and gather you from the west. Isaiah 43:5

I am learning a lot as I write these messages of encouragement, and one of the things I'm learning is how often God told His people not to be afraid. In almost all cases the reason He told them to not be afraid, was because He was with them. I'm realizing more and more that no matter what I do or where I go, God is with me, just as He was with the Israelites. I am amazed at His patience with them and grateful He has just as much patience with me.

For most of my life, my mother has been my spiritual guide, and she has proclaimed many times the promises of God regarding her children. When I am troubled, I always know I can call Mom, and she will have the words to say that I need to hear. She, like God, has been patient with me.

This past Christmas a strange thing happened—Mom arrived for her annual Christmas visit, and she needed *me* to encourage *her*! Though she is spiritually strong, Mom is not infallible, and she gets discouraged just like the rest of us. I had begun to write these devotionals just prior to her arrival for the holidays, had printed the first forty five or so, put them in a binder, and wrapped them up as a present for her. She was so elated and uplifted by this endeavor of mine and by the things I was writing that it renewed her spirit and re-energized her. I had the words *she* needed to hear.

I knew Mom would be excited about what I was writing, but I had no idea how much she needed them. It just goes to show how God can use you in the most incredible, unexpected ways.

February 28

This is what the Lord says—he who made you and formed you in the womb, and who will help you: Do not be afraid, O Jacob, my servant, Jeshurun, who I have chosen. Isaiah 44:2

I am not doing much research as I write these devotionals, because I want them to be simple, and more than that, I want them to be what I think, not what others think. But my curiosity got the best of me, and I had to look up Jeshurun.

I have noticed over the years as I read the Bible, that God tended to rename people quite often. Jeshurun is one of those times, and until now, I had no knowledge of it. Jeshurun is a poetic name for Israel and can mean the people of Israel or the land of Israel. The patriarch Jacob was renamed Israel by God, and I think in this verse God is merely referring to Jacob as Jeshurun in an affectionate or possibly complimentary manner.

No matter the name though, I think the key to this verse is the last four words; *that I have chosen.* God knew Jacob before he was even born, and he knew us before we were even born. He chose us and put us into His plan for the world and His Kingdom beyond it.

Think on that and do the best you possibly can today at everything you do. You never know when a seemingly unimportant thing you say or do will have a tremendous impact on things and people you encounter. It could be as simple as smiling at someone you pass on the street.

Love God and allow His love to show in all you say and do. You are created in His image!

March 1

"Do not tremble, do not be afraid. Did I not proclaim this and foretell it long ago? You are my witnesses. Is there any God besides me? No, there is no other Rock; I know not one." Isaiah 44:8

The passage this verse comes from is one that speaks of man's building idols to worship rather than worshiping God.

It seems strange to me the people of Israel, with all the wonders God showed to them, would build and worship idols. But then, we do the same thing many times. We might not build idols from stone or wood or other materials, but we let *things* of this life become our focus and our god.

Money and possessions too often become our focus. We get so wrapped up in obtaining wealth and "things" we forget the reality is it all belongs to God, and what we have is only ours to use while we are here on this earth. We never really own anything.

It has been my experience that the less I try to gather, the more that seems to come to me. I am amazed that as I go about my days, God constantly provides over and above what I need. I'm not rich by any stretch of the imagination, but I always have more than I need, and no matter how much of it I give away, it seems to keep multiplying and coming back to me. I look around sometimes and wonder where all this stuff keeps coming from!

My point is we need to focus on God and not let "things" become our focus. God will provide everything we need if we just love Him and put Him first and foremost in our lives.

March 2

"Hear me, you who know what is right, you people who have my law in your hearts: Do not fear the reproach of men or be terrified by their insults. Isaiah 51:7

This passage deals with salvation, which, to me, is what God is all about. He tells throughout Isaiah 51 how nothing, not even this planet we live on, will last forever, but His salvation is forever.

He tells us in this verse not to be concerned with what men have to say because to quote one of my favorite sayings, "it just doesn't matter." If we have God in our hearts and do our best to live our lives the way He wants us to, the things of this world are of little consequence.

Sometimes I struggle with that concept—I'm sure you do, too—because I start wondering why we are even here if what happens here doesn't matter? When I start thinking like that things get all messed up in my mind. It is only when I turn my attention back to God and trust that He knows why we are here and He knows what He is doing that I can feel at peace in this crazy, mixed up world.

As for knowing what is right, we all know what is right. Some of what we know is right comes from how we were raised and some comes from what we learn as we go along. But many times I think we *just know* in our heart what is right or wrong, because that is how God made us. I also believe as we love God more and are filled with His Spirit, He gives us a sure knowledge of what is right and what is wrong.

The main thing is we should not let the opinions or attitudes of others stop us from doing what we know is right. We should not only do our work as if we are doing it for the Lord, but we should live our lives as if we are living it for Him as well. *His* opinion of us is truly the only opinion that matters.

March 3

"Do not be afraid; you will not suffer shame. Do not fear disgrace; you will not be humiliated. You will forget the shame of your youth and remember no more the reproach of your widowhood." Isaiah 51:7

As I read this verse, I at first thought, *now this is good,* but when I came to that last part about not remembering the reproach of your widowhood, I thought, *what?*

This is one of those passages in the bible that is not so easy to understand. I have learned not to spend too much time trying to figure these things out, because it seems when I am ready to understand them or need to understand them, God opens my mind to what He wants me know.

Therefore, I am not going to try and come up with an explanation for what is being said in the verse or try and tell you what I think it means. Instead I am going to concentrate on the part I *do* understand, which is that God is again telling us no matter what the situation might be, it is not the opinions of those around us that are important. God forgives us and loves us unconditionally, and *that* is what matters.

He loves us unconditionally!

It doesn't matter how many silly things we did in our youth. (I can't even begin to count mine), God forgives us and loves us. He loved us then, He loves us now, and He will love us tomorrow and forever.

Love Him back.

March 4

"In righteousness you will be established: Tyranny will be far from you; you will have nothing to fear. Terror will be far removed; it will not come near you." Isaiah 54:14

Throughout chapter 54 of the book of Isaiah, God talks about righteousness and its power over the things of the world. He tells us—His people—to not be afraid, because our righteousness will establish us. I believe our righteousness is simply our trust in Him. But more than that, our righteousness is His love for us.

I don't think God is guaranteeing we will never have troubles or enemies, but I think He is saying we will be able to overcome anything that comes against us if we love Him as much as He loves us and put our full trust in Him. Sure, we will have trials and tribulations in our lives. But if we face them without fear, knowing nothing they can do to us will prevent us from spending eternity in the loving embrace of our heavenly Father, what power do they have over us?

Too simple? Maybe. But I think that is the key to God—simple love. Love is not complicated, and I don't think God is complicated either. Love cannot be taken, it can only be given and received.

God loves us—He gives us His love freely. It *is* that simple. We complicate it by thinking we have to earn His love, when all we have to do is receive it.

I believe there is only one thing God wants us to do in return for His love.

I'll say it again; I can't say it enough: Love Him back.

But you know what? He will still love you even if you don't love Him.

March 5

"Do not be afraid of them, for I am with you and I will rescue you," declares the Lord. Jeremiah 1:8

God told Jeremiah to go and tell the people what God wanted them to hear. Throughout the book of Jeremiah, God warns the people of Judah that they are trying His patience with their idol worship and wicked ways.

He told Jeremiah not to be afraid when telling the people these things. Jeremiah was one of God's appointed prophets, and God assured him He would be with him and rescue him from trouble.

It was through his faith and devotion to God that Jeremiah was able to do what was asked of him. He could boldly go forward and tell the people of Judah they must change their evil ways and return their attention to the Lord. I'm sure many people were angry with him for doing this.

Like the people of Judah that Jeremiah was sent by God to speak to, we are a people and a country founded on Godly principals. A *minority* of people in this country are attempting to remove God from our lives by taking Him out of our schools, our jobs, our government institutions and even off of our currency.

We cannot stand by and let this happen. We must take a stand and insist on—demand—our right to worship and pray when and where we want to. Don't be afraid to speak your mind about such things. God is with us, and he will rescue us from those who come against us. It's like I said yesterday, do what you know is *right*. But…. don't allow your *rights* to be taken from you!

March 6

Like a scarecrow in a melon patch, their idols cannot speak; they must be carried because they cannot walk. Do not fear them; they can do no harm nor can they do any good. Jeremiah 10:5

That's kind of funny that God would compare an idol to a scarecrow! But in reality, it's not funny at all. To think people can build something out of wood, metal or any other material and worship it as a God is not only not funny, it is rather sad.

In my way of thinking, an idol has even less power than a scarecrow. At least a scarecrow can perform the feat of scaring off the birds and protecting the garden. An idol, on the other hand, can't do anything—unless you allow it to.

By that, I mean if you allow anything—cars, houses, food, anything material—to be more important to you than God, then it could be said you idolize that thing and perhaps even worship it. And please don't confuse "idolize" with merely wanting to have nice things. There is a big difference! But if you allow anything or even a group of things or all things to be your complete source of happiness, then you are in danger of them controlling your life. When we do that, it becomes so easy to believe we can control our lives on our own and don't need God.

I believe we should put God first in our life. We shouldn't let *things* become our idol.

March 7

"So do not fear, O Jacob my servant; do not be dismayed O Israel," declares the Lord. "I will surely save you out of a distant place, your descendants from the land of their exile. Jacob will again have peace and security and no one will make him afraid." Jeremiah 30:10

Sometimes when I read something, one word will jump out at me and have tremendous meaning. In this passage of scripture, that word was "security." Isn't that what we all seek? I know it has always been a key element in my life. We strive to get the best job and make the most money so we can have nice things. But more than the nice things, most of us want to have money in the bank so if things go wrong, we are able to continue on unabated.

Doggone it! There it is again! Fear! I go around telling myself I'm not afraid of anything, and then suddenly I realize I <u>am</u> afraid. Afraid something will go wrong or break down and I can't afford to fix it because I don't have enough money in the bank. I don't have security.

But! I am getting better all the time! More and more I am learning to not worry—be afraid—of something going wrong or breaking and not having the means to repair it. I'm learning to trust that things won't break, and if they do, God will provide me the means to fix them. And you know what? He usually does!

Simple! (I'm really beginning to like that word)

March 8

Gedaliah son of Ahikam, the son of Shaphan, took an oath to reassure them and their men. "Do not be afraid to serve the Babylonians, he said. "Settle down in the land and serve the king of Babylon and it will go well with you." Jeremiah 40:9

I like this! What this verse says to me is no matter where we are or who might be our boss, king or ruler of any kind, we will be okay if we are where the Lord wants us to be. It tells me even when it appears the worst has come, we are still under the protective wing of God.

I often let myself become discouraged about my job. It's a good job—in many respects, a wonderful job—yet I am often troubled because I am instructed to do things that just seem wrong. Most of the time it is simply that I am required to do things that are extremely inefficient and costly, and since I work for a government agency that means, in my opinion, we are being wasteful with taxpayer dollars. That really bothers me, and I have often thought about leaving and finding another job because of it.

Let's continue to keep it simple. According to today's scripture, if I settle down in this job I have and serve my employer, it will go well with me. Now, that *is* simple.

Whatever your circumstances today, settle down into them, do your best and it will go well with you.

March 9

"Do not be afraid of the king of Babylon, whom you now fear. Do not be afraid of him," declares the Lord. "For I am with you and will save you and deliver you from his hands." Jeremiah 42:11

We are lucky in this country in that we have never really had to fear our leaders. I know some of you might be shouting, "Bull," to that, but I'm talking about the fear of being physically punished or killed for believing in God. I am well aware that some of the actions of our leaders are pretty scary sometimes.

I read some novels recently about England back in medieval days, and it was horrifying what took place at back then. No wonder the founders of our country fled from there! According to the books I read, when a new king or queen would take the throne, they would institute their religious beliefs, and if you did not believe as they did and professed it openly, then off with your head! Thousands of people were tortured and killed because of their religious beliefs and practices each time a new ruler took the throne.

It is all quite confusing to me, since it appeared that all the people in England at that time believed in God. The kings and queens, though, insisted the people believe and worship exactly as they—the king or queen—did.

I thank God I live in this country where I can worship Him in any way I choose. And even though sometimes it seems like the wrong people are winning and making the rules, I know God is in charge, and He will deliver us from the hands of the bad guys.

March 10

"Do not fear O Jacob my servant, for I am with you," declares the Lord. "Though I completely destroy all the nations among which I scatter you, I will not completely destroy you. I will discipline you but only with justice; I will not let you go entirely unpunished." Jeremiah 46:28

Throughout the Old Testament times, God punished His people. Then, to put it simply—in my own words, He must've gotten tired of constantly having to discipline us, so He devised another plan. Actually, I tend to believe He had this in the plan all along, because the prophets of the Old Testament foretold of it—the coming of Jesus Christ.

I try sometimes to compare this to us raising our children, but I can find no parallel. I think of how we struggle to get our children to do the right things and how sometimes we feel like they just won't ever get it right, but then… what do we do? What can we do? Wouldn't it be nice if we could bring in this perfect kid to live with us and demonstrate to our children how they should behave? Ah, but see, our children would react to little-mister-perfect just like the people reacted to Jesus. "By golly we need to get rid of this kid!" they would say. And so you see where that story is going…

But the fact is, God had a plan for us, and knowing we could never be perfect—far from it, in fact—He sent His son to bear our sins on the cross.

Knowing God loved us so much he would allow His son to die a horrible death on the cross for us, is punishment. It hurts me to imagine what Jesus went through for us. His pain is my discipline.

"Thank you God."

March 11

You came near when I called you, and you said, "Do not fear."
Lamentations 3:57

The book of Lamentations is a short book that consists of five chapters, each a poem believed to have been written by the prophet Jeremiah. It is a sad book, in that it tells of the destruction of Jerusalem by the Babylonians. God allowed the destruction because the people of Jerusalem had turned to idols and other ungodly things. Yet in this verse, Jeremiah speaks of God's love and faithfulness to His chosen people.

None of us are perfect—we never will be—and God knows this. Though He may be disappointed in us at times, He is always waiting patiently for us to confess our sins and shortcomings. And I believe when we do, He forgives us, and it is forgotten. God does not hold a grudge or keep a list of what we do, whether it is good or bad.

Some will disagree with that assessment, but I believe if you really consider God and His gift of grace to us through His Son, Jesus Christ, you will eventually come to the same conclusion.

God loves each of His children unconditionally. No matter what your circumstance today, call out to God, confess your shortcomings to Him and profess your love to Him.

He will come near and remove your fears.

March 12

"I will make your forehead like the hardest stone, harder than flint. Do not be afraid of them or terrified by them, though they are a rebellious house." Ezekiel 3:9

The Lord was sending the prophet Ezekiel to speak to the rebellious people of Israel. I believe His encouragement to Ezekiel that his forehead would be harder than stone was because Ezekiel feared the people would attack him when he spoke the words the Lord had given him to speak.

From what I have read, it was the people of Israel that had heads harder than rocks. God had shown them miracles and wonders and promised them the world, so to speak, and yet they went on worshiping idols and living ungodly lives. They were stubborn, and determined to do it *their* way.

Sound familiar?

It sure does to me!

The people of Israel remind me of myself when I was a teenager (I'm sure many of you can relate to this). I was the smartest person on the planet back then, and my parents knew absolutely nothing. But strangely, as I grew older and actually did start to gain knowledge, my parents seemed to get smarter and smarter. I laugh as I look back at how stubborn and hard-headed I was.

Move out of your rebellious house today. Listen to what God has to say. Just like our parents, God seems to get smarter every day.

March 13

Then he continued, "Do not be afraid, Daniel. Since the first day that you set your mind to gain understanding and to humble yourself before your God, your words were heard, and I have come in response to them." Daniel 10:12

Wow!

When I read the Old Testament, I often wonder what it has to do with us today. But then I read a verse like this, and it all seems to make sense!

The angel speaking to Daniel tells him he has come in response to Daniel's desire to gain understanding. Daniel's desire for understanding was accompanied by his humbling himself before God.

I get it!

This is what I am trying to do—understand—and I believe the key to it is merely to humble myself to God and love Him. To me that means, just like I talked about yesterday, I have to realize I don't know what it's all about, take my seat in God's classroom and begin to learn that my Father knows so much more than I do.

If we love God and seek God, He will hear our words, and He will come in response to them.

Awesome!

March 14

Again the one who looked like a man touched me and gave me strength. "Do not be afraid, O man highly esteemed," he said. "Peace! Be strong now; be strong." When he spoke to me, I was strengthened and said, "Speak, my lord, since you have given me strength." Daniel 10:19

After being encouraged and strengthened by the angel, Daniel was ready to hear what God had sent the angel to tell him.

Daniel was just like you and me. He was just trying to understand and follow God's will for his life. Sometimes he was confused, sometimes he was scared and many times he just didn't understand.

I know so many times in my life I feel worn out and think I just don't have the strength to keep going. I start thinking I have done all I can do, and I'm tired of trying. I don't understand why I continue to do what I think I should do, and still seem to be spinning my wheels and going nowhere.

Ding!

I, I, I, I… Look back at that paragraph and note how many times "I" appear in it. How many times did God appear in it? … … DING DING DING DING!

When you feel like you are at the end of your rope, let go.

And let God.

March 15

"Be not afraid, O land; be glad and rejoice. Surely the Lord has done great things." Joel 2:21

Joel and the other Old Testament prophets continually warned Israel of the destruction their wicked ways would bring upon them, and at times the people made attempts to repent. Unfortunately, their attempts were usually efforts to keep the laws of the Lord and do works in His name. The reality was that those things were not what God wanted from His people. I believe what He really wanted—still wants—is for them to love *Him* instead of their idols.

In the coming months, after the "do not fear" verses, these daily encouragements will be based on verses regarding "love." I believe love is the key. God is love. God created us in His image so He would have someone to share His love with. He desires our fellowship and love. Nothing else we can do is of greater importance.

I know each of us must go about the business of the day. We must work, raise our children and attend to the matters of this world. God knows this, too.

I believe today and every day, before we set out to do what the world requires of us, we should take a moment to just say, "God, I love you. Thank you for loving me."

March 16

Be not afraid, O wild animals, for the open pastures are becoming green, the trees are bearing their fruit; the fig tree and the vine yield their riches. Joel 2:22

When I first read this, I was surprised to think that even animals can have fear. But then I thought that was pretty silly, because obviously they have fear. I just tend to think their fears are based more around things like being chased and killed by another animal or man than such things as having enough to eat or drink.

My little dog, Dockers, worries and frets all the time, mostly about where I am or where I'm going. Her entire world, it seems, is based on being with me. Of course, part of that is she knows where I am is usually where the food is. She depends on me to provide her food and water, and as long as she knows I am there, she is able to relax and rest, knowing I will take care of her.

You can probably see where I'm going with this line of thought.

As long as we draw near to God and know He will provide for our every need, what is there to be fearful of? Unlike my little dog, we have to go to work and then go to the store and buy our food, clothing and so on. If we do our part, and do it knowing God is there and will take care of us, we should be able to go through each day without worry and sleep restfully each night.

Be not afraid today. Our Father has seen to our needs, and He is with us.

March 17

On that day they will say to Jerusalem, "Do not fear, O Zion; do not let your hands hang limp." Zephaniah 3:16

When I came to this verse, I had to admit I had never heard of the prophet Zephaniah or this book in the Old Testament. But then, I told you from the get-go I was no scholar and was not learned in the scriptures.

My lack of knowledge led me to do a little research on Zephaniah, and what I discovered was that he was a confident follower of the Lord, and his writings show that. He begins his book with, "The word of the Lord..." and finishes it with, "... says the Lord."

One of the statements Zephaniah makes in this passage intrigues me, and I wonder what the reference is when he says, "Do not let your hands hang limp." It probably has to do with a custom of the day, but I wonder if perhaps it is indicative of a show of despair and hopelessness.

I picture an athlete—a boxer comes to mind—that has just been defeated. Tired and beaten, his arms hang limp at his sides. Defeat is beyond fear. When we feel defeated, we feel devoid of strength, and our will to fight leaves us. But that is when we should turn to God, for He has promised to renew our strength. As long as we have the strength to whisper, "God help me," we are not defeated.

If you are facing a challenge in your life today, don't give up.

Give *it* up!

Give it up to God, and watch what He can do. He is a powerful God, and He loves you!

March 18

"This is what I covenanted with you when you came out of Egypt. And my Spirit remains among you. Do not fear." Haggai 2:5

Over and over, God told the people He was with them and encouraged them not to be afraid. He never gave up, in spite of their unfaithful ways.

This little jaunt we've taken through the Old Testament has taught me a lot. I have a new respect for the lessons and stories told in the times before Christ, and I have gained a better understanding and appreciation for how much God loves us.

Maybe that was the intent—His plan—to show us how patient He can be and how far He is willing to go to prove His love for us. I'm convinced, and I realize more than ever His Spirit is among us, and we have no reason to fear.

The Lakota Indians believe winter is a time of cleansing, and spring is a new beginning. Winter has come and now stubbornly leaves us with perhaps a final cool breath across our faces. God is with us. We have nothing to fear. Let's celebrate that fact and begin anew each day as though it were the first day of spring.

I think it fitting that in a few days we will move into the New Testament verses that tell us not to be afraid. Now we will see what Jesus—the one who cleansed us—and the apostles have to say about fear. It will be the spring of our daily encouragements and perhaps.... a new beginning.

March 19

"As you have been an object of cursing among the nations, O Judah and Israel, so will I save you, and you will be a blessing. Do not be afraid, but let your hands be strong." Zechariah 8:13

God has continued to love His people in spite of all they have done, and in this verse He tells them He will save them from the troubles they have endured. He tells them they will be a blessing.

These types of passages continue to show me the awesome extent of God's undying love for His chosen people. I use the word "chosen" purposefully here, because I believe God chooses us, not the other way around. We do have to make a choice, though, and He gives us the free will to do so. I suppose there are some who do not come when He calls them, and I imagine that must cause God much sorrow.

In this particular passage, God also tells His people to not be afraid and to let their hands be strong. I find it interesting that He says "let" your hands be strong. The people were about to begin building a temple for the Lord, and I think possibly they did not feel they were up to the task. It seems to me God is telling them they are already strong, and they just have to believe in themselves.

I believe you and I have been saved by Jesus, and we are well able to do what God wants us to do. "Let" yourselves be strong today. God is with you, and you are well able.

March 20

"So now I have determined to do good again to Jerusalem and Judah. Do not be afraid. Zechariah 8:15

God had been angry with His chosen people for many years, and now He had decided to forgive them and give them another chance. Again, as He had done so many times before, He told them He was going to do good things for them and they should not be afraid.

I can remember times when I was a child, and I had done something wrong. I knew I would be punished, and I usually was. In those days, Dad's belt on our backside could be expected if we did something outside the rules he had set for us. The rules were usually common sense things, designed to keep us from getting hurt or hurting someone else, or things to teach us to be fair, honest and do what was right.

Sometimes, when a father disciplines a child it causes the child to fear the father, but in most cases the child knows their father still loves them. But even so, when the father calls to them not long after they have been punished, they are sometimes fearful of him. I'm fairly sure that's how God's people felt when He would call to them. They had done bad things, and continued to do bad things, and still God wanted to forgive them and do good things for them. Yet they remained fearful of Him.

Most fathers love their children no matter what they've done and punish them in hopes they will no longer do things that are wrong. God—our heavenly Father—loves us more than any earthly father ever can, in spite of anything we've done. Many times we have plenty of reasons to fear God, but I don't believe we should ever fear Him because we are afraid of being punished. If we fear God at all, it should be a fear that we have disappointed Him after everything He has done for us.

Accept God's unconditional, unwavering love. He loves you no matter what.

Love Him in return, without fear.

March 21

> *But after he had considered this, an angel of the Lord appeared to him in a dream and said, "Joseph, son of David, do not be afraid to take Mary home as your wife, because what is conceived in her is from the Holy Spirit."* Matthew 1:20

We move into the New Testament today, and we start out with a bang! I mean, can you imagine what must have been going through Joseph's mind when he received these words?

First off, an angel was speaking to him in a dream. That had to be hard to accept. Then, the angel tells him his wife, he'd not yet had relations with, was pregnant. Yikes! And she was pregnant by way of the Holy Spirit! Excuse the expression, but, Oh—my—God!

The amazing thing is Joseph, apparently with little consternation regarding all this, did as the angel of Lord told him to do in his dream. That, my friends, is faith! Joseph must have known he would be subject to much gossip and condemnation, but he trusted that God would see him through it.

As we go through the New Testament verses that contain the phrase, "do not fear," I am sure there will be other instances where great faith and trust in God are displayed. I can think of no instance before or since Joseph's experience that is more important or had more impact on our world.

Our part in God's plan can never be as big as the one Joseph played, but it is no less important. And our degree of faith should be no less than Joseph's.

Seek God's will for your life, and He will direct you. When He does, don't be afraid. Love Him and trust Him, and He will prepare the way before you.

March 22

"So do not be afraid of them. There is nothing concealed that will not be disclosed, or hidden that will not be known." Matthew 10:26

This is the first verse on my list where it is Jesus who says, "Do not be afraid." It is a momentous time for me with regard to writing these encouragements. The words of Jesus, to me, are the most important words ever spoken by any man. I want more than anything to understand them and live by them as much as is humanly possible. I trust, as I said in the beginning of this book, God will author what I write, and I will be merely the instrument He uses.

The words Jesus speaks in this verse from the book of Matthew are as simple as it gets, though at first reading their intent may elude you. To me, the words of our Savior simply say God is all knowing and He sees everything. Nothing we say, do or think is hidden from God.

After writing that last sentence, I sat and stared at it for quite some time. God's omnipotence is a concept that will make anyone who loves Him stop and think.

Remember when you were a child and at times it seemed like your parents had eyes in the backs of their heads? They could be facing the other way while you were rolling your eyes at the back of their head, and they would say, "Don't roll your eyes at me, young man." Spooky, wasn't it?

To know God sees and hears our every sound and movement should not be spooky, and we should not be afraid. Actually, we should take comfort in it. For if we love God, we will do His will, and He will be with us—not to keep us from doing wrong, but to help us do His work. He watches over us every minute of the day.

March 23

Do not be afraid of those who kill the body but cannot kill the soul. Rather be afraid of the one who can destroy both soul and body in hell. Matthew 10:28

In the tenth chapter of Matthew, Jesus is giving instructions to His disciples prior to sending them out, with His authority, to drive out evil and heal every sickness and disease. He tells them to not be afraid three times in His instructions to them.

This verse is of particular importance to me and you, as I'm sure it was to the disciples. Jesus was telling them—and us—not to be afraid of death of the body. My belief is that what He means by this is we should not be afraid of what men can do to us, because our souls will live forever with Him after our earthly bodies are dead and buried.

This concept is one that makes it difficult for some to accept Christianity. To many people, life on this earth is all there is.

I heard someone say—I've heard it more than once—that it seemed to them it would be better to believe there is a God, than to believe there isn't, die, and find out you were wrong.

I will say with confidence I believe God wants more of a commitment than a better-safe-than-sorry attitude. If you believe in God simply because you're afraid not to, then you do not love Him. I hold firm to my belief that what God desires most from us is our love.

Love God, and fear nothing. He is with you now and will be with you always.

March 24

"So don't be afraid; you are worth more than many sparrows."
Matthew 10:31

Jesus again tells His disciples to not be afraid as they go forth to do God's work. He tells them how God cares even for the smallest and least valuable of His creations, such as the sparrow. He says God knows the number of hairs on each man's head.

Wow! That is hard to comprehend! Can you imagine how hard it would be to count the hairs on somebody's head?

Even though Jesus uses this as an illustration of how important the disciples are to God, I believe it is true. I believe God knows each and every minute detail about every one of His children.

He knows how He put us together, and He knows what part we will play in His plan.

Today, know that you are important to God, He has a plan and you are a part of it.

Seek Him and love Him, and He will do His perfect will through you.

March 25

But Jesus immediately said to them, "Take courage! It is I. Don't be afraid. Matthew 14:27

This is an awesome story! A story of faith that turns into a story of fear and doubt.

I cannot fault Peter for losing faith as he walked across the water to Jesus. His faith in Jesus allowed him to step out, but then his fear overwhelmed him, and he began to sink. How many times has that happened to you? I can attest that many times I have begun to move forward, filled with faith and ready to do something, only to meet up with discouragement or problems that either stopped me cold, or at the very least, delayed me considerably.

I can also confess it happens much too often. I am too easily discouraged, and maybe I don't give up, but I stay in my discouraged state and grumble that I can't do what it is God wants me to do. Usually, though, I somehow become inspired to get on with the task, and when it is done, I look back, and I'm amazed at how easy it actually was.

I am learning not to be so quickly discouraged, and I'm trying to face my difficulties and challenges more positively, knowing God will see me through them. I'm not even close to accomplishing this lofty goal, but I'm working on it.

My encouragement to you today is to recognize when troubles assail you and you start to be discouraged, you can stop and picture Jesus holding a helping hand out to you and saying, "Come."

Jesus wants to help you.

Let Him.

March 26

But Jesus came and touched them. "Get up," He said. "Don't be afraid." Matthew 17:7

It must have been a frightening time for the disciples. They would see Jesus do miraculous things, see angels and hear the Lord's voice booming in the heavens. And on top of that, the high priests and some of the people wanted to harm or kill them and Jesus. Jesus had to constantly reassure them and encourage them to not be afraid.

We are, no matter how we try not to be, much like the disciples when it comes to fear and a lack of faith. We get caught up in the troubles of the day and forget we have Jesus walking beside us to help with whatever we might encounter.

There have been times in my life where I was overwhelmed by the things of this world and allowed myself to become terribly discouraged and defeated. I was afraid I could not overcome my dire circumstances. Sometimes that feeling would take me into the depths of despair for days and even weeks. I would become listless and begin to lose my will to keep trying. Eventually, though, and it always seemed to happen in an instant, I would snap out of it, and on most occasions I would attack my problems with a vengeance, or sometimes I would simply throw them aside and forget about them.

After reading this short verse in Matthew, I can imagine all those times when I snapped out of my woes, it was because Jesus had touched me and said, "Get up. Don't be afraid."

If the world is dragging you down today, let Jesus touch you. He's right there beside you, you know.

March 27

The angel said to the women, "Do not be afraid, for I know that you are looking for Jesus, who was crucified." Matthew 28:5

I cannot even imagine what must have been going on in the minds of Mary Magdalene and the other Mary when the angel told them this, and then continued with, "He is not here; He is risen." It says they hurried away from the tomb, afraid, yet filled with joy, and ran to tell His disciples.

I don't see anything in the scriptures that says they even questioned what they had been told. It simply says they hurried away to tell the disciples. Now that is faith.

Too often we are hesitant to accept the promises of God. He tells us to ask, and it will be given, but yet we hesitate to even ask. He tells us, seek and you will find, and we are afraid to look for the good things He has promised us. He tells us He is with us always, and we continue to try and do things on our own without Him.

We need to learn to believe what God tells us and receive what He offers us. We are God's children—His family—He loves us and wants us to be happy. I believe our love for Him is all He wants in return. If we love Him, we believe His promises, and more than that, we believe *in* Him.

March 28

Then Jesus said to them, "Do not be afraid. Go and tell my brothers to go to Galilee; there they will see me." Matthew 28:10

The two Mary's run smack into Jesus, and it amazes me when the first thing He says in the verse previous to the one above is, "Greetings."

Are you kidding me? "Greetings?"

I almost think this was a display of Jesus' sense of humor. I can almost see him trying not to bust a grin.

Did Jesus have a sense of humor? I think He did. He was human, wasn't He? I heard a preacher the other day saying how he thought Jesus had a sense of humor, and He probably laughed often. The preacher talked about how when Jesus and the disciples went fishing they were probably just a bunch of guys out fishing. I agree. They were probably a lot like me and my buddies out fishing on the lake, joking and relaxing; enjoying the day and the time together—without the beer, of course.

My point is, I think Jesus had a sense humor, and I don't think He wants us to go around all serious and stern, never laughing or having fun. In fact, I think He wants us to smile at everyone we meet and tell them we hope their day is going good.

"Greetings."

That cracks me up!

March 29

Ignoring what they said, Jesus told the synagogue ruler, "Don't be afraid; just believe." Mark 5:36

This might be the best "do-not-fear" verse I've read so far. It is so simple and to the point!

Jairus, the synagogue ruler, has just been told his daughter has died. Jairus had sought out Jesus in hopes Jesus could heal his sick, young daughter. Jesus was on His way to Jairus' house when the news came it was too late. The men that delivered the message told Jairus there was no use bothering Jesus anymore. Jesus ignored the messengers and told Jairus, "Don't be afraid; just believe."

Jesus brought Jairus' daughter back to life.

When troubles come, our first reaction is usually to do as the messengers that came to Jairus suggested to him; give up and say, "What's the use?" Our first reaction *should* be to turn immediately to God and ask for His help. This might not cause things to happen exactly like we want them to, but I tend to believe they will go our way much more often if we have faith first instead of faith as an afterthought.

Many verses in the Bible are quoted often to encourage people. I'm sure all of you can bring one to mind. I have to wonder why the simple words of Jesus in Mark 5:37 aren't standard fare. They are a devotional/encouragement on their own.

I encourage each of you as you start your day, today and every day, to say, "I will not be afraid; I will just believe!"

March 30

Immediately He spoke to them and said, "Take courage! It is I. Don't be afraid." Mark 6:50

Picture yourself in a boat with all your fishing pals and imagine you've been trying to row the boat ashore for hours against the wind. All of a sudden, there's a man standing on the water beside the boat.

I am quite sure my buddies and I would be climbing over each other to get to the other side of the boat and possibly get out! Probably be screaming like little girls, too!

But Jesus just told them to buck up, and then He got in the boat. All it says is they were amazed.

I'm amazed! They had just seen Jesus feed five thousand people with five loaves of bread and two fishes. What was so amazing about Him standing beside the boat? He made blind men see and crippled men walk! He healed the sick and brought the dead back to life! You think He can't walk across a lake? Come on, fellas!

We are much like the disciples, in that we can watch, as time after time, Jesus works miracles on our behalf and for those around us, then the next big crisis or challenge comes along, and we panic. Oh, Lord, how will I ever get through this? I can't do it!

In Philippians 4:13, Paul says, *"I can do all things through Christ who strengthens me."*

So can we! Jesus is right there with us all the time. Let Him get in your boat, car, house, or wherever you are, and He will strengthen you and help you.

March 31

But the angel said to him, "Do not be afraid Zechariah; your prayer has been heard. Your wife Elizabeth will bear you a son, and you are to give him the name John. Luke 1:13

I tend to think Zechariah had not seen an angel of the Lord prior to this time, and I certainly can't blame him for being startled. To top that, the angel then tells him he and his wife are going to have a son. They're both getting up there in years, so Zechariah is a bit skeptical. The angel explains to Zechariah that he was sent by God and because Zechariah did not believe what he told him, he would not be able to speak until his son was born. Say what? (No pun intended)

I wonder what that was all about. I mean, you would think Gabriel—the angel—would have laid out the rules before he told Zechariah about having a son. Especially if there were heavy penalties involved based on Zechariah's response!

That's like somebody you've never seen before coming into your office, wearing a Peter Pan outfit, and telling you your boss is giving you a free trip to Disney World. You respond with, "You're kidding me, right?" The messenger shakes his head sadly and says, "No, I'm serious, but since you didn't believe me, you will have to wear a blindfold while you're there."

There are many things in the Bible I don't understand, but in the interest of keeping things simple, I'm going to believe God had a reason for what He did. Many times, things that happen in our lives don't make perfect sense to us, but when all is said and done, we can usually look back and see that most of it really didn't matter anyway. All that mattered was the end result.

April 1

But the angel said to her, "Do not be afraid, Mary, you have found favor with God." Luke 1:30

What an incredible encounter this must have been. It seems at first that Mary is not quite sure about the angel or what he wants from her. Then after he lays out this incredible plan God has for her life and her son, Jesus, Mary says, "I am the Lord's servant. May it be to me as you have said."

To Mary, it was that simple. God said it, so that's the way it would be.

So far, I have not had a visit from an angel bringing me specific instructions as to what God wants me to do with my life. What I do have is the Bible and my belief God sent His son, Jesus, to live on this earth, be crucified and then rise again in order that we might have everlasting life. Maybe it's more complicated than that, but I'm a simple man and prefer to keep it all within my limits of understanding. I figure if God wants me to know more than that, He will make it clear somehow.

For now, I believe, I love God, and I do my best to do what is right according to what I know.

I am serving the Lord the best way I know how. As He chooses to reveal Himself to me, it will be as He says.

April 2

> *But the angel said to them, "Do not be afraid. I bring you good news of great joy that will be for all the people.* Luke 2:10

It's the middle of the night, and you're in the country watching over your small herd of sheep. Suddenly it's as bright as day, and an angel is speaking to you.

Run for your lives, boys!

Nope. After the light went out, and the angel was gone, the shepherds said, "Let's go on into town and check this out."

The angel brought "good" news. Has any news ever been more fantastic?

The news was of "great" joy; unbridled, uncontainable, totally awesome joy.

News for "*all*" the people. *All the people!* The angel brought news for you and me, our children, our relatives and friends.

This was the ultimate gift from God to us, and He did it simply because He loves us and wants to be with us.

He wants us to love Him.

April 3

And so were James and John, the sons of Zebedee, Simon's partners. Then Jesus said to Simon, "Don't be afraid; from now on you will catch men." Luke 5:10

Jesus had filled the boats of the fishermen so full they began to sink. The fishermen were astonished, and Simon Peter fell before Jesus and proclaimed himself to be a sinful man. I believe he was humbled and perhaps even fearful of the powerful man of God, Jesus.

I have known men of power in my life, but obviously none who could compare with Jesus.

One of the best men I ever encountered was the justice of the peace in the small Arizona town I grew up in. His name was Billy Meck, and I would guess when I was ten years old, he was probably fifty, give or take a few years. He taught a Sunday school class for boys at the church our mom took us to on Sundays.

We liked Mr. Meck a lot, because he was a not only a nice man and good teacher, but he took us fishing! It was part of the lesson he was trying to teach us youngsters, and we kind of understood, but not really. He was trying to teach us to be fishers of men as well as fishers of fish. He wanted us to go out and tell others about Jesus so they could know God like we did. To tell the truth, we were only ten years old and weren't really ready to go out telling folks about Jesus. But you know what? I still remember Billy Meck, and I still remember what he taught us forty-eight years ago.

We all have a part to play in the bringing of others to Christ; some preach, some just let their light shine, some share what they know by teaching. No matter what you might perceive your part to be, don't be afraid of it. Just throw out your net and see what Jesus puts in it.

April 4

> *Hearing this, Jesus said to Jairus, "Don't be afraid; just believe, and she will be healed."* Luke 8:50

Just believe; so simple, yet sometimes so difficult to do.

In this case, Jairus' daughter was dead, and all her relatives were wailing and mourning for her. Jesus told them to stop wailing and told them the girl was not dead, but asleep. The people laughed at him!

This illustrates to me that Jesus was indeed just a man. The people saw Him as this young teacher who was revolutionizing their way of believing and living. They also heard of His many miracles, and yet, when confronted with it, they were unable to accept what He was saying. I can see them looking at one another grinning, or more likely, due to the dire circumstances, scowling at one another; all of them thinking what a foolish young man He was.

Jesus never missed a beat, He just took the girl's hand in His, and said, "My child, get up."

I believe Jesus can do all things for and through us if we have faith and believe in Him, but too many times, we get so involved in what is going on in this crazy, mixed up world, we forget to do the simplest thing; have faith.

I am learning that those times are when I must "be still."

The problems or difficulties you face today may seem insurmountable to you. Love God, have faith and know you can do all things with His help.

Just believe!

April 5

"I tell you, my friends, do not be afraid of those who kill the body and after that can do no more. Luke 12:4

In Luke's account of this story, Jesus encourages the disciples, and I find it interesting that He refers to them as His friends. The song, "What a Friend We Have in Jesus," came immediately into my mind.

The song was originally penned sometime prior to 1855 by an Irishman—Joseph Scriven—as a poem to encourage his mother. He called it *Pray Without Ceasing*. It was put to music in 1868 by a musician—Charles Converse—who titled it, *What a Friend We Have in Jesus*. It has become one of our most cherished hymns.

Do you ever get a song in your head and can't get rid of it? I do. My youngest son does, too, and I used to aggravate him by purposefully singing a few lines of a really obnoxious song when he'd be around. He'd get so annoyed at me, because he knew he'd have that dumb song in his mind the rest of the day. My favorite was the theme song from The Beverly Hillbillies.

But how about getting a song like *What a Friend We Have in Jesus* stuck in our mind all day? I don't know about you, but I could deal with that!

What a friend we have in Jesus
All our sins and grief to bear
In His arms He'll take and shield thee
Thou wilt find a solace there

I can't say it any better than that. Put *that* song in your mind and heart today.

April 6

"Indeed, the very hairs of your head are all numbered. Don't be afraid; you are worth more than five sparrows." Luke 12:7

Jesus was trying to convince the disciples they had nothing to fear because God was with them and loved them. He explained how God loved even the sparrow that was worth very little; and therefore, He surely must love them because they are His people.

God loves us and wants the best for us. Of all His creations, we are His favorite. He loves us more than the birds, the animals or all the fish in the sea. We're number one!

I remember times as a child when I wanted attention from my mom or dad, and for whatever reason, they were too busy and had no time for me at that particular moment. It made me so sad. I'd sit on the other side of the room watching longingly and wishing they could just take a few minutes and talk to me or play with me.

But God is never too busy and is always there if you need Him. In fact, He's there whether you need Him or not. Sometimes it's us that don't have time for Him. Can you envision God sitting across the room from you right now, looking at you longingly and wishing you would take time to talk to Him? Maybe you have a problem on your mind, and He wants so much to help you with it—if you would just ask Him. Maybe you're excited and happy about something good going on in your life, and He wants to share it with you!

Take time to talk to God today. He might be missing you.

April 7

"Do not be afraid, little flock, for your Father has been pleased to give you the kingdom." Luke 12:32

In Luke 12: 32-34 Jesus talks to the disciples about what is important. More precisely, He speaks to them about what is *most* important. In verse 34 He finishes with, *"For where your treasure is, there your heart will be also."*

These verses have been interpreted and discussed since the time they were spoken. Some believe they should be taken literally, and we should sell or give away everything and serve God.

I disagree with that interpretation. I believe what God wants is for us to put Him, and loving Him, first. Everything else is second. I believe God wants us to be comfortable and enjoy our lives, as long as we recognize that without Him we have no future. … … Whoa! That might have come out a little stronger than I intended it to. But, hey, it's true!

Our treasure should be our God. He should be what and who we love more than anything there is. This world can offer fleeting pleasures, but God offers a love and happiness that will last forever.

Set your eyes and heart on what is truly a treasure. I'm telling you, folks, it's the best bargain in town!

April 8

"Do not be afraid, O daughter of Zion; see, your king is coming, seated on a donkey's colt." John 12:15

The disciples did not understand at first that Jesus sitting on the donkey's colt was a fulfillment of Prophesy. They realized it only after Jesus was glorified. Jesus was gaining followers, and His popularity was growing rapidly. He knew this was only the beginning of the end.

Was it the end? Yes, it was the end of Jesus' life as a man here on earth, but in reality it was the beginning. After all, isn't that why we count years as BC and AD. We started over after the death of Jesus Christ!

Jesus did not worry or fear as He approached the time of His crucifixion. I believe this was the most important lesson He was sent to teach us; not to fear death—of the body. He knew without a doubt He would rise again and then go to be with God the Father forever. He wants us to live our lives the same way He did; without fear, full of faith, and knowing when our job here is done, we will spend eternity with Him and God.

I'm in!

Live honorably today, loving God and doing your very best at whatever you do. Do your work as unto Him, for ultimately He will be your reward.

April 9

"Peace I leave with you; my peace I give to you. I do not give to you as the world gives. Do not let your hearts be troubled and do not be afraid." John 14:27

Complete and perfect peace; that is the peace Jesus is talking about. His peace in His own life was due to the complete and unwavering belief he had a part to play in God's plan and He would play it perfectly. And after His part was played, He would spend eternity with His Father... in perfect peace.

He gave us that same kind of peace when He died on the cross for us and then rose again on the third day. He gave it to us not as the world gives, which to me means He gave it to us with no strings attached, and we did not have to pay anything for it. You cannot obtain anything from this world unless you pay for it one way or another. And even then, the world will sometimes take it back from you; especially when that thing is love.

So many times, I have been loved by someone, only to have the love lessen or be taken away entirely because I did something the one who professed to love me did not like or approve of. That's not the way God does it. His love is the same every moment you live, and you can't make Him love you any less or any more by doing something He approves or disapproves of.

Accept the gift of peace Jesus gave to you. Go into your day knowing that nothing you can say or do will cause His love for you to waver. I'm betting you will have a great day if you do.

April 10

One night the Lord spoke to Paul in a vision. "Do not be afraid; keep on speaking, do not be silent. Acts 18:9

Paul was preaching the message that Jesus was the Christ to the Jews in Corinth. When they opposed him and became abusive toward him, he was ready to quit and go on to someplace else. But God spoke to him in a vision and told him not to be afraid, to keep on speaking. He stayed for over a year and a half before leaving for Syria to continue his teaching.

I can relate to Paul's situation in a way. I have been in situations where I'd had all I could take of a job, a town, a relationship, and was ready to move on to something else. Many times I did move on, and regretted it later; sometimes I moved on, and it turned out to be a good move.

I believe the key is to seek God's will prior to making a move that will impact our lives in a big way. I know many people are unhappy with their jobs and would like to move on and find a better one. The problem with that is we usually leave one set of problems for another. The thing is, I believe you must examine where you are and determine if it is where God wants you to be. Sometimes a simple procedure such as making a list of the good things and another list of the bad things and comparing them will help. Many times, the good things far outweigh the bad.

Today, look to God and seek His direction in the decisions you make. He has a plan, and you are part of it. Though it may not seem like it, sometimes God needs you to be right where you are.

April 11

Last night an angel of the God whose I am and whom I serve stood beside me and said, "Do not be afraid, Paul. You must stand trial before Caesar, and God has graciously given you the lives of all who sail with you." Acts 27:4

Paul and some other prisoners were aboard a ship and encountered a tremendous storm that went on for days. It became obvious to all those aboard the ship it would not survive the storm. Paul was visited by an angel of the Lord and told that he and the men would survive even though the boat would not.

Do you ever feel like you are in a sinking ship? I know I do! Sometimes it seems like the storms of life are raging, and your life is falling apart around you. You begin to wonder if you will ever see the good times and sunshine again. And sometimes, to top it off, you know—like Paul knew even after he survived the storm he must stand trial—there is another storm waiting for you when you get through the one you're in.

If Paul had not had faith, if he had not believed what the angel had told him, he and the other passengers might have given up, and there is no telling what might have become of them. But Paul believed, and so they survived and went on to the next part of God's plan.

A favorite saying of believers in Jesus Christ is, "This too shall pass." The phrase is not found in the Bible, but I do believe it is Godly in its simplicity. I believe with God's help and love, we can weather any storms this life may bring. The storm will pass. The sun will come out.

Let me put a song in your mind today, *"Oh, let the sunshine in, face it with a grin."* Remember that one? I hope you hear it all day!

April 12

But even if you should suffer for the sake of righteousness you are blessed, "And do not fear their intimidation, and do not be troubled."
1 Peter 3:14 NASB

I suppose this is the ultimate we can do for God; suffer because we believe in and worship Him. I think it is something most Christians—especially those new in their faith—fear the most.

I cannot tell you the thought does not cross my mind on occasion, "What will people think when they find out I am writing these daily encouragements." Some will no doubt judge me; others will laugh and talk about what a sinner I am. Some will be downright angry at me for having the gall to think I can talk about God and Jesus.

All those things can be hurtful, but none of them make me fearful. I do not consider myself righteous, but I do consider myself blessed. The things people will say or think about me are their way of trying to intimidate me, and I will not be intimidated. I am blessed with the ability to write, and I feel these daily encouragements will help some who read them.

I have decided I will not suffer, nor will I be troubled, no matter what others may say or do. I am confident what I am doing is a good thing and the words I write will encourage many who read them.

Don't let what others say, or what you perceive they might think, keep you from doing what you know is right. Seek God, love God, and do what you know He would have you do.

April 13

When I saw Him, I fell at His feet as though dead. Then He placed His right hand on me and said, "Do not be afraid. I am the first and the last. I am the Living One; I was dead, and behold I am alive forever and ever! And I hold the keys of death and Hades." Revelation 1:17

I'm going to confess to you right now, there is no way I can begin to explain the things that are said in Revelations. That is except for four words that appear in this verse; *"Do not be afraid."*

I hold firmly to the promise that if I believe Jesus died on the cross and was raised on the third day I will live with Him forever when my days on this earth are done. I believe if God wants to reveal to me what the book of Revelations is telling us, He will. Until He does, I will continue to do what I believe to be right and have faith God is with me.

Many people are afraid of God. Whether they are afraid because of things they have been taught, or things they have read, they are nonetheless afraid. Why? I believe most people who are afraid of God, are afraid because they don't understand and accept one key thing; God loves them.

On April 16 these encouragements will begin to be based on verses in the Bible that speak of love. As I said in a previous writing, I believe love and fear are direct opposites. It is, in my opinion, difficult, if not impossible, to love someone you are afraid of. So if you love God, how can you fear Him?

Above all else you do or think, love God and put Him first in your life. He will do the rest.

April 14

> *"Do not be afraid of what you are about to suffer. I tell you, the devil will put some of you in prison to test you, and you will suffer persecution for ten days. Be faithful, even to the point of death, and I will give you the crown of life."* Revelations 2:10

If you profess to be a Christian and your government says you will be thrown into prison for doing so, what will you do? This is where your love of God is put to the ultimate test. Will you deny your love for Him in order to continue living your life the way you choose?

Unfortunately, many folks are fair-weather believers. They can boldly profess their love of God when there are no consequences and can easily say they believe in God as long as it doesn't affect their daily lives.

I can think of no good way to illustrate this point. It's just too blatantly simple. If you believe in God and believe Jesus died and rose so you might spend eternity with Him if you but believe in Him, then I believe you will do whatever you have to do. No suffering, no persecution, no threat, even the threat of death, will sway you.

A very interesting thing jumps out at me in this verse. Jesus says, *"The devil will put some of you in prison."* I believe this answers the often asked question; "Why do bad things happen to good people?" Answer: Because the enemy wants to destroy you. And the more you love God and put your trust in God, the more the devil hates you and he wants to see you eliminated. But by standing fast in your faith and continuing to love God no matter what the circumstances, you show the world God is in control.

Satan is a thief and a liar! Ignore him!

Stay focused on God! Do not be afraid! Be faithful! Love God! Your reward will be the crown of life!

April 15

Then Jesus said to them, "Give to Caesar what is Caesar's and to God what is God's." Luke 12:17

Tax day, the day everyone looks forward to each year. Not!

Many people are a nervous wreck by the time this day rolls around. Why? Because many of them will have to fork over a portion of their hard earned cash to the government, that's why. The government takes taxes out of our pay checks; we pay sales tax; we pay property taxes; we pay extra taxes on gasoline and many other items. When is enough, enough?

I quit concerning myself with that question a long time ago. Enough will never come. We will always pay taxes, and there is no use getting worked up about it. The more money you make, the more they're going to try and get. People who make lots of money, and even people who make very little money, spend much of their time and energy trying to figure out ways to keep from paying taxes. Why is everybody obsessed with not paying taxes? They all want the things taxes pay for: roads, schools, bridges, etc., but they want somebody else to pay for it.

If the people of this world would spend even half as much time thinking about and loving God as they spend thinking about and loving money, the world would be a much better place.

I've often said—maybe I've said it in one of these encouragements already—the key to happiness is to not want anything.

Keep your lives free from the love of money and be content with what you have, because God has said, "Never will I leave you; never will I forsake you." Hebrews 13:5

April 16

Dear friends let us love one another, for love comes from God. Everyone who loves has been born of God and knows God. 1 John 4:7

Today, these encouragements will begin to be based on verses that speak of love. In my initial perusing of verses that deal with love I came upon quite a few in Chapter Four of the New Testament book of 1 John. They seem to be a good beginning for this portion of encouragements.

I have said throughout my encouragements that were based on not being afraid that love is the key. Loving God, loving ourselves and loving others. John says in this verse love comes from God. I agree. John also says those who love are born of God and know God. Again, I agree.

I have to confess, though, I did not always agree. In fact, for many years in my young adulthood, I professed there was no such thing as love. I attribute those thoughts and proclamations to the rebellious and frightened young man I was. A lot of my youth was unpleasant and painful, and as I began life on my own, which included a family to support at a young age, things were tough. And instead of turning to God, I got mad at Him. Why was life so hard? Why wasn't He helping me? The thing is, though, all the while I was denying the existence of love, I knew God loved me. And even after all the mistakes I've made, I know He *still* loves me.

As time goes on, I am learning more and more about love, and I try to love everyone just as they are, not as I wish them to be. That's how God loves us. As I write these daily encouragements based on love, let me start by saying two things to you:

God loves you. And I love you.

April 17

Whoever does not love, does not know God, because God is love.
1 John 4:8

That statement, God is love, has always fascinated me. I can't quite get my mind around the concept and explain exactly what it means, yet I understand it.

God is love – love is God. So simple and yet so profound.

Some definitions from the online Miriam-Webster dictionary define love as: (1): strong affection for another arising out of kinship or personal ties. (2): affection based on admiration, benevolence, or common interests.

Those definitions seem to me to fit the love God has for us and we should have for Him. They also seem to be in accordance with how I define my love for others.

God's love for us can certainly be defined as a strong affection arising out of kinship. He is our Heavenly "Father,"—kinship. Our love for God should also be based on our admiration for Him and our common interests with Him.

We could discuss the meaning of love and God's love for days and days and probably not accomplish the feat of defining either one. But for the sake of simplicity, let's begin by believing we are created by God, and God is love. *We* are created in the image of God, and therefore, *we* are love.

Any way we try to look at it, and anyway we try to define it, we must agree love is the key to God and His kingdom.

God loves you. Love Him, love yourself and love others.

April 18

> *This is how God showed his love among us: He sent His one and only Son into the world that we might live through Him.* 1 John 4:9

God sent Jesus to show how much He loved us. The kind of love we share with God is called "agape" love, while the kind of love we share with one another is referred to as "phileo" love. Agape love requires a relationship with God through Jesus Christ and is a love that gives and sacrifices, expecting nothing in return. That is how God loves us; unconditionally and expecting nothing in return.

Phileo love, on the other hand, is an emotional kind of love that can be experienced by believers and non-believers alike. It is often translated as "brotherly love."

God wants us to be able to share agape love with Him *and* with one another. But trying to do so by the power of your will is sure to end in failure. Agape love can only be possible through the power of God and faith in Jesus. Even Christians must abide in God to truly experience His agape love and succeed in returning it to Him and others.

I can't say it often enough, and you will read it many times in the coming months, the key to peace, joy, happiness, and life in general, is love. First and foremost, you must believe God loves you unconditionally. Secondly, you must love Him the same way. No holds barred.

April 19

> *This is love: not that we loved God, but that He loved us and sent His Son as an atoning sacrifice for our sins.* 1 John 4:10

I can hardly grasp the reality of what God has done for us. It is huge! Knowing we could not save ourselves, He sent His Son to take all our sins upon Himself. This is a miracle! It's bigger than healing the sick or raising the dead. It's more than walking on water or feeding five-thousand people with five loaves and two fish. It is the ultimate demonstration of God's power and love.

We are forgiven!

We are loved!

So what's the problem today? Why do we live in fear? Why are we sad?

If you ask me, self-imposed guilt is the culprit. Many of us—I'm just as guilty as anyone—spend the majority of our waking hours dwelling on our fears and insecurities. Everyone has them, but not everyone realizes they don't have to keep holding on to them. In John 3:17, Jesus said, *"For God did not send His Son into the world to condemn the world, but to save the world through Him."* And in Romans 8:1 Paul tells us, *"Therefore, there is now no condemnation for those who are in Christ Jesus."*

We condemn ourselves! We feel guilty about things we've done, said, or thought. God tells us over and over and over He loves us, and we sit off in a dark corner, telling ourselves he must be talking to someone else because we are not worthy of His love. Stop it!

You are forgiven! God loves you! Believe it!

April 20

Dear friends, since God so loved us, we also ought to love one another.
1 John 4:11

I'm sure you will agree with me when I say some people are hard to love. Many times we have neighbors, co-workers, even relatives, that are just downright hard to contend with—much less, love! And I am not going to tell any fibs, I struggle a lot with this.

On the other hand, some folks are quite easy to love. Those are usually the ones who love us, too, though, right? Uh-huh. Those are the easy ones. Them and the ones we call, "like-minded." You know what I mean; you're a soccer fan-they're a soccer fan, you're a Democrat-they're a Democrat. It's easy to love one another when it's convenient, too. Such as, if you're in a good mood, things are going your way, and you only have to see them for a few seconds as you pass them on the sidewalk.

Let's get back to the hard ones. How do we do that? How do we love the ones that bring us down with their surly moods; the ones that are just plain mean-spirited? You just love them. You don't have to agree with them or put up with them. Give them your best smile (genuine smile), tell them, "How ya doin'" and "Hope you have a nice day," then be on your way. But as you're going on your way, ask God to bless them and help them to understand His love.

I've been around people that were hard to love and seen them change, and I've been around some that never change. It's not our job to change them. We just have to love them, and let them see through our actions that God loves them.

Pick one person you know that is hard to love, start loving them and see what happens.

Oh, come on! God's going to help you!

April 21

No one has ever seen God; but if we love one another, God lives in us and His love is made complete in us. 1 John 4:12

This goes along with something I mentioned yesterday, when I said we have to let people see God is love through our actions. If people see us loving our spouses, sons, daughters, family, and friends in an agape way—unconditionally and expecting nothing in return—they will see the joy and peace that kind of love can bring, and they will want it, too.

God is love. By demonstrating His love in our lives, we make His love complete, in that we love Him and one another completely and unconditionally.

There will probably never be perfect peace in this world, but there will be everlasting joy, love and peace when we finish our part of God's plan on this earth and go to spend eternity with Him. I can't even imagine what that will be like, but I like to hope there will be golf courses that are finer than anything I've ever seen, and there won't be any scorecards!

Seriously, there are some who will never give their lives to God. They will never know the love of God and never be able to share true agape love with anyone. That is why, many times, rich people are miserably unhappy. Their money and possessions has become their God. They love their money and possessions more than anything, but, sadly, their money and possessions can't love them back.

I encourage you to start with the ones you care about most and begin to love them unconditionally, expecting nothing in return. I bet that love comes back to you big-time!

April 22

And so we know and rely on the love God has for us. God is love. Whoever lives in love lives in God, and God in him. 1 John 4:16

That one statement, *"whoever lives in love lives in God,"* is pretty doggone simple and to the point, don't you think? It seems so simple, in fact, I can't think of another way to put it, other than to say we *must* love if we desire to be a part of God's plan. "Desire to be," being the key phrase.

I also believe a bad person can be a part of God's plan unwittingly and even unwillingly. Sometimes God uses unlikely people and circumstances to forward His plan. A nonbeliever can be put in our path, or allowed to be in our path, to teach us something God wants us to know in order for us to accomplish our part of His work. Instead of judging these bad folks or being angry at them, we should be amused by them (and love them). For in spite of all their angry, defiant posturing, their denying the very existence of God, and whatever various, foolish actions they may perform, they are doing His work.

A circumstance or event may be tragic when it is happening, but in its wake we will sometimes find we've learned from it. I have had instances in the past where what appeared to be the utter destruction of my personal world turned out to be a blessing in disguise. I am learning to endure and plow through troubles, knowing victory, in one form or another, awaits me on the other side of almost every situation.

In the end, it all comes back to love. When troubles or evil people come into your life, continue to love God and love others. Live in love, and you live in God. And as Paul said in Romans 8:31, *"If God is for us, who can be against us."*

If you live in love, you live in God, and no foe or situation can stand against God!

April 23

In this way, love is made complete among us so that we will have confidence on the day of judgment, because in this world we are like Him. 1 John 4:17

Once again, a much debated and discussed topic is stated so very simply. This verse tells me if we love completely, as God loves us, then we are like Him and will spend eternity with Him.

Many Bible scholars and religious folks will try and tell you that is not enough. They will dissect and interpret verse after verse that tells us we must do this and do that, and then do this and then do that, and on and on they go! I believe we are saved by grace, and when we profess Jesus is Lord and allow God's love to be in us, we're done. God does the rest. We are, after all, saved by grace, not by what we do or not do.

I must re-emphasize to you I am no expert in the field of religion, and I don't claim to be knowledgeable in the ways and desires of God. I am merely telling you what I believe in hopes it will encourage you.

In essence, what I am doing with these daily writings is loving and encouraging each person that reads them. Actually, I can go a step further and say I love those that choose not to read them also, by merely writing them, thereby offering my love and encouragement to anyone who chooses to accept it.

I encourage you today to know if love is in your heart, God is there also. And conversely, if God is in your heart, love is there also.

How cool is that?

April 24

> *There is no fear in love. But perfect love drives out fear, because fear has to do with punishment. The one who fears is not made perfect in love.* 1 John 4:18

That's what I'm talking about!

If anyone reading this is near where I am today, could you stop by and see me? I have a tremendous need to high-five somebody after reading this verse!

If you have read my encouragements based on not being afraid, you have to know this verse excites me tremendously. It says it all!

There is no fear in love! If you love unconditionally, expecting nothing in return, what is there to be afraid of? On the other hand, if you love expecting something—anything—in return, even love returned, you will, in most instances, be afraid of being rejected and disappointed. Rejection is the punishment brought upon you because of your fear.

How then can we define "perfect love?" My definition would be that perfect love is the love we feel when it comes through us from God. If we first love God with all our heart, He will love others through us.

God loves you unconditionally, and He will never reject you or disappoint you.

There is no fear in love!

April 25

If anyone says, "I love God," yet hates his brother, he is a liar. For anyone who does not love his brother, whom he has seen, cannot love God, whom he has not seen. 1 John 4:20

If you believe Jesus died on the cross and rose again so we can spend eternity with Him and our Heavenly Father, then we are brothers.

In today's verse, God does not tell us we should love those we are like-minded with or those who do things the way we believe they should be done. He doesn't tell us we should only love our brothers in Christ. What He does tell us here is if we truly love God, we will love our brothers. Not by our own volition, but by God loving through us with His perfect love. If we try to love on our own without God, we will fail.

That might sound complicated to you, but it always comes back to the one simple fact: Love God. If you do, He will take care of the details.

Love God first today, and I believe you will begin to see your brothers, who don't necessarily think and do as you do, will start to appear more loveable to you. Shoot, it might even start to work on some of the bad guys!

April 26

And He has given us this command: Whoever loves God must also love his brother. 1 John 4:21

The key word in this verse is, "must."

God doesn't tell us if we love Him, He would appreciate it if we love our brothers, also. He says we *must* love our brothers.

I'm no different than many of you. When I first hear the word "must," my rebellious nature rears its ugly head, and I want to find a way around whatever it is I've been told I *must* do.

In this case, I have to take a look at what God is saying, and all of a sudden the rebel in me is nodding his head and saying, "Hey, I see what He's saying!"

What I believe John is saying is not we must, as in we have to, but we must, as in it only makes sense that we do. We don't love our brothers because God says we have to, we love them because when we first love God, He places within us the ability to love others.

So you see, we are not being *ordered* to do anything, we are simply being told if we love God, then by His grace we *will* love others.

Works for me!

April 27

And a voice from heaven said, "This is my Son, whom I love; with Him I am well pleased." Matthew 3:17

I can remember times when I was growing up and my dad was proud of something I'd done. I can also remember times when he wasn't pleased with what I'd done. The thing was, my dad seemed to remember my failures as much or more than he remembered my accomplishments. I can't remember any specifics, but a for-instance would be: "Hey, dad, I'm going to wash your car for you." "Okay, son, but don't scratch it like you did last summer." He didn't remember all the times I'd washed the car well since the summer before, he only remembered the time I did it wrong.

We tend to do this in many of our personal relationships. Our spouse, child, relative or friend can be a wonderful companion most of the time, but one little slip-up and suddenly they are the scourge of our life. And oftentimes, we store that incident in our memory banks and remind them of it when they slip up again.

God, fortunately for us, does not operate that way, and if we love Him, neither will we. God forgives us when we make mistakes, and when we commit to love God, we will forgive others when they make mistakes.

Today, just do one thing; accept the fact that God loves you unconditionally. Do that, and He will let His love shine through you to everyone around you.

April 28

> *"You have heard that it was said, 'Love your neighbor and hate your enemy.' But I tell you: Love your enemies and pray for those who persecute you, that you may be sons of your Father in heaven. He causes His sun to rise on the evil and the good, and sends rain on the righteous and unrighteous.* Matthew 5: 43-44

Again, we are confronted with the task of loving those we would rather not love. We must look to God as our supreme example and take note of the fact that we—most of us—were not worthy of His love and forgiveness, yet he gave it to us anyway.

One of the most difficult things is to not judge people. If you judge them, you are expecting something from them—that they do as you think they should—and; therefore, you do not love them the same way God does.

Jesus points out that our enemies live beneath the same sun and rain we do. This goes back to what I've said before; even our enemies and trials can be a part of God's purpose and plan. And as I have said before, we don't have to embrace those who come against us, but we do have to love them. But remember, God will do the loving through us if we love Him.

I must tell you that as I write these messages, the question often arises; how can I talk about and expound upon one subject—love—approximately 250 times, without being repetitive? The answer is, I can't. Sometimes, I believe we need to hear the same thing—the same positive thing—day after day. I know I have read or heard things over and over for years, and then one time, it is written or spoken in just the right way and "ding", I suddenly understand.

Hopefully, you won't get bored with the subject of love, and one of these days, you will hear a little bell—maybe you already have—and are able to shout, "Hey! I get it!"

April 29

If you love those who love you, what reward will you get. Are not even the tax collectors doing that? Matthew 5:46

The point of this verse is it is easy to love those who love us. It is easy, for instance, for me to love my wife and my mother because they love me and think I can do no wrong. It should therefore be easy for me to love God because he loves me even more than those two do. And that's a lot, let me tell you.

But loving those that don't love us is a challenge. I know I've hurt people and disappointed people throughout my life, and it's hard for some of them to love me because of the things I've done. I also know I can be abrasive at times, and my sarcastic sense of humor can hurt folks. I'm working on those things, but in many instances, the damage has already been done, and all I can do is ask the people I've hurt to forgive me and try to show them I really do love them. But sometimes, I don't want to love them.

That's where God comes in. I don't want to love those people because they think I'm a bad person. They think the things I've said and done are unforgiveable. So I say, "that's fine with me," and go on down the road. But God says, "No, love them regardless of how they feel about you!"

And I say, "God, I can't do that! Can you help me to do it?"

God says, "Deal! Let's do this!"

April 30

"No one can serve two masters. Either he will hate the one and love the other, or he will be devoted to the one and despise the other. You cannot serve both God and money." Matthew 6:24

Oh, boy. This is the one that gets most of us. How do we live in this world that revolves around money and possessions and put God first in our lives? We are bombarded on a daily basis with the need to make more money so we can buy more stuff or to put money in the bank so we can be secure for the future. The answer is simple: put God first, love God more than money, possessions or anything this world might offer you.

I look at it this way; the things of this world are temporary. Nothing we own will go with us when our days on earth are done and we go to live for eternity with God. Every possession we have is on loan from God. Every good thing He allows us to enjoy is His. It doesn't matter if it is money, houses, cars or golf clubs, we are only using it because God loves us and wants us to enjoy our time here.

I believe the key is not to want anything. Like Paul said to the Philippians in verse eleven of chapter four, "… for I have learned to be content whatever the circumstances." If we can be content with what we have and stop wanting more, then we will be truly happy. But the world encourages us to want more. Our economic system has become a dog chasing its tail—a vicious cycle of spend and sell that has to continue or chaos will set upon us. We don't have to be a part of it. Let the dogs spin. We can slide to the side and be content with what we have, all the while knowing the things of this earth have no meaning and are temporary. God does not recognize "economic crisis".

Love God, not things. Things are temporary. God is forever!

May 1

"Here is my servant whom I have chosen, the one I love, in whom I delight; I will put my Spirit on him, and he will proclaim justice to the nations." Matthew 12:18

These were the words spoken by Isaiah, the prophet in the Old Testament. God had foretold of the coming of Christ long before He sent Him to atone for our sins. Jesus was the way God chose to bring us close to Him. He had given us free will, and we could not handle the responsibility. Jesus, God's chosen one—the one in whom He delights—came to proclaim justice for us.

I may not have dissected that correctly in the eyes of Biblical scholars and the religiously educated, but that is the way it seems to me.

God sent the "one" He loves, so we all could love Him. By accepting Jesus and the grace He bought for us, we are now able to love God without fear. We can love Him with agape love—unconditionally.

God is not asking us to do anything to repay Him or thank Him for sending His Son to atone for our sins. He is merely asking us to love Him. I'm telling you, it is that simple. There is nothing we can do to gain God's love or increase it. Jesus did it all over two-thousand years ago.

All you *have* to do today is love God and let Him love others through you. When your first priority is to love God, your light shines bright, and others are drawn to you like moths to a porch light. People are attracted by the light and comforted by the warmth that is the love of God emanating from you when you are in tune with Him and His plans.

God loves you unconditionally. Love Him the same way. He'll do the rest.

May 2

> While h*e was still speaking, a bright cloud enveloped them, and a voice said, "This is my Son. Whom I love; with him I am well pleased. Listen to him!"* Matthew 17:5

Jesus had taken three of His disciples to the top of a mountain. He was transfigured before them and was talking to Moses and Elijah, who had suddenly appeared. And the three disciples did what?

They told Jesus they could build shelters for Him, Elijah and Moses. Don't get me wrong, I think they were probably awed by what was going on and thought they must be there to serve these Holy men. They probably talked to each other and decided they should do something besides gawk at the scene before them.

Then God said, "Would you three just *listen!*"

We do the same thing so many times in our lives. God wants us to listen and learn, and what we do is scurry around trying to *do* things to please Him. We need to recognize that, sometimes, all God wants from us is our attention focused on Him. He's not impressed by the things we do; He is impressed by what's in our heart.

This morning, or sometime during the day, be still for a few moments, focus on God, and just listen. I believe if you do, God will be well pleased.

May 3

'Honor your father and your mother,' and 'love your neighbor as yourself.' Matthew 19:19

Jesus was talking to a young, wealthy man when He quoted these two commandments. The young man had asked Jesus what he must do to have everlasting life. Jesus told the young man other commandments he must obey also, and the man said he had obeyed them all, then asked Jesus what else he should do. Jesus told him to sell or give away all his possessions and come follow Him. The man went away, sad.

I believe this story is an illustration of the fact that it doesn't matter what we do—obey the commandments, good deeds, etc.—if we do not follow Jesus. I believe good deeds –works—and holy living mean nothing if we do not completely surrender our lives to the Lord.

By complete surrender, I mean accepting Jesus as the only way to eternal life and having complete faith that He is in charge of each and every step you take. If you give yourself over to Him, He will do the things He needs done through you.

Today, try focusing your attention on God. Don't think about what you have to do to please Him; just love Him. I believe if we can learn to do this, a peace like nothing we've ever known will settle upon our lives.

May 4

> *Jesus replied: "'Love the Lord your God with all your heart and with all your soul and with all your mind.' This is the first and greatest commandment."* Matthew 22:37-38

This is what Jesus told the Pharisees in answer to their question, "Which is the greatest commandment in the law?"

That drives home the point I am trying to make with these writings based on love.

Loving God is the beginning, the middle and the end of our earthly life. It is everything forever in our eternal life.

I think it is important to note that the word "all" is used three times in this statement Jesus makes to the Pharisees; "*all* your heart, *all* your soul, and *all* your mind." With your every fiber, loving God should be your first effort.

Please don't be confused and think that by this, Jesus means we should do nothing all day except sit and love God. Surely, it would make for a strange world if we all did that. I believe what He is telling us is to Love God "all the way," not just halfheartedly. For instance, if you are going to hit a baseball with a bat, and you don't concentrate on the effort of making contact—bat to ball, you will either miss the ball completely or not hit it squarely. The same can be said about loving God: if you don't give it your best effort—your all—you will not make good contact with Him.

Love God first and with all you've got. Imagine the solid crack of the bat meeting the ball and watch as it soars out of sight.

May 5

"And the second is like it: 'Love your neighbor as yourself.'"
Matthew 22:39

Would all of you reading this that don't love yourself, please raise your hand?

In case you are wondering, I did not raise my hand. Today.

I have to admit there are times—too many times—when I do not love myself. But I am most happy to tell you those times are becoming fewer as I begin to grasp the enormity and totality of God's love.

My point is if we do not love God first, this second of His commands is impossible. Yes, impossible. Why? Because we cannot love ourselves or our neighbor if we do not first love God. To try and love our self or our neighbor without loving God first is to try and <u>do</u> it on our own. Loving God first allows Him to love us; we, then, love ourselves, and as a result, we can love our neighbor with the love of God that lives within us. That sounds complicated, doesn't it? Kind of like the "who's on first" routine by Abbot and Costello?

Take it back to step one—the greatest commandment; the only thing we have to commit to; loving God. He will take care of the rest.

May 6

Because of the increase of wickedness, the love of most will grow cold. But he who stands firm to the end will be saved. Matthew 24:12-13

Sometimes it seems we are in the time Jesus was talking about as He explained to the disciples what the signs of the end of the age and His second coming would be. The world around us seems to become more loveless and cold with each passing day.

But is it? Or are the ones that would have us turn our attention away from God trying to convince us that it is?

There is so much good around us, but the media makes a tremendous attempt to show us only the bad. And, unfortunately, a large portion of our population is quite eager to believe all they see and hear on the old boob-tube. I have a simple solution: turn it off.

Personally, I can hardly watch the things on television any more. Part of the reason is that I live in a place—Central Texas—where the weather outside is much too nice for me to want to be inside watching television, but mostly it's because there is just too much junk on it these days. It's gotten so bad, in my opinion, that one can almost change the popular quote "the love of money is the root of all evil," to "the love of television is the root of all evil." But in reality, what drives them to put the things on television they do is, you guessed it, money.

Don't let your love grow cold. In this time when wickedness seemingly runs rampant, look to God, not to the world. He is still in charge!

May 7

"He had one left to send, a son, whom he loved. He sent him last of all, saying, 'They will respect my son.'" Mark 12:6

Jesus used examples—parables—to teach people. In this parable, Jesus compares the actions of the chief priests, the teachers of the law, and the elders He is speaking to, to the actions of evil men in His story. The men He is telling the parable to understand what He has told them, and it angers them. They want to have Jesus arrested for condemning them in this manner.

This—the anger of learned men—was all part of God's plan. If they had accepted Jesus for who, and what he was, and Jesus had not given His life so we might be saved, what would have become of us? I surely can't answer that question, and I doubt anyone can. It would all be conjecture.

My point, though, is the men who ultimately crucified Jesus did so not knowing they were being used by God. God uses even unbelievers to accomplish His ultimate plan. His plan was to send His Son, whom He loved, as a last resort to save His people—us.

God's ultimate plan is for us to spend eternity with Him, loving Him and being loved by Him. Our part is simply to love God. He will take care of the details.

May 8

"But I tell you who hear me: Love your enemies, do good to those who hate you," Luke 6:27

Jesus said, "But I tell you who *hear* me." It seems to me when He said that, He was indicating not everyone will hear what He has to say. I can definitely relate to that.

I spent much of my life, and will probably spend some of it in the future, not hearing what God was telling me. I did not hear because I was not listening. I had my mind on me and not on God. I thought—much like I thought when I was a teenager and my dad was none too bright in my opinion—I knew it all and could do it on my own, without God. And so, I did not seek Him and His instruction.

I can remember typical conversations with my dad during my teenage years. One of His favorite things was to tell me what I thought about whatever subject we were arguing about. For instance, he would say, "You think you're so smart, don't you?" I would reply with my own question: "How do you know what I think?" In a way, my dad did know what I thought about many things because he had been there and done that, as the saying goes.

On a much larger and complete scale, God knows *exactly* what we are thinking. He hasn't been-there-done-that, but He has certainly seen it all before. In fact, there is nothing we can do, say or think that God hasn't seen or heard before.

Seek what God has to say today, and listen to Him.

Hear Him.

May 9

"If you love those who love you, what credit is that to you? Even 'sinners' love those who love them." Luke 6:32

    I believe the point Jesus is trying to make with this and the verses that follow is we are to love everyone unconditionally, expecting nothing in return, and we are to do it regardless of whether or not they love us. If we love only those who love us, we are doing so because we can do it without fear of rejection. Ha! So we're back to the "fear" thing!

    Yes, we will probably revisit the "fear" thing often, for I believe many times it is the reason we do not love. We fear if we go out on a limb and love someone first, we are setting ourselves up for a big fall. That is why I believe we must first love God and love others second. Once we understand God is with us, and it is Him loving others through us, the fear of failure will be gone.

    Remember, God *is* love. If He is in us, then *we* are love, and loving others is not a choice we make but something that comes from within.

    First step: Love God

May 10

But love your enemies, do good to them, and lend to them, without expecting to get anything back. Then your reward will be great, and you will be sons of the Most High, because he is kind to the ungrateful and wicked. Luke 6:35

I do not know where I got the idea—perhaps it came from this verse—but I long ago began to use one of the principles in this verse; when I would loan money to someone, I would tell them it was not a loan, but a gift. If they chose to pay it back, that would be good, but they didn't have to. Many of them paid back what I loaned them, some of them didn't.

But most of those I made that deal with were friends. If someone I did not care for were to ask me for a loan, I don't know if I could offer the same deal to them. That would be difficult to come to terms with. I would definitely have to give the situation to God and let Him handle it.

You know what that means, don't you? It seems to me to mean if I am willing to give the situation over to God and let Him make the decision for me, then I'm going to loan the money, or whatever it might be, to that person. Because that is what God would do.

Man! Sometimes this stuff is hard to swallow! It's like taking medicine that tastes bad. You know it's what you need to do, but you are hesitant to do it.

Here's what I think we should do. Let's you and I do the easy part: love God. He will do the rest through us.

I can do that!

May 11

When they came to Jesus they pleaded earnestly with him, "This man deserves to have you do this, because he loves our nation and has built our synagogue." So Jesus went with them. Luke 7:4-6

The elders who approached Jesus had been sent by a centurion (a Roman officer) to ask Jesus to heal his servant, who was sick and about to die.

It is interesting to me that this—the New International Version—translation of the Bible uses the word "so" to start the 6th verse. That would indicate to me Jesus was going to heal the centurion's servant because the messenger he had sent told Jesus he deserved it. In other translations, the word used to start the 6th verse is, "then", or "and", which makes more sense to me. I don't think it made any difference to Jesus what the centurion had done to deserve the healing of the servant. I believe Jesus' only concern was that the servant be healed. He didn't need a reason to do it.

I don't want to get started trying to interpret different translations of the Bible. That is far from my intent with these writings. But I felt it necessary to point out this one for the reasons stated in the preceding paragraph.

Jesus ultimately healed the centurion's servant, and He did so because of the centurion's faith. In most recorded cases of healings performed by Jesus, the only requirement was faith. Can we tie faith to love for the sake of maintaining our theme in these writings? I think we can do that quite easily. We have determined that God is love, correct? So if we have faith in God, then we have faith in love. Therefore, the centurion's servant was healed because the centurion loved God.

Simple!

May 12

"Two men owed money to a certain moneylender. One owed him five hundred denarii, and the other fifty. Neither of them had the money to pay him back, so he canceled the debts of both. Now which of them will love him more?" Luke 7:41-42

Jesus uses this parable to demonstrate to Simon that those who have sinned much will love God more when He forgives them than those who have sinned little.

Well… that explains why I love God so much!

It's like those contests they have at class reunions where they give a prize to the person who traveled the greatest distance to be at the reunion. I never win those contests, but I always have to travel a good distance to be at the gathering. And that's about how it is with me and God. I know there are others that have done worse than I have and drifted farther from God than I have. But I also know I have done a pretty good job of wandering from place to place not heeding His direction for my life.

As a result, now that I have turned to Him and seek His guidance in my life, my love for Him is huge! I am constantly amazed at how He sat patiently on that rock, watching and waiting for me all the time I was wandering around on the other side of the river. And I wasn't just wandering in an aimless, innocent way. I was doing things that I know broke His heart to watch, yet He never stopped loving me, and He never gave up on me. I was His, and He knew I'd come home.

My love for God is tremendous. I love God unconditionally, and I want nothing more than to be able to serve Him in whatever way He wants me to serve. I am reminded just now of a line from an old country song by, George Jones. I hear God singing those lines to me now; *Walk through this world with Me, go where I go.*

I'm going.

May 13

"Therefore, I tell you, her many sins have been forgiven—for she loved much. But he who has been forgiven little loves little." Luke 7:47

I have been forgiven so much by God! I am a sinner! I am the person God sent Jesus to atone for. I wish it wasn't so, but it is! I am the typical sinner God looks down upon and sadly shakes His head. But I love Him! And He loves me!

And… I love much!

Those of you that know me know I am a loving person. I am a servant. I care not what you can do for me, I care only about what I can do for you.

And so, I know what love is. Love is God. God is love.

How can we then not love each other? How can we not love one another unconditionally? This is a mystery to me.

If I love you unconditionally, expecting nothing in return, and you love me in the same way, who gets hurt? Who wins?

Answer: Nobody gets hurt, and everybody wins.

The key is to love *unconditionally*, expecting *nothing* in return.

Try it.

May 14

> *"Woe to you Pharisees, because you give God a tenth of your mint, rue and all other kinds of garden herbs, but you neglect justice and the love of God. You should have practiced the latter without leaving the former undone.* Luke 11:42

I think what Jesus was trying to convey to the Pharisees was that their tithing and good works were of no value if they did not first love God. The way of the world is to make us think things are the key to happiness. And while I agree that things—possessions—are nice, and things can bring comfort and happiness, things are of no value if God is not at the center and forefront of our lives.

Likewise, we sometimes think if we do good things and follow God's commandments, living a moral and decent life, we can *do* our way into His good graces. God doesn't work that way. Your supervisor at your job might accept that as perfectly good operating procedure, but your supervisor, in most cases, could care less what you think of him. He just wants you to do your job and do it well. And even though you might think he's the greatest guy or gal in the world and you simply adore him or her, if you don't do your job, he/she will probably look to replace you.

That is the good news about God; all He wants is for us to love Him. Anything else we do is second in importance to God. And in my opinion, if we love God first, doing the right thing will get to where it is automatic with us. God will work through us to accomplish His plan for our lives and the lives of those around us.

Today and every day, start the day by saying, "I love God."

May 15

"Woe to you Pharisees, because you love the most important seats in the synagogues and greetings in the marketplaces." Luke 11:43

Pharisees were known for their strict observance of rites and ceremonies of the written law. By what we read about them in the Bible, they appeared to think of themselves as celebrities, too. In our country, we should be able to relate to the celebrity the Pharisees thought they were. We have always been, and seem to becoming more so, a people that places men and women of fame high on a pedestal. And many of those we place there, start thinking they are the cat's meow.

In a 2008 football game, a well known and accomplished college quarterback wore a Bible verse in the eye-black under his eyes during what was deemed a very important game. To me, it was a refreshing thing to see a person of his stature taking the opportunity of being on a big stage to show his love for God. Unfortunately, our society has become one that looks down upon Christians that do such things. Non-believers bemoaned the sports arena was no place for God. Their *important* event was tarnished by such blatant disregard for what to them was important: the game.

Yet if a player scores a touchdown and wants to do some foolish dance in the end zone, those same people are outraged when the player is fined and/or punished for a frivolous—"fun"—display to self-acknowledge his conquering of the opposition.

Getting back to the point, if we love God, it will show. We won't have to paint it on our face, sit in the best seats, or receive accolades in the marketplace. Our love will show because God will put a huge smile or grin on our face no opposition has the power to erase.

I'm wearing one now!

May 16

"For God so loved the world that He gave His one and only Son, that whoever believes in Him shall not perish but have everlasting life.
John 3:16

I think this has to be the most quoted Bible verse ever, and it pretty much says it all. But to me, the most important thing it says is God so loved us. He made the ultimate sacrifice to show us just how much He loves us, and all He asks in return is we believe in what He did for us.

And what is the reward for merely believing He sent Jesus to atone for us? It is we will have everlasting life with our heavenly Father. It seems like a pretty good deal to me!

I will be the first to admit none of this is as easy as I make it sound. In fact, at times it seems overwhelmingly difficult. Some days we just can't seem to find the strength and faith within us to smile and say, "What a glorious day the Lord has made!" The world has brought us down, and we can't find a reason to get back up. I am learning when I run into days like those, I sometimes just have to hang on until the feeling passes. It's weird sometimes, too, because the feeling of dread or despair seems to come out of nowhere.

I have an ace up my sleeve for times like those, though. I have a partner—my precious wife and best friend, Sherry—who is always there to encourage me and help me to see through the situation. I like to think I do the same for her when the roles are reversed.

I hope you have someone like Sherry in your life, and if you don't, I pray God will send a special friend to you soon.

May 17

The father loves the Son and has placed everything in His hands.
John 3:35

God had an ace up His sleeve, too. And when He sent Jesus to die on the cross for our sins, He played it. He knew all along He would have to play the Jesus card because He knew man could not be saved unless He did. And fortunately for us, God wanted us to be with Him for eternity. So He played His trump card because He loved us so much, and He could not see spending eternity without us. How awesome is that?

I want to love like that! I want to give everything I have to God and my family and friends so we can all be together with God forever. If loving unconditionally is what it takes, then I want to do it! And I truly believe if I just focus on God and love Him with all I've got, He will put that kind of love in me. In fact, I will go a step further and say I think that kind of love is already in me; it just needs to be unleashed. The world has bound the love that exists in me and you, and if we will simply turn from the things of this world and lift our faces to God, He will remove our bindings and set the love within us free.

Wow! I think I'm onto something!

May 18

"But I know you. I know that you do not have the love of God in your hearts. John 5:42

The Jews did not believe Jesus was the Son of God and wanted to kill Him. Jesus told them they did not believe Him because they did not have the love of God in their hearts.

Everything keeps coming back to the love of God doesn't it? Before I began writing these encouragements, I had made statements to the effect that God's love and our loving Him in return was the key to understanding Him, but as I read these verses and write about what they are saying to me, that fact keeps getting larger and larger.

I'm beginning to think that is why God impressed me to write these encouragements; so I would fully understand His love.

Well, it's working! Man! It is working big time!

I will let you in on another tidbit of information. Remember those bad days I talked about in an encouragement a few days ago? Well, I was having one today, and the more I write, the better I feel!

Go figure!

May 19

Jesus said to them, "If God were your Father, you would love me, for I came from God and now am here. I have not come on my own; but He sent me. John 8:42

The Jews argued to Jesus that God was their Father, yet they refused to believe Jesus was sent by God. Jesus explained it very simply to them when He told them if they truly knew God and he was indeed their Father, they would love Him.

I believe what Jesus is saying here, is if we do not first love God, we cannot believe He sent Jesus to die on the cross for us. That makes perfect sense to me. How can we believe in Jesus if we don't believe in God?

I remember back in the sixties when it became popular with some to proclaim God was dead. I was amazed then, and even more amazed today, that anyone could have thought such a thing. If God were dead, then love would be absent from our world, for He is love. Love would be dead!

Can you imagine a world completely devoid of love? Now, there is a horror movie for you!

I cannot imagine being in a world where God and love do not exist.

May 20

The reason my Father loves me is that I lay down my life—only to take it up again. John 10:17

In this chapter of John, Jesus is trying to explain to the Jews they can only gain eternal life with God if they believe God sent Jesus to die for them and He would be raised on the third day. Some of the Jews thought this man Jesus was demon-possessed and raving mad and wondered why anyone would listen to Him.

The Jews who could not believe Jesus were those who knew nothing of God but what the laws said. They did not love God; they professed to love Him because they were obeying His laws. They did not understand that by fulfilling prophesies and sending His Son, God was seeking their love.

I believe the rules are what keep a lot of people away from God and Jesus. All they see is what will be required of them by the laws and rules of whatever church might be trying to attract them. In my opinion, the best way to invite people to know Christ and God is to tell them all God wants them to do is love Him. Tell them if they do just that one thing—love God—they have done their part, and God can then begin a work in them and take care of all the details.

I believe it is that simple. God loves us, and all He wants in return is for us to love Him.

May 21

For they loved praise from men more than praise from God.
John 12:43

I think this verse just about says it all when it comes to living in this world. Way too often, we are concerned with what those around us think and say, and we forget that the only one who really matters is God.

We let the same thing happen in our personal relationships, too. We are often more concerned about what our friends think than what our spouse thinks. And unfortunately, we might even put our friend's needs in front of those of our spouse.

I've made many mistakes in my relationships, and I have to admit I am a slow learner. But one thing I have learned is the best way to make a relationship work is to do your best to out-love the other person, and do it expecting nothing in return. If you can truly commit to that, and you want nothing for yourself and all for the one you love, you cannot fail. I say this with one very large qualification; the other person must love you, also. They may not be as committed as you in the beginning, but if they love you, they will respond and eventually you will both be doing your best to out-love each other. And *that* is a recipe for success.

Love unconditionally! Give it all you have!

After all, that's how God loves you!

May 22

> *It was just before the Passover Feast. Jesus knew that the time had come for Him to leave this world and go to the Father. Having loved His own who were in the world, He now showed them the full extent of His love.* John 13:1

I do not pretend to know what all that Jesus said or did means, but I do know what He did at this gathering was wash the feet of the disciples. From things I have read and been taught, I believe the act was symbolic, and He was washing their feet to symbolize the complete forgiveness He was about to give all mankind.

In the days when Jesus walked this earth there were no paved roads or concrete sidewalks. Men wore sandals or went barefoot, and though they might have bathed recently, their feet were usually dirty when they arrived at their destination. The washing of His loved ones feet was an act of servitude, and Jesus asked that when He was gone they remember to act the same way toward each other as He was acting toward them.

I can almost feel the sad love coursing through Jesus as He knelt before His disciples and washed the dust and mud from their feet. I can imagine His touch was gentle and yet firm. Perhaps an unnoticed tear traced down His cheek. A tear quickly wiped away with the towel He was using to dry the feet of those who had so faithfully followed Him on His earthly walk.

Those were our feet Jesus was washing. It was for us He gently wiped away the mud and dust. The tear he might have wiped away… was for you and me.

He asked for nothing in return. Only that we believe.
And He hoped…. we would love Him.
I believe.
I love Him.

May 23

"A new command I give you: Love one another. As I have loved you, so you must love one another." John 13:34

Jesus commanded us to love one another as He loved us. He didn't suggest we do it; He didn't ask us to do it; He commanded us to do it. I believe He commanded us to love one another much the same way a mother tells her children, "Be nice to your brother!"

Jesus wants us to love each other the way He loves us; unconditionally.

I know I repeat that a lot, but I just can't help believing it is the key to God and His kingdom. The phrase, "God is love," keeps coming back into my mind over and over until it is as if it's my only thought. Like a song I can't get out of my mind, it keeps playing again and again. If there's not a song called God is Love, maybe I should write one.

But for now, I want to encourage you to obey the command Jesus gave us. Love one another.

Love without asking anything in return.

May 24

"By this all men will know that you are my disciples, if you love one another." John 13:35

Again, Jesus drives home the point that love is the key by pointing out to His disciples all men will know they are His disciples by the fact they love one another and they love their brothers in Christ.

That is how the world will know we are followers of Christ—if we are full of God's love. If we are truly filled with God's love—with God—then it will show. It won't be a concerted effort on our part to love one another; it will just *be*.

I think this is what Jesus is saying. I don't think he is actually ordering His disciples and us to do anything—obey commands, love, etc.; I think what He is saying is if we love Him and love God, love will be what we are, not what we do.

God is love. God created us in His image.

We are love.

May 25

"If you love me, you will obey what I command." John 14:15

Jesus does not say if we love Him we *have* to obey what He commands. He says if we love Him, we *will* obey what He commands. This says to me we do not have to make a choice to do as Jesus commands, but rather if we make the choice to love Jesus, we will do His commands without even thinking about it.

I'm telling you, the more I read about it and the more I write about it, the more convinced I become God has set this up so that it is easy! All we have to do is commit to loving God, and the rest will fall into place!

God is love! Love is God! We are created in His image! We are love!

So get out there and love!

May 26

"Whoever has my commands and obeys them, he is the one who loves me. He who loves me will be loved by my Father, and I too will love him and show myself to him." John 14:21

I am not going to pursue translations and word uses, but John uses the word "command" many times in his recounting of the things Jesus said. I wonder if many of those times the word is not used in the sense Jesus *orders* His disciples and us to do them, but, rather, *desires* we do them. It seems to me to love God is the highest and most important commandment for a reason, and the reason is because if we first love God—completely—we will do the rest of His commandments without even thinking about them. They will be in us as they are in God, and we will do them automatically.

What I'm saying is I believe Jesus is not telling us to obey His commands/commandments because we love Him, He is saying when we love Him we will obey, and that is how people around us will know we are His followers. It's kind of like the chicken and the egg question—which came first. Only in this situation, I believe it is easy to tell which should be first—loving God.

I am increasingly (as you can plainly see) of the opinion loving God is our number one assignment, and if we don't accomplish it, then everything we try to do is of our own accord and of little consequence.

The first of the Ten Commandments tells the people of Israel, "You shall have no other god's before me." I believe the other nine commandments can become so important we forget the first one; and thereby, we are worshipping God's commandments instead of loving Him.

Concentrate on the one thing today—loving God. Make it your priority every day and see what happens.

May 27

> *Jesus replied, "If anyone loves me, he will obey my teaching. My Father will love him, and we will come to him and make our home with him."* John 14:23

Notice the first thing Jesus says in this verse—if anyone loves me; then the second—he will obey my teaching. I don't think He said those things in that order by accident. I think He is clearly saying what I have been telling you for several days now. (Oh come on now! It has not been weeks!)

I guess when it comes to loving God, I'm like a dog with an old sock; I won't let go! I just think it's too big and too important to let go. I think it is *the* answer!

Actually, I can remember a time when I was younger thinking it was pretty arrogant of God to make loving Him the greatest commandment. But then one day I realized God wasn't commanding us to love Him, He was simply telling us we should do it first. If we don't, nothing else we do will make much difference.

It's so simple, and Jesus says it very plainly in today's verse, "If you love me, you will obey my teaching." And—here's the bonus—if we love Jesus, God will love us, and they will both come to live with us! How can you turn down a deal like that?

There I go again; up on my soapbox, rambling on about loving God.

Y'all let me know when you want me to stop!

I'm going to go love God some more today. Care to join me?

May 28

He who does not love me will not obey my teaching. These words you hear are not my own; they belong to the Father who sent me.
John 14:24

    Jesus reiterates what He said in John 14:23 in this, the very next verse, but He adds that the words He speaks are not His own, but the words of His Father who sent Him. I believe Jesus wants it made perfectly clear He is nothing, and can do nothing, without God. We are the same in that respect. I think what Jesus is saying to the disciples—and to us—is if they love Jesus, they love God. And if they love Jesus, and therefore love God, they will obey the teachings of Jesus who was sent by God.

    Jesus said His words belong to God. Why? Because Jesus loved God with all His heart, soul and mind, and everything Jesus does is an act of His Father working through Him to accomplish His most important plan—the saving of His people.

    None of this could have happened if Jesus did not love God completely. God could not have spoken through Jesus if Jesus had not loved Him. God's plan could not have come to pass if Jesus had not loved Him. Do you see what I'm saying?

    It is the same for you and me. God's plan for our earthly lives, and for our eternal lives, depends on one thing—loving Him. All the rest will fall into place if we do that one thing.

    God is waiting—He's on the edge of His seat—and I can see Him smiling as we walk toward Him, grinning broadly and shouting, "I love you, God!"

May 29

"You heard me say, 'I am going away and I am coming back to you.' If you loved me, you would be glad that I am going to the Father, for the Father is greater than I." John 14:28

One of my favorite sayings is "That's the same thing, only different." It's a way of saying twelve is the same as a dozen, or two words mean the same thing.

It seems to me Jesus said many times, if you loved me, you would _____. And I don't think He is telling us to make a list and make sure to do all those things to prove we love Him. I think what He's saying is we will do those things as a result of loving Him.

Jesus living in this world, dying on the cross, rising on the third day, then leaving us to be with the Father, was God's plan. It was one of the major parts of God's plan. I am grateful for what Jesus did for us, and I am grateful I am part of God's plan.

I might be repeating myself in these encouragements to you, but I think this thing about loving God is worth repeating. I think loving God is literally the key to *everything*. Try to look at them each day as being the same, only different.

And though each day is different, if our love for God is constant—as His is for us—each day will also be a day filled with the same joy as the days past and the days to come.

Ain't it cool?

May 30

But the world must learn that I love the Father and that I do exactly what my Father has commanded me. "Come now; let us leave." John 14:31

Jesus was trying to explain to the disciples why He must leave them. They loved Him and understandably did not want to see Him leave. His explanation to them was simple; He had to go because He loved the Father, His Father, and thus He had to obey His Father's command.

We will never be perfect as Jesus was. We will never be able to obey God as Jesus did; the simple reason being we are human, and we are fallible. I'm not even sure we can love God as much as Jesus did. I am still searching for the release button that will let loose all my love toward God. I know it's here somewhere.

We are constantly barraged with the things of this world and told how important they are to us. Jesus was tempted, too, but He loved God so much and had such faith in God's plan for His life and ours, He could not be tempted beyond what He could endure. God would not allow Jesus to fail. The success of His part in the plan had way too much riding on it.

My encouragement to you is when temptation comes—and it will come—listen for the voice of Jesus saying, "Come now; let us leave," and turn away from the things of this world. Keep those five words handy. Focus on how much God loves you.

Come now; let us leave.

May 31

"As the Father has loved me, so have I loved you. Now remain in my love." John 15:9

If you have ever been so fortunate as to have a son, you know the pride that can well in you when he does something really good. Your pride and love overwhelm you at those times. And even when your son does something he shouldn't, you still love him just as much as when he was doing the good thing. Imagine having a son like Jesus. Wow! You could throw away that *Parenting For Dummies* book!

But even more, can you imagine having a son who loves you as much as Jesus loves God? Now, all you good sons out there, please don't take offense at what I'm saying, but no matter how much you love your dad, I don't think you can love him more than Jesus loves God. In any case, to have a son who loves you that much would be an incredible blessing.

The key to the relationship between God and Jesus was they knew their love for each other had no bounds. They did not have to expect anything from the other in return for their love, because they had complete faith it was already there.

Unconditional love is what God and Jesus shared. Unconditional love is what They give to us.

Love them the same way. You can't lose!

June 1

If you obey my commands, you will remain in my love, just as I have obeyed my Father's commands and remain in His love. John 15:10

Jesus tells his disciples—and us—they must follow His example and love Him as He has loved His Father. I believe He is saying by loving Him as much as He loved God, we will obey His commands. And what is the number one command? Love God.

I can't emphasize enough that this one theme keeps coming back to me time and time again.

It's not only that we should love God, but loving God is the first step toward Him.

It makes me think of when I was a child and a strange dog would approach. I was told the worst thing I could do was to be afraid because the dog could tell I was afraid. Taking it a step further, I thought, if the dog could tell I was afraid, it could probably also tell if I was friendly. I have found when a dog is suddenly in front of me, if my instant reaction is to smile and say, "Hey there, buddy! How you doin'?" the dog will usually accept that I am friend, not foe, and come to me with tail wagging.

My point is my first reaction to the dog was the important one, just as our first step toward God is important. If we approach God with fear or uncertainty, we are approaching Him without love, for I believe love is the opposite of fear, and in unconditional love there can be no uncertainty.

God is waiting for you. His arms are open wide, and He loves you unconditionally. Know you can go to Him today and every day, loving Him with all your heart, and He will never hurt you or let you down.

June 2

My command is this: Love each other as I have loved you. John 15:12

As I have said before, loving God is easy, because we can do so knowing He loves us unconditionally. Loving each other, as Jesus commands us to do, is not so easy to do. We are most times cautious about loving others because we are afraid they won't love us in return.

Therein is the problem: we are expecting something from them. When God loves us, He doesn't expect anything in return. Although I'm going to go out on a limb and say God has a trick up His sleeve. You see, He knows we will love Him back. He knows there can be no other response to His unconditional love than to return it. If we love God, and God is love, then we become part of God and love.

Another dog story comes to mind, but this time the dog is chasing its tail. But maybe that's a good comparison. God's love is like a dog chasing its tail, in the sense it is a continuous circle of sheer joy. When a dog chases its tail, I think it knows it can't catch it, but it loves the chase. Chasing after God and loving Him should be the same way. No matter how much we love Him, we know He loves us more, and there is tremendous joy in trying to catch up with Him in that regard.

Chase God's love today; experience the joy of knowing you can't possibly love Him as much as He loves you. Then watch as the love you share with God begins to spread to those around you.

June 3

Greater love has no one than this, that he lay down his life for his friends. John 15:13

Jesus told the disciples he could no longer call them servants, and because they knew everything He had learned from His Father, He could now call them friends.

I believe in this passage Jesus was telling His disciples—His friends—He was about to make the ultimate sacrifice for them by laying down His life so they could spend eternity with the Lord.

Occasionally, we hear stories of men or women who sacrifice their own lives to save the life or lives of others. I always wonder what I would do if I were in a situation where I could throw myself in the path of danger in order to save another's life. I tend to believe I could do whatever I had to do, especially if it were a loved one or a friend, but one can really never know until the moment is upon them.

Jesus knew His whole life he was going to arrive at a moment in time where He would lay down His life for us. Yet He did so without a second thought. He did so because He loved God and us.

Love God, Jesus, yourself, your family, and your friends.

Love is everything!

June 4

This is my command: Love each other. John 15:17

It's short and sweet, and I think this verse should be one we keep at the very edge of our mind. It's short, to the point and yet so powerful, as Jesus tells us in no uncertain terms He wants us to love each other.

In his autobiography titled, "I Am Third", the great Chicago Bears running back, Gayle Sayers, explained the book's title; God is first, everyone else is second, and he (Gayle Sayers) is third. Although I am not sure if I am in complete agreement with the second and third portion, I do believe Mr. Sayers had the number one thing correct. I wonder if maybe I would say second and third should be a photo finish, with loving yourself ahead by a nose.

My reasoning is I believe we must love God first, or we will not be capable of truly loving ourselves or others. But then I think if we don't love ourselves, how can we love others? Then again, based on all I read in God's word, if we truly love the Lord, He will instill in our hearts a love for our own self and others.

Reading and writing about these verses on love—especially God's love for us—has made a change in me and the way I look at those around me. Be still for a moment today and look at something beautiful God has made, and let your love flow toward God. I think if we could allow that to become a daily habit the world would begin to change before our very eyes.

June 5

I have given them the glory that you gave me, that they may be one as we are one: I in them and you in me. May they be brought to complete unity to let the world know that you sent me and have loved them even as you have loved me. John 17:22-23

Jesus says, "that they may be one as we are one: I in them and you in me." This is a key point I have not yet stressed in these encouragements. That point being there is only one way to God and it is through the acceptance of Jesus as our Lord and Savior. We cannot bypass Jesus and go straight to God. I accept that as a given fact.

The next thing Jesus says is He wants us to be in complete unity, to let the world know God sent Him and loves us as He loves His Son, Jesus. I am sad to say there appears to be little or no unity among God's faithful today. I say this because, even though there might be unity within one group of believers or church, they are, in many cases, not in agreement or unified with most other groups of believers.

Rather than go off on a tangent that will edify no one, I will simply say this: we must purpose in our hearts to love *all* our brothers in Christ, no matter how many or how large our differences might be. I have said for years it troubles me to see so much division and disagreement among believers in Christ, but I hope somehow they are all correct.

If you disagree with your fellow believers, do it with love and understanding. (I did not say with love and *condescending*.) Agree to disagree, but do so with the love of God in your heart. As I stated above, the main thing is that we believe in Jesus and what He did for all of us, and through Him, we are one with Him and share the love of God.

Love others. You don't have to be in total agreement to be in unity.

June 6

> *"Father, I want those you have given me to be with me where I am, and to see my glory, the glory you have given me because you loved me before the creation of the world.* John 17:24

I believe Jesus was telling God He wants us to experience the love God has for Him, His Son. Jesus knows and feels the complete, unrelenting and passionate love God has for Him and wants us to experience that love, too.

I know—at least I hope—every one of you has experienced the feeling of being in love with someone; a feeling that if you could not be with them, you would not know what to do. You were—or are—so in love with the person you would do anything for them.

That is the kind of love God and Jesus share and they want to share with us. Jesus says God knew He would love Jesus even before God created the world. The plan! It always comes back to "the plan." God's plan! God wrote the screenplay for the world and eternity, then He created it. He is writer, producer and director and knows what part each of us will play.

The story is one that includes every possible theme; drama, horror, comedy. But most of all, it is a love story; a love story that will make you weep with joy. Because you see, if you play the part God has assigned you, the story never ends. When you realize how completely and unconditionally God loves you, joy and peace will be yours.

Love lives forever.

June 7

I have made you known to them, and will continue to make you known in order that the love you have for me may be in them and that I myself may be in them." John 17:26

In this verse, Jesus says He has made God known to us *and* He will continue to do so. He is relentless in the pursuit of the task God has set before Him; that being the salvation of God's people.

Jesus knew He was part of God's plan, and He knew there was no margin for error built into what He must do. In fact, Jesus was sent to atone for the margin of error we had stretched to the limit and continue to abuse to this day.

Believe me, if we had to play our parts without retakes, I, for one, would be in trouble. I assure you, the cutting room floor is cluttered with wasted film with my image on it.

But thanks to Jesus—the star of this play we are all performing in—we can try, try again until we get it right. Jesus plays His part so magnificently he covers our bumbling and stumbling until we learn our parts. He carries the show!

As I said previously, the play of life is a never ending saga of many facets, but the overlying theme is love. Jesus is the leading man, and though He outshines us all, He continually points us out to the Director—God—and says, "They are stars as well."

June 8

Then the disciple whom Jesus loved said to Peter, "It is the Lord!" As soon as Simon Peter heard him say, "It is the Lord," he wrapped his outer garment around him (for he had taken it off) and jumped into the water. John 21:17

To most who read this verse, the first thing they notice is the reference to "the disciple whom Jesus loved." This is one of the often discussed and debated mysteries of the Bible. I have not studied it and have little knowledge of it, so I will not try to explain or discuss it. My opinion is Jesus loved all the disciples equally and loves each of us equally. He has no favorites.

Sometimes, people—good people—begin to think they are a better Christian than others and, as a result of those thoughts, begin to act in a very un-Christian manner. Even Christian leaders are susceptible to this. We must all be careful when we begin to understand God and His plan for our life, we don't begin to think we are better than those who do not yet understand.

I believe the best way to remain humble in whatever station you might find yourself is to always remember that without God, and without His love within us, we cannot do His bidding. We are merely the vessels God uses to carry His love to the world, and we are nothing without Him.

As the love for and of the Lord increases in your life, always remember your part in God's plan begins with loving Him. When you love God, He can then use you to do the things He needs done.

He is the potter, we are the clay.

June 9

> *When they had finished eating, Jesus said to Simon Peter, "Simon son of John, do you love Me more than these?" "Yes, Lord," he said, "you know that I love you." Jesus said, "Feed my sheep." Again Jesus said, "Simon son of John, do you truly love me?" He answered, "Yes Lord, you know that I love you." Jesus said, "Take care of my sheep."*
> John 21:15-16

    Chapter 21 of the book of John tells of the third appearance of Christ after His rising. Some of His disciples had gone fishing, and when Jesus appeared to them, He filled their nets with fish. They had fished for quite some time and caught nothing before Jesus appeared to them. They then had breakfast with Jesus, after which He asked the questions of Simon.
    I believe the questions Jesus asked Simon Peter were the questions He asks each of us He has chosen to follow Him; "Do we love Him?" I also believe the commands that followed Simon's answer—"Feed my sheep", and "take care of my sheep"—are what we are also commanded to do.
    First, as always, we must love the Lord. Then by His power and grace, we will feed and care for His people. We will feed them by imparting the wisdom and understanding to them God has placed within us. We will take care of them by demonstrating the love of God through our actions—actions not of our own doing, but done by God who lives within us and through us.
    We are nothing, have nothing, and can give nothing if we do not first love God. When we love God and become love, having been created in His image, then, as it says in Philippians 4:13, "*I can do everything through Him who gives me strength.*"
    Love God and be strengthened.

June 10

The third time he said to him, "Simon son of John, "Do you love me?" Peter was hurt because Jesus asked him the third time, "Do you love me?" He said, "Lord, you know all things; you know that I love you." Jesus said, "Feed my sheep." John 21:17

I can easily relate to Simon Peter's reaction to the repeated question, "Do you love me?" I can also imagine that deep down inside, Simon Peter knew not only did Jesus know he loved Him, he knew every single time he had denied or doubted Him.

I have been given chance after chance in my life and have doubted and denied Jesus so many times they cannot be counted—by me. But Jesus knows every one of them.

The good news is He doesn't keep count, nor does He keep a record. Jesus came to do the perfect will of His Father, so that we might follow Him and spend eternity with Him. God already knew we would follow, and He knew each and every stumbling step we would take along the way. I believe even those stumbling steps were used by God—if not to show us the way, perhaps to show someone else the way *not* to go. How can we say someone in our past, having seen our mistake, did not follow in our footsteps, and thus was saved the heartache and disappointment we went through because of our error.

God's plan is multifaceted beyond our understanding.

I believe we are required to understand just one thing; God is love.

I believe we are required to *do* just one thing; Love God

Love God, and then I believe you will fully know, and experience, the love of God.

June 11

Jesus did many other things as well. If every one of them were written down, I suppose that even the whole world would not have room for the books that would've been written. John 21:25

The last verse of the book of John does not contain the word love, but to me, it speaks loudly and clearly of it. In this last verse of John's testimony regarding the life of Jesus on earth, he tells us he has but scratched the surface of what Jesus did while He lived as a man among us. I believe John's statement in this last verse of his book is a declaration of love; a love that is in awe of the Son of God.

As I read the Bible, and as I write these words of encouragement to myself, my family, my friends and my fellow believers, I, too, wonder at what is not said in this Holy document called the Bible. How many miracles did Jesus perform that are not told? How many stories in the Old Testament remain untold? I think we will know. I think when we leave this world and spend eternity with the Lord and all those that have gone before us, we will have the opportunity to talk with Moses, Paul, John and all the others and hear their stories. And they will hear ours.

They will listen, and nod their head sadly, but with understanding, as we tell the stories of our misspent youth. They will smile and pat our shoulder when we tell of the time we were called to the Lord—perhaps the gleam of a tear will appear in their eye at the telling of that one.

There will be time to know all the untold stories, but for now we must fulfill our destiny—our part of God's plan. We must put our attention not on the things that were—the past—but things of now. All that matters is now—this very moment—and all we must do at this very moment is love God. God alone knows what the moment after will bring.

June 12

To all in Rome who are called by God and called to be saints: Grace and peace to you from God our Father and from the Lord Jesus Christ.
Romans 1:7

The first chapter of the book of Romans speaks strongly of God's wrath toward men who have turned from Him and are living wicked and sinful lives. Paul gets pretty down and dirty in his description of what those who do not choose to follow God's plan are and what they will reap if they do not repent and love God; death.

We could read much of what Paul says in the first chapters of his letter to the Romans and become terrified. Terrified that we have blown it, and there is no hope for us due to the bad things we have done in our lives. But we must read the whole letter, because after Paul tells us what our punishment could have been, he tells us what God did for us when He sent Jesus to take our sins upon Him so that we could gain life eternal.

This is a problem we face as we try to understand God and what He wants from us. We read, or hear, only part of the message and jump to quick and incorrect assumptions. This is why I have come to the conclusion, based on everything I have read and heard—all of which I believe is filtered by God so I understand it—that all I am required to <u>do</u> is love God. Works—what we do—are of no value or consequence if we don't love God. If the things we do are not done by the power of God's love working through us, they are merely dust in the wind and will pile one upon the other to form mountains of wasted time.

Works without God contain no love. Love God, in His image be love, and let Him work through you.

June 13

And hope does not disappoint us, because God has poured His love into our hearts by the Holy Spirit, whom He has given us. Romans 5:5

What is the Holy Spirit? I believe it is the spirit of God working through us when we love God. Until God reveals a different definition to me, I will go with that.

What is hope? Webster defines it as, "to desire with expectation of fulfillment." That seems to fit with the hope Paul speaks of in Romans, chapter 5. What is it we are hoping for? Well, in my case, I hope I am doing God's will, and my life on this earth will have purpose. And I must tell you that though I do not perceive myself to be finished, I believe my life has had purpose. If the things I write and send to you today encourage even one person, then I believe my life has had purpose. If one person sees me today and their life is affected in a positive way according to God's will, my life has had purpose.

Am I no longer hoping for anything? No, I'm *still* hoping I am doing God's will, and my life on this earth will *continue* to have purpose. I cannot know when my last line will be spoken or my last scene will be played. I can only know God will tell me when that time is come.

I do not fear that time, but I do cherish this time I have been given to do the things I do; to write, to love and to give what I have to give.

God loves you. Love Him so that His Spirit will dwell in you, and cause you to love yourself, and love others.

June 14

But God demonstrates His own love for us in this: While we were still sinners, Christ died for us. Romans 5:8

Once again, it all comes to something short, sweet and simple. God loved us so much that even though we are sinners, He sent His Son, Christ Jesus, to die so we could be forgiven and spend eternity within His love.

I think about my life and the things I've done, and I am awed that God would still love me this much. But through no doing of my own, He chose me to be His companion and friend, and He selected you also to be in that special group. The only requirement to be a member of God's loving family is to love Him and accept His love. By believing He sent His Son to die on the cross and rise the third day, you have done all that needs to be done; and thereby, God knows you love Him. God did the rest when He sent Jesus, and what is left to be done, He will do through you as you love Him.

It may sound like I have succeeded in complicating what started out as simple, but just remember the key to it all; love God.

We like to joke that on our little nine-hole, pasture-pool golf course we have only one rule; get back to the house without hurting anyone. God's course has only one rule; love Him. Do that one thing, and I am quite sure no one will be hurt.

June 15

And we know that in all things God works for the good of those who love Him, and who have been called according to His purpose.
Romans 8:28

There it is! That's what I'm talking about! That verse says everything!
"We know." Not we *think*, but we *know*!
"That in all things." Not just *some* things, but *all* things.
"God works for the good." He is working for our good!
"Of those who love Him." I can say *our* good, because *we love Him*!
"And who have been called." He chose us!
"According to His purpose." According to His purpose—*the plan*!
Any questions?

June 16

Who is he that condemns? Christ Jesus, who died—more than that, who was raised to life—is at the right hand of God and is also interceding for us. Who shall separate us from the love of Christ? Shall trouble or hardship or persecution or famine or nakedness or danger or sword? Romans 8:34-35

No one and nothing can separate us from God once we profess our belief in the fact Jesus died and rose again in order that we might have eternal life with our heavenly Father. Even those of us who fall away for a time and return to our sinful ways remain tied eternally to our Lord and Savior. He is, no doubt, saddened by the fact loving Him is not our first priority during those times, but His love for us does not change because of our actions.

And when you examine your own inner feelings, you will most likely have to admit that even when our minds are not set on loving God, there is that string—that tie to Him—that continues to tug at our core, pulling us back to Him.

I remember my brother saying one time that we—he and I—would never be able to stray very far from the Lord because the faithful prayers of our mother would prevent it. I thank God for those faithful prayers, and I thank God for placing me in this world under the tutelage of one of His most faithful and loving servants—my mom. She was instrumental in God's plan for my life and the lives of many others.

I believe each of us has someone, or perhaps a multitude of people, in our lives that assist God in holding us to Him. That, among other reasons, is why we cannot be separated from Him.

Once we commit to God and accept His call, we are His forever.

June 17

No, in all these things we are more than conquerors through Him who loved us. Romans 8:37

More than conquerors. What does that mean?

I believe it means we can not only conquer anything that might try to separate us from the love of God, but those things cannot even come near us. God is with us and stands for us; therefore, those things are powerless against us.

Like the mother's love for her children, God's love is undying and steadfast. He will let nothing separate His children from Him. He is our strength and our shield when the enemy comes. If anything or anyone should attempt to take us from Him, He will stand between us and the enemy and inform them we are His, and He will not let us go.

We cannot be conquerors, much less more than conquerors, of our own accord or strength. Without God's love, we are weak and cannot stand against any foe. But by loving God and combining our love for Him with His for us, nothing can defeat us.

It makes me think of when we were in grade school and kids used to taunt each other with, "My dad is stronger than your dad!"

Well, our Father is the strongest of all!

June 18

For I am convinced that neither death nor life, neither angels nor demons, neither the present nor the future, nor any powers, neither height nor depth, nor anything else in all creation, will be able to separate us from the love of God that is in Christ Jesus our Lord.
Romans 8:38-39

Nothing.

No person, no *thing* can cause God to stop loving you.

Some of you might remember the movie, "Love Story." One famous line from the movie was, "Love means never having to say you're sorry." I've thought about that line many times in relation to love between two people and came to the conclusion it was not going to work—not in my case at any rate. Because I made too many mistakes and hurt the people I loved, and if I never said I was sorry, they would not think too highly of me.

God never has to say He is sorry.

In retrospect, whoever came up with that line was correct. God's love is a perfect love, and if we love Him, our love will be perfect as well. I believe when we truly and completely love God, we become the embodiment of His love and will never again have to say we are sorry to our loved ones.

Wouldn't that be awesome? Isn't it awesome to know God's love is so complete and so utterly immoveable He will never have to say He is sorry?

I want to love like that!

June 19

Just as it is written, "Jacob I loved, but Esau I hated." Romans 9:13

God didn't have to choose you. He doesn't choose everyone. In Romans 9: 21 Paul says, *"Does not the potter have the right to make out of the same lump of clay some pottery for noble uses and some for common use?"*

There are evil men in this world. God created them. They are for common use by Him.

By this I mean to say I believe God uses everyone to complete His plan, but not everyone is called to Him and His love.

Now I'm a bit confused. Does God love those He made for common use—those who will not return His love? Surely, He does.

I can't explain this, so I will leave it for another day when God reveals the truth of it to me.

I will, however, thank God that He chose me to be for noble use.

He chose you, too! He loves you!

June 20

> *As he says in Hosea: "I will call them 'my people' who are not my people; and I will call her 'my loved one' who is not my loved one."*
> Romans 9:25

God is a forgiving God. In these words from the book of Hosea, I believe He is referring to the Israelites and saying even though they have fallen away from Him, they are His, and He will take them back. Even though they have worshipped idols, God cannot turn His back on those He has chosen. He waits eagerly for them to turn from their sin and love Him.

I think of children who have been drawn into the wicked ways of the world in spite of their parent's good teaching and best efforts. Peer pressure and the lure of worldly things can be very enticing to young men and women as they begin their journey into adulthood. Their bodies crave the pleasures that have been awakened in them, and their minds are open to the powerful suggestion of things they have been told will harm them. They are filled with curiosity.

Parents are then confronted with a dreadful decision. They must decide whether to let their child go into the darkness and trust that God will bring them back into the light, or should they resist and fight to keep their child from the dark? Sadly, in most cases, parents find the choice is not theirs. They must let their children wander into the wilderness and trust God to return them safely.

My mother believed God would return me; He did. We—those of us who are parents—must believe likewise.

If you are a parent whose child has wandered into the darkness, keep your light—your love—on them. They will come back.

June 21

As far as the gospel is concerned, they are enemies on your account; but as far as election is concerned, they are loved on account of the patriarchs, for God's gifts and His call are irrevocable. Romans 11:28

There are so many religions in this world, it boggles the mind. And too many times, religions look at other religions as the enemy because their beliefs are so at odds. This often results in hatred and war between people who love God. I don't mean war between nations—though that is often the case as well—but I'm talking about war between individuals.

A war doesn't have to be fought with weapons—guns, knives, and the like; wars can be fought with words.

I am saddened when I see men, who profess to love God, attacking the method other men, who love God, use to teach or proclaim God's love. The one feels the other is wrong in His interpretation and teaching of God's word and deems Him the enemy because of it. I've said this before: I hope both of them are correct in their own way and in the eyes of God.

My feeling is it will take many varied instructors to explain God's love to the many varied people of this world. There are myriads of cultures on this planet, and surely, God knows this will require myriads of messages.

In that regard, if the things I write are encouraging to you and bless you, that is wonderful. If they are not, that is okay, too. Someone out there is saying the same thing I am—God loves you—in a way that will touch your heart and make sense to you. I believe God will put that person in your path.

Because…. He loves you.

June 22

Love must be sincere. Hate what is evil; cling to what is good.
Romans 12:9

Is your love for God sincere? What is sincere?

One definition of sincere is: not hypocritical. Ah, how we love to throw that word about when talking about religion. I believe that is one thing Christians around the world fear most—being deemed a hypocrite.

But look at what Paul says; *"hate what is evil; cling to what is good."* Don't you think what he is doing is telling us how to be sincere? I think that is exactly what he is trying to do.

God hates sin, wouldn't you agree? And God loves what is good.

God is good; I'm sure you have heard that many times. And God can in no way be construed as evil; I think we can all agree on that. So God is love, God is good, and we cling to Him. We love God sincerely. This sincere love of God will result in His love being in us, and that will cause us to hate what is evil.

Once again, God has made it all so simple for us; all we have to do is love Him sincerely. He'll take care of the details.

June 23

Let no debt remain outstanding, except the continuing debt to love one another, for he who loves his fellow man has fulfilled the law.
Romans 13:8

This is an often quoted verse and is usually used to encourage people to stay out of debt and live within their means; something that has become increasingly difficult to do in this world today.

I don't know about you, but I get at least one piece of mail a week offering me a credit card or a loan. These offers are sent out to everyone, even those who are unemployed. And too often, we decide what the heck and accept this easy money. Then another letter comes, and we take advantage of it. Soon, many of us find we owe more than we can pay, and we wind up going deeper and deeper into the devouring pit of debt.

My advice to you is—and I learned the hard way—just say no!

Owe no one anything except love. Love is not something you borrow and have to repay. Love is something you give freely, expecting nothing in return. Wouldn't it be nice if that was how the banks operated? We'd get letters in the mail with money in them and a note saying, "No need to repay this, it's a gift, and we want nothing in return." Woo-hoo!

But returning to the real world; do your best to stay out of debt. Most of the time, we borrow, not in order to buy things we really *need*, but rather to buy things we *want*.

Love God. He will provide for your every need.

June 24

The commandments, "Do not commit adultery," "Do not murder," "Do not steal," "Do not covet," and whatever other commandment there may be, are summed up in this one rule: "Love your neighbor as yourself." Love does no harm to its neighbor. Therefore love is the fulfillment of the law. Romans 13:9-10

All of the Ten Commandments God gave to Moses are good, and we will obey them, but God made it easier for us by wrapping them up in a neat little package called "love." He probably saw we were having such a hard time keeping up with ten things and decided maybe we would do better if we just had to keep up with one. It was a trick of sorts, though, because He attached the ten things to the one.

It works for me!

All I have to do is love God, and when I do, He puts it within me to do what He wants me to do. I like that!

That includes loving my neighbor as myself, which is sometimes harder than obeying the Ten Commandments. Harder, that is, if I try to do it without first loving God. Some people are very hard to love; some are mean, some are grouchy, and some are just plain evil. If I had it my way, I would not love them. But God loves them, so since I love God, I guess I love them, too. It's really kind of easy, though, because all I have to do is love God, and then He loves others through me. I'm sort of the middle man in this operation.

Loving God is so cool.

June 25

If your brother is distressed because of what you eat, you are no longer acting in love. Do not by eating destroy your brother for whom Christ died. Romans 14:15

In the fourteenth chapter of his letter to the Romans, Paul speaks to them, and us, about passing judgment on others that do not believe exactly as we do. This is a problem which, as you can see, has existed since the beginning of mankind. Is Paul saying if we do something that our brothers in Christ don't agree with, we don't love them? I don't think that's what He's saying. I think if you read the entire fourteenth chapter of Romans, you will agree what He is saying is to not let our differences cause us to not love one another.

This goes back to the different churches and beliefs I mentioned earlier this year, and it appears Paul agrees, or perhaps even confirms, my hope they are all correct in their own way. And we should love all our brothers in Christ regardless of our differences.

Our part of God's plan is not to pass judgment on others because we disagree with their interpretation of God. Our part of the plan is to love Him, and by loving Him, allow Him to use us to do His will.

I remember an intersection in Charlotte, North Carolina that was most confusing. Three roads came together at the intersection, and all three had the same name.

The roads that lead to God are much the same. They are all different, they come from all directions, but they are all named love, and they wind up at the same place.

June 26

> *However, as it is written: "No eye has seen, no ear has heard, no mind has conceived what God has prepared for those that love Him."*
> 1 Corinthians 2:9

That, my friends, is hard to comprehend. For just a moment, think about the most beautiful thing you have ever seen and the most amazing sound you have ever heard. Imagine then that what God has in store for you is far more beautiful than anything your mind can perceive.

How deeply have you loved another? Can you recall the feeling? It was awesome, wasn't it?

Can you imagine then what awesome love God must have in store for you?

Can you imagine you are capable of returning that love to Him and to others around you?

It boggles the mind to think what lies ahead; God's perfect and everlasting love.

June 27

What do you prefer? Shall I come to you with a whip, or in love and with a gentle spirit? 1 Corinthians 4:21

That's a good question. I'm sure many of you have heard the phrase, "spare the rod, spoil the child." I think this is what Paul is saying to the followers of Christ in Corinth. He is asking if they would rather he pat them on the rear and say the wrong things they do are okay, or would they rather he come down hard on them, so they get the message loud and clear.

I'm not advocating that anyone should use physical punishment to get their child's attention and thereby cause the child to behave correctly. I do believe parents today have gone too far to the extreme in the opposite direction. Although, I quickly admit I am certainly no expert in childrearing.

That said, what about us—adults who are doing things we know we shouldn't? Does God come to us with a whip or in love, with a gentle spirit?

I think it is the latter of the two, simply because God loves us; and therefore, we can be assured that is the way He comes to us. I also believe God comes to us with a gentle spirit and knows He does not need a whip to get our attention. I do think sometimes God allows us to go through hardships we bring upon ourselves when we make poor choices. In that case, we are wielding the whip, He merely allows us to "learn-the-hard-way."

Some lessons can't be learned the easy way, and sometimes we have to learn the hard way. But no matter how difficult or easy the lesson, God never stops loving those that love Him.

I *try* to learn something every day. I *know* God loves me every day.

June 28

> *Now about food sacrificed to idols: We know that we all possess knowledge. Knowledge puffs up, but love builds up. The man who thinks he knows something does not yet know as he ought to know. But the man who loves God is known by God.* 1 Corinthians 8:1-3

I think what Paul is doing here, is using the example of food sacrificed to idols as an example to state his point that knowledge without God is useless. I believe Paul is saying that by loving God, we will truly understand His principles.

The more I read the Bible, the more I agree with Paul. When I began the task of writing these daily encouragements for us, I began with verses based on having no fear. I learned a lot from those verses, but when I finished with those and began writing based on love, it was as if a door were opened.

I have long believed, and even stated at times, that the key to God was love. But it seems the more I read about it, the easier it becomes to love God. And the more I love God, the more I seem to understand. No, I am not puffed up because I feel like I understand God more than I used to. I am awed by it. I am awed by the fact that when I love God, He seems to open my eyes, my ears and my heart to what He has to say to us and how much He loves us.

Love God sincerely then stand back, because the door that will open to you is enormous, and it opens to reveal a universe of knowledge and love that is vast and awesome.

June 29

If I speak in the tongues of men and angels, but have not love, I am only a resounding gong or a clanging symbol. 1 Corinthians 13:1

Chapter thirteen of 1 Corinthians is known as the Love Chapter. In this chapter of his first letter to the people of Corinth, Paul tells them in every way he can think of, if they don't have the sincere love of God and Christ in their hearts, then nothing they do will be of consequence.

In this, his first example, he tells them—and us—if they do not have love, nothing they say will mean anything to those who hear it. They might as well be sounding a gong or clanging a symbol.

Some of you might remember a TV show from some time back called "The Gong Show." It was kind of like today's show, "American Idol," only without the chance to go on to stardom for the winners. A person would come on stage and perform their act, and if they were so bad the judges and audience did not want them to continue, a loud gong would sound, and they would have to leave the stage. The gong on "American Idol" is Simon Cowel's berating criticism.

My point is, if we speak without love, we will surely hear the loud gong, and we might as well not continue. But if we have the love of God within us, He will speak through us. And as you know, God is love, and so what we say will be said in love and understood.

Love God. Allow Him to use you to spread His love to those around you.

June 30

If I have the gift of prophesy and can fathom all mysteries and all knowledge, and if I have faith that can move mountains, but have not love, I am nothing. 1 Corinthians 13:2

Paul tells the people of Corinth it doesn't matter how much they understand, how much they know, or even how much faith they have. They can have all that, but if they do not have love, they are nothing.

What is love? Right! God is love! So, if you ask me, what Paul is saying is it doesn't matter how much you know about God, or how much faith you have, if you do not love God it is all worthless. God's knowledge and power cannot be used through people who do not love Him. That makes perfect sense to me!

It makes me think of the commercials I see on TV for dating services. They tell us if we use their service they will find a perfect match for us. Someone who thinks like us, knows the same things we know, and likes the same things we like. Great! So we find the perfect match, and then we love them. Right? That is possible, but my point is even with all that knowledge and common ground, the relationship will not work if the two people that are brought together do not choose to love each other. It will all be useless information.

Likewise, we can learn all there is to learn about God and Christianity, and we can agree what God has to offer us is good and will benefit us, but it will be of no use to us unless we love God.

Love God; He will provide the knowledge you need, and that knowledge combined with your faith and love, can move mountains.

July 1

If I give all I possess to the poor and surrender my body to the flames, but have not love, I gain nothing. 1 Corinthians 13:3

"*If I give all I possess to the poor?*" Just as Paul goes on to say, if it is not done in God's perfect love, then it will mean you just gave away all your stuff! Nothing more.

All you will have done if you give all you possess to the poor, without first loving God and the act being done through you by Him, is attempt to buy God's approval. I'm quite sure God doesn't work that way.

Remember, God's greatest desire is for you to love Him. If you love Him, and then are quite certain He wants you to give all you have to the poor, give it to them. If you are only doing it because you think the world will think highly of you, then I suggest you hold on to your belongings, because most of the world is going to think you're some kind of nut.

I think it's pretty plain God is not interested in what we can do for Him. He has the situation quite well in hand.

Just love Him. That alone is a full time job!

July 2

Love is patient, love is kind. It does not envy, it does not boast, it is not proud. 1 Corinthians 13:4

Though I could not have told you where to find it in the Bible, this has always been one of my favorite verses.

I want to be patient; with God, with my loved ones, and others. I know I'm not patient most of the time. But, man, I want to be.

I try not to envy others for what they are or what they have. I'm better at this than I am at being patient, but I could be better.

As for boasting, I'm not much of a boaster. I do it, but usually in a joking manner. I'm certainly not one to think I have a lot to boast about. (Wait… am I boasting about not being a boaster?) DOH!

And love is not proud. That's same as boasting, if you ask me.

But what is Paul saying when he tells us what love is, and what love is not? I believe he's telling us love is perfect in humility, and we are nothing without God. For God is love; and therefore, if we love God and become as He is and do His perfect will, we are love, and we will be patient and kind, never envious, boastful or proud.

Paul is telling us to love God because God is love, and when we sincerely love God, we will begin to live as He would have us live.

I think this loving God thing is going to work out just dandy!

July 3

Love never fails. But where there are prophesies, they will cease; where there are tongues, they will be stilled; where there is knowledge, it will pass away. 1 Corinthians 13:8

I like this verse for its simplicity. It seems complicated after the first sentence, but it's really not. Paul could have used any of hundreds of examples to emphasize the first sentence, and I think that was all he was doing. The verse could have literally been left at three words.
Love never fails.
If you have talent, gifts, brains, money; it will not last. Love—God—will last forever. How many times can I repeat God is love? I don't believe I can say it enough. I am so utterly convinced it is the secret, the truth, the way, I don't know if I will ever be able to stop saying it.
God never fails.
Love never fails.
Awesome!

July 4

And now these three remain: faith, hope and love. But the greatest of these is love. 1 Corinthians 13:13

If you've been reading these encouragements for long, you should know that in my opinion, this verse is a no-brainer. Of course love is the greatest of these! God has never been referred to as faith or hope. Maybe he has been referred to as one or both of those things, but I *know* He is love; and therefore, nothing can be greater than love.

Without faith, though, could we love God? It seems to me we must have faith in Him, or we cannot love Him.

If we did not have the hope of spending eternity with God, would there be any reason to love Him? I can't see where that would make any sense.

So I agree the three are necessary, and I definitely agree love is the most important.

We must have faith in order to justify hope. When we love God, we allow our faith to keep the light of hope within our sights. As our love grows, our hope burns brighter, and our faith becomes stronger.

I envision the three—faith, hope and love—as a whirlwind of power set in motion by the hand of God. He spins us like a child would spin a top from a string, and His joyous laughter fills the heavens as He watches our faith, our hope and our love for Him spin joyfully out of control.

July 5

Therefore, my dear brothers, stand firm. Let nothing move you. Always give yourselves fully to the work of the Lord, because you know that your labor in the Lord is not in vain. 1 Corinthians 15:58

Standing firm as we work for the Lord can be difficult, if we attempt it of our own accord. If we love God and let Him do His work in us and through us, it ain't no thang!

It makes me think of those reporters that go out to report on hurricanes. They stand there with their microphone, leaning into the rain and wind, telling us how hard the wind is blowing. Well, duh! I always wonder what they are trying to prove by "braving" the storm in order to report on it.

Doing God's work on our own can be much like the experience of those reporters. We will no doubt face storms of controversy and winds of criticism and doubt. But we don't have to *brave* those things—or any things—to get God's work done. Our first step should be to love God, then put our hope and faith in him, knowing He will work in us and through us to accomplish His plan. He will calm the storm and part the seas so we can do what He wants done. He will pave the way.

So if you feel as though you are leaning into the wind in your walk with God, be still for a moment. Fill your heart, mind and soul with love for God. After you've done that—even though the storms might continue to rage—He will walk in front of you and shield you from them.

July 6

Do everything in love. 1 Corinthians 16:14

Everything?
That's what it says. *Everything.*

I can just see Archie Bunker, eyes heavenward, whining, "Ah, jeez Louise, Lord! How'm I gonna do dat?"

It seems an impossible task—to do *everything* in love. Going to work, paying the bills, raising the children, dealing with all the things life will throw at us today. We have to do *all* those things in love?

No. We don't *have* to. But they will be much easier to deal with if we do.

And the kicker is we don't *have* to do it to get it done. Say what?

Nope. All we have to *do* is love God. (Like you didn't see that coming!)

If we make our first priority—more than that, our *only* priority—loving God, He will fill us so full of joy and love that all those things that once seemed like drudgery will start to slide off our backs and become easy.

It's all about attitude, I reckon. God is love. If we love God, He will fill us with faith, hope and love, and we will begin to wonder what it was about the things we do each day that used to bother us.

July 7

Now instead, you ought to forgive and comfort him, so that he will not be overwhelmed by excessive sorrow. I urge you therefore to reaffirm your love for him. 2 Corinthians 2:7-8

Many times, lack of forgiveness can cause the destruction of a relationship. A person who has done wrong and is not forgiven by the one he wronged can suffer from immense self-condemnation. When we are guilty of un-forgiveness, we do not have to look far to find an example of how we *should* be acting. Another no-brainer, don't you think?

God sent Jesus to die on the cross and rise on the third day to forgive us *all*. For *everything*!

How then can we refuse to forgive someone for a wrong done against us? Who do we think we are?

I know some things are hard to get over, and maybe in our human state we cannot forgive the one who wronged us, but I believe we have to. We not only have to forgive, but we have to love them.

I just heard Archie Bunker whining again. Yes, it seems impossible—it can even seem unfair. After all, we didn't do the wrong, the other guy did!

Well…. Did God sin, or did we?

Who forgave who?

Case closed.

July 8

Christ's love compels us, because we are convinced that one died for all, and therefore all died. 2 Corinthians 5:14

All mankind died on the cross with Jesus? If you believe Jesus died so you could be cleansed of sin and spend eternity with Him, then the answer is yes. And the offer of eternal life was extended by Him to all mankind. If we choose Jesus, we die with Him, in that our sins are hung upon the cross with Him.

But what is the key part of the verse Paul writes to the believers in Corinth?

"Christ's love compels us."

Christ's love—God's love—for us is so fully and utterly demonstrated by the extent of what They did for us on the cross we cannot begin to fathom it.

Just think for a moment that in order to save your family from sure death, you would have to send one of your children to die. You can't even imagine what that would be like, can you? Imagine you are the child who must go out and be killed by the enemy so the rest of your family can live. Some can say they would gladly do it—but, I think not many.

Jesus went to the cross for us and died for us. He did so because he loves us, and God loves us. Nothing you or I can do will repay them. How then can we not be compelled to love them? How can we not love them unconditionally?

I can't think of a good reason not to love God. Can you?

July 9

> In *purity, understanding, patience and kindness; in the Holy Spirit and in sincere love,* 2 Corinthians 6:6

Paul suffered many hardships as he traveled and took the news of salvation to God's people. He was beaten, imprisoned and spent many a sleepless and hungry night. Yet he never wavered in his love for God and Jesus. In spite of all he endured, he continued *"in purity, understanding, patience and kindness; in the Holy Spirit and in sincere love."*

What was the key? How was Paul able to do that?

Sincere love for God. There is no other way.

If Paul had merely been hired to go out and preach the gospel of Christ, he could not have endured the hardships he endured. He would have called the home office and told them to find another sucker! And perhaps, the supervisors that had hired him would have tried to sweeten the offer and said, "There's a huge bonus in it for you if you hang in there and continue to spread the good word."

"What good is a bonus if I'm in prison or dead?" Paul might ask.

But Paul wasn't working for men. He was working for God, and he knew what the bonus was if he completed the job—his part of the plan. The bonus was eternity with the Boss—a boss that loved him so much, He had sent His Son to pave the road before him.

Paul loved God sincerely and was willing to do anything for Him. *Anything.*

July 10

Since we have these promises, dear friends, let us purify ourselves from everything that contaminates the body and spirit, perfecting holiness out of reverence for God. 2 Corinthians 7:1

Is this verse telling us we must attempt to be perfect? I don't think so at all. Paul is exhorting the people of Corinth to purify themselves from things that contaminate the body and spirit, thus perfecting holiness out of their reverence for God. Paul knows the people of Corinth cannot be perfect, he knows that like him, they are sinners. Why would he tell them they must be perfect?

I believe what Paul is telling the people is to love God—to revere Him. God has given them and us the promise of everlasting life with Him. I also believe if we love God, the things Paul is saying we should do will become automatic, and we won't have to *try* and do them We will become purified when our love and reverence for God overflows and washes everything from our lives that contaminates our body and spirit.

We can *do* nothing; except, that is, love God. Then God's love will shine through us like a lighthouse in a world filled with the haze of sin and wickedness. Those who are lost will be drawn to us and know where we are, there is God's love—the light.

Jesus did it *all* for us, expecting nothing in return.

The only thing *I* want to *do* is love Him and our heavenly Father as much as I possibly can and by doing so, place myself at their beck and call.

July 11

> *But just as you excel in everything—in faith, in speech, in knowledge, in complete earnestness and in your love for us—see that you also excel in this grace of giving.* 2 Corinthians 8:7

In previous verses, Paul has told the Corinthians how the people in Macedonia had helped him and his fellow teachers. The people in Macedonia had shared what they had with him even though times were tough, and they had little to share. He is asking the people of Corinth to do likewise. He is not demanding anything of them, nor is he attempting to make them feel as though it is their duty to share with him and his band of teachers. He is *asking* them to share with others out of love.

I do not believe we should share with others so we can be seen as good by God and others. I believe we should share because we love God and others. If we give out of a sense of duty or because we think it is required of us, there can be no joy in it. Like most other things we try to *do*, if we do not give with the love of God in us and working through us, giving is merely a chore we must accomplish.

I also believe when we give material things or our time, we are giving our love—God's love. And when we love God, we are giving ourselves to Him, and He then allows us to have stewardship over material things while we are on this earth. He puts it within our hearts to share what He has given us with others, whether it is love or possessions.

Anything and everything we own is on loan to us from God. If we love Him, I believe He will place much within our reach so it can be distributed as He requests and desires.

July 12

I am not commanding you, but I want to test the sincerity of your love by comparing it with others. 2 Corinthians 8:8

I am concerned that this verse, in this translation of the Bible, can easily be misinterpreted. I do not for one second think Paul was attempting to test the love of the people of Corinth by comparing it to the love of those from another town. I just don't think Paul would do that.

I think what he was doing when making this statement—and I do not profess to know in any certainty—was indeed comparing the two towns—Macedonia and Corinth—and bragging as to how generous and loving the people of both cities were.

And what was he not commanding? He was, as we talked about in yesterday's encouragement, not commanding, but *asking* the people of Corinth to share with him and his fellow teachers and be hospitable to them when they arrived in their town.

I don't think God demands we share, and I don't think He tests our love. I don't think Paul, being the faithful, loving servant of the Lord he was, would either.

God made the ultimate sacrifice for us and asks for nothing in return. He desires only that we love Him and accept His invitation to spend eternity with Him.

I have responded to His R.S.V.P request and will be attending.

You're going, too, aren't you?

July 13

Therefore show these men the proof of your love and the reason for our pride in you, so that the churches can see it. 2 Corinthians 8:24

Paul was sending other teachers and church leaders to Corinth ahead of him. He wanted the people of Corinth to treat them well when they arrived. Paul was proud of the people of Corinth and wanted the men from other churches to see why. Paul knew the people of Corinth would treat the men well, but I think he was the kind of guy who knew building the people up with kind words would be better than *demanding* their services.

I have found this tactic works well in almost any instance. I've seen people in supervisory positions who yell and demand things of their people, and they often do not get the best effort from the workers. Then I have seen supervisors who constantly praise and encourage their team, and in most cases the results and performances they receive are considerably better.

I believe God is like the supervisor that encourages and compliments. He does not demand we do things His way, but instead, offers us everything He has and asks only that we love Him and do the very best we can. He'll even provide the training and give us minute by minute instruction.

That is…. if we are paying attention.

Love God and listen for His instruction. He's the best teacher ever!

July 14

Each man should give what he has decided in his heart to give, not reluctantly or under compulsion, for God loves a cheerful giver.
2 Corinthians 9:7

I say amen to that!

These days, too many churches, evangelists and so on seem to be focused on money. In my opinion this turns more people away from God than anything churches do in today's world. I believe if they would preach the word of God, while loving God, they wouldn't even have to ask for money. God would put it within the hearts of those who love Him to give. I believe a church operating upon the premise of sincerely loving God as the number one priority will not be able to give the money away fast enough. There will be so much of it coming in they won't be able to handle it all.

People who love God and know the fullness of His love will give all they have. They will give their time, their hard work, their money; they will give it *all* because God will fill their hearts with a love so large and bless them so much they won't be able to stand it if they don't give some of it away.

I believe in prosperity. I believe if you love God He will supply all your needs and then some. And the then-some will start piling up, and God will put somebody in your path that needs some. That person will see the light of God's love in your eyes, and he will want some, then you will give him some, and then God will add some more. And pretty soon that person's needs are met, and God will multiply them some and then some more! And there it goes again!

Whew! I had no idea how I was going to end that! I was getting dizzy! But the point is; love God, and He will bless you some!

July 15

So I will very gladly spend for you everything I have and expend myself as well. If I love you more, will you love me less? 2 Corinthians 12:15

Paul was a pastor and teacher of the gospel of Jesus Christ. He was willing to give everything he had and all his energy for the sake of the gospel. It meant everything to him. He loved God, Jesus and others with every ounce of his being. He suffered severe hardships and still would not budge in his thinking. He loved God no matter what. He loved Jesus no matter what. And he loved God's people and asked nothing in return, only what God placed in their hearts to give.

Are you and I capable of such sincere love?

I believe the answer is yes, but not of our own strength and volition.

But if we love God and yearn to love Him more and more with each passing day, we will be capable of love beyond our wildest imagining.

That's what God's love is! It is beyond our comprehension. It is so vast and powerful I cannot, as a mere man, begin to describe it. I think I would have to make up new words, and sights, and sounds, and feelings.

Try and imagine what the touch of God must be like; His lips on your cheek; His arm around your shoulders; His hand in yours.

I can't even begin to imagine what awaits us.

July 16

Finally, brothers, good-by. Aim for perfection, listen to my appeal, be of one mind, live in peace. And the God of love and peace will be with you. 2 Corinthians 13:11

How often can you say you are truly at peace? Peace is too often an elusive thing for us. It seems even when times are good, we often find something to fret about, or start thinking there is something else we need.

I have found more peace since I began writing these daily encouragements than I think I have experienced in all the days before I started them. That ratio, my friends, is not a good one. I have been writing these for forty* days, and the days before I began to write them number some twenty thousand or so.

To what can we attribute the peace I am experiencing? My first guess would be that I am spending my days loving God first, and He, in return, is spending more time with me. The truth is He has always been near, but now He sits beside me as I write and encourages me. He looks over my shoulder, sometimes nods in agreement, sometimes chuckles at the funny things I say—or even the serious things I say that I don't get quite right. Sometimes I think I see a tear of sadness when I write something sad, and other times I see a tear of joy. Always I feel His love. And His love comes with peace. I feel His peace as I write.

I have so much to be thankful for; so much to give. So much love I want to share.

---

*I need to point out to readers that I began writing these daily encouragements on December 14, 2008, and wrote several encouragements each day thereafter until the book of 365 encouragements was completed. This particular encouragement was actually written on January 22, 2009, thus, the 40 day reference.

July 17

I have been crucified with Christ and I no longer live, but Christ lives in me. The life I live in the body, I live by faith in the Son of God, who loved me and gave Himself for me. Galatians 2:20

These bodies we walk this world in are merely vessels God has placed our souls in until we leave this earth to be with Him. When I think of how large and awesome God is, I am stunned that he chose to come among us, as one of us, to show how much He loved us.

I think if I didn't have faith in God's love for me, this world would devour me. There is so much going on around us that wants us to look away from God and wants us to go down the wrong path. But the more we keep our eyes on God, and the more we make loving Him our first priority, the more those things become less and less important. Their lure becomes less alluring.

Have you ever done something that upset your spouse or even a good friend—something that hurt them? Did it make you feel bad? I know I have—too many times. In some cases the memory of it still causes me to cringe and feel sad and ashamed. I want so much to be a good husband, father, relative and friend to those who love me, and yet—human that I am—I sometimes fail. And when the failure is large, I wonder can they ever forgive me. Some do, some don't, and in many instances, I can't blame those who don't. I thank God for those that do.

But God always does. He always forgives; always loves; never gives up.

I want to be able to love like that.

July 18

> *For in Christ Jesus neither circumcision nor uncircumcision has any value. The only thing that counts is faith expressing itself through love.*
> Galatians 5:6

Many churches and people today are concerned more about what they believe and how they think others should believe, than they are about what God wants. They spend too much time teaching and trying to obey the rules, and not enough time loving God.

Have you ever watched a football or basketball game where the officials seem to be picking apart every situation and stopping the game every few seconds to call a penalty and enforce a rule? When that happens, a coach, player, or fan will invariably shout at the officials, "Let them play, you're messing up the game!"

Sometimes we get so bound up in what we perceive God's rules to be we forget the most important thing; loving Him. I agree with what Paul says to the Galatians in chapter five, verse six; *"The only thing that counts, is faith expressing itself through love."*

We can try to obey and live by all the rules, or we can accept God's grace and by loving Him, and with Him living in and through us, live our lives His way.

I believe God is shouting from the heavens to all those who attempt to officiate His people: "Let them play, let them love Me, you're messing up My plan!

July 19

You, my brothers, were called to be free. But do not use your freedom to indulge the sinful nature; rather, serve one another in love.
Galatians 5:13

Christ died for our sins, and we are forgiven when we sin. We are, in essence, free to sin. But this does not mean we should go on our merry way doing as we please, knowing God will forgive us.

What does Paul tell the Galatians regarding this? He tells them no, don't use the freedom Christ bought for us to continue sinning; serve one another—the same way Christ served us—in love.

We humans are sinful in nature. We are tempted at almost every turn, and many times we succumb to the temptation. We sin every day. Sometimes our sin is small, and sometimes it is large. Some days we sin many times, sometimes we sin very few times. But we sin, and small sins are the same as large ones in God's eyes, and many sins are the same as a few sins to Him.

When my construction crew and I are faced with a task which seems daunting—one that challenges our abilities to complete it within the budget and time constraints allowed—I tell them all we can do is the best we can do each day, and our goal should be to make progress each day.

I believe God asks no more than that from each of us. I also believe He will assist us if we have faith in Him and love Him. He will assist us, not only in living a life that is pleasing to Him, but He will assist us with those tasks which seem daunting in our jobs, our relationships and our lives.

One freedom we have that is not bound by rules or law is the freedom to love God. Do your best to Love Him today, and I believe He will place it in your heart to serve one another in love.

July 20

The entire law is summed up in a single command: "Love your neighbor as yourself." Galatians 5:14

Everything always comes down to the one thing; love. No matter how much we might read and study God's word, no matter how many translations there may be, all of it will circle and twist, and when the dust settles, the one thing left is love.

"Love your neighbor as yourself." If everyone did that, what a world this would be.

Unfortunately, we will probably not see such a world in our time here on earth, but won't it be a sight to behold when we go to spend eternity with God?

Imagine for a moment a certain person you are in disagreement with at this very moment. Think about whatever it is you are in disagreement with them about. Is the thing that comes between you and the other person so important? Is it so important you can spend time dwelling on it and dealing with it, when the time could be spent loving God—and them? If they finally come over to your way of thinking regarding whatever it is that has come between you, will you love them then, and will they love you? In so many cases, when we really examine our differences with others, those differences mean virtually nothing in the larger scheme of our lives.

Turn your thoughts from the things that come between you and your neighbor. Look toward God and love Him. *That* is what matters! When you concentrate on loving God, you will love yourself because He loves you. When this happens, you will begin to see your neighbor through God's eyes.

I think you will discover your neighbor isn't so bad after all.

July 21

But the fruit of the Spirit is love, joy, peace, patience, kindness, goodness, faithfulness. Galatians 5:22

As you are all well aware by now, I like to keep things simple—that way *I* can understand them. I believe God likes to keep things simple, too. Man tends to complicate Him.

The Holy Spirit, or the Spirit, is God dwelling within us when we love God and believe He sent Jesus to live among us, die for us, and then rise on the third day to prepare a place for us with the Lord for eternity.

When a seed is planted and a tree grows, it bears fruit. I believe when we love God, the Holy Spirit—God—dwells within us, and we bear fruit. Paul lists some of the fruit we bear in this passage to the Galatians. Notice the first fruit of the Spirit in His list to them is love. I don't think for even a moment that was an accident.

I am convinced that without love, none of the others in the list could exist. We might try to force them, and we may even experience a degree of success, but until we first love God, I think we will merely go through the motions.

The really cool thing is when we do bear fruit, there are seeds within the fruit, and when we plant those seeds, the process begins again, and someone else will grow and bear fruit.

Keep it simple. Love God. He grows a mighty fine orchard.

July 22

For He chose us in Him before the creation of the world to be holy and blameless in His sight. In love He predestined us to be adopted as His sons through Jesus Christ, in accordance with His pleasure and will—to the praise of His glorious grace, which He has freely given us in the One He loves. Ephesians 1:4-6

He chose us... before the creation of the world.
Now *that* is a plan!
Imagine you are at work, and you have a plan for the day. You arrange your tools, check your drawings and documents, and then you begin. God did that, and we are the tools He chose to use for His project. How cool is that?
It makes me think of childhood games on the playground when we would choose sides for a game of football, baseball or whatever might be the game of choice that day. The ones doing the choosing were usually the oldest, biggest, or smartest. For various reasons they were in charge, and as a result, they got to choose who would be on their team. They usually—but not always—chose players who could best help them to play the best game and win. I remember the exultant feeling of being chosen, especially if chosen by the person I thought was most capable of leading us to victory.
God chose us! Before the game even began, before the stadium was even built, he chose us to be on His team! I feel like pumping my fist in the air, jumping for joy and shouting, "Yes!"
By golly, I think I will!

July 23

For this reason, ever since I heard about your faith in the Lord Jesus and your love for all the saints, I have not stopped giving thanks for you, remembering you in my prayers. Ephesians 1:15-16

Do you suppose there is someone out there giving thanks for you or me? I think deep down inside each of us, we hope there is. We want to be of importance; we want our lives to mean something—to someone.

When I was a young boy, I dreamed of being a hero. I don't know why. Maybe I watched too much television and wanted to be like the Lone Ranger or one of the many heroic characters played by John Wayne. But for whatever reason, I used to imagine I would happen upon a scene where someone was in dire straits, and I would come fearlessly and valiantly to their rescue. I feel pretty silly when I recall those childish thoughts.

I think inside us all there is a yearning to be honored and recognized for our efforts. The thing is, we are honored and recognized every day—by God. Since the day we entered this world, God has been watching every move we make, and even when we were going the wrong way, He knew where we would end up. God knew His plan for us and never doubted we would do what He needed done.

We are the supporting cast in this great endeavor of God's. And though the Star will surely shine with or without us, we are recognized and honored by the One that wrote the script. We will each speak our lines, play our parts, and perhaps even save the day on occasion. God will then honor us by inviting us to the awards ceremony that will follow, and we will celebrate in eternity with Him and Jesus.

Today, practice the most important line you will ever say, "I love you, God."

July 24

But because of His great love for us, God, who is rich in mercy, made us alive with Christ even when we were dead in transgressions—it is by grace you have been saved. Ephesians 2:4-5

When the world was not yet in existence, when it was still a vast vacant lot, God chose us. He said, "You will be on my team, and I will give you my Son as a coach to show you how to play this game, so no one can defeat you."

The game was rigged! Thank you, God!

Why did God chose you and me to be on His team? Was it because we could speak eloquently, write well, or because we looked the part? I don't think so. I believe God gave each of us talents and abilities that would be useful in the fulfillment of His plan. Some of us can do one thing, and some of us can do another, but it all comes together in the way God wants it to come together.

But the point here is God did not choose us because we could do those things, He chose us because He loved us. He included us in spite of all the wrong we had done and in spite of our lack of talent or ability. He knew all along we had what it takes to fulfill our part of His plan.

We are all sinners, but God has given us grace—salvation—in spite of our sinful ways.

The only ability necessary to be a member of God's team is the ability to love Him. He will supply everything we need to be victorious.

July 25

> *I pray that out of His glorious riches He may strengthen you with power through His Spirit in your inner being, so that Christ may dwell in your hearts through faith. And I pray that you, being rooted and established in love, may have power, together with all the saints, to grasp how wide and long and high and deep is the love of Christ, and to know this love that surpasses knowledge—that you may be filled to the measure of all the fullness of God.* Ephesians 3:16-19

What an awesome prayer! And the last line tops it off grandly! How awesome would it be to be filled to the brim, to have every fiber of our being bursting with the fullness of God?

I believe we will find out. Maybe we won't—probably we won't—find out while we live on this earth, but I am certain we will find out how awesome God's complete love will feel when we go to be with Him after our jobs on earth are complete.

I believe we can experience God's love while we are here doing His bidding, too. I'm not sure we can feel the full extent of it, because I believe, as Paul says, "It surpasses our knowledge." We have no words to describe it, nor do we have experiences to compare it to.

I want all God can reveal to me now! I want to experience all the love he will allow on this earth, and I believe the way to do that is to love Him! I don't know how really, but I believe He will show me how.

It's kind of like pouring the pieces of a puzzle out onto the table. You're not sure how it will all fit together, but you are confident it will, and so you put the first two pieces together and begin.

In this puzzle that is life, the first two pieces are your love and God's love.

Put them together… and begin. If you've already done so then keep adding pieces—love—and watch God's love begin to grow and take shape in your life. The end result—the completed puzzle that is life on this earth—will be more beautiful than anything you can imagine.

July 26

Be completely humble and gentle; be patient, bearing with one another in love. Ephesians 4:2

And once again, eyes heavenward, Archie Bunker –the epitome of you and me—whines, "Ah, Jeez, Lord."

But is it really so hard to be humble? I think not, if we remember one thing: without God, we are nothing, and can do nothing. Our first duty is to love God, allow His love to live in us, so He can work through us using His love. So being humble is really quite easy. All the things Paul exhorts the Ephesians to be should come easy to us. That is, if we allow God to *be* these things through us and don't attempt to *do* them on our own.

Loving God is definitely the key, because if we don't do that first, we are trying to do all the things we think He wants us to do, but He is not within us. If He is not within us, all the works we do are just motions.

Imagine a situation where God wants to save a person from being hit by a car. You—a person that is *not* a part of God's plan—and a man who *is* a part of God's plan are standing beside each other on a street corner, and you both see a man about to walk into oncoming traffic. You reach for the man's sleeve, but it is just beyond your grasp. The person who is a part of God's plan reaches out and grabs the man's sleeve and pulls him back to the curb, preventing him from being hit by the car. You tried to do it on your own. The person beside you did what you couldn't because God was working through him. The person that was going to walk in front of the car was a part of God's plan and God used another person that was part of His plan to save him from being harmed.

Love God. Let Him use you in His plan.

July 27

Then we will no longer be infants, tossed back and forth by the waves, and blown here and there by every wind of teaching and by the cunning and craftiness of men in their deceitful scheming. Instead, speaking the truth in love, we will in all things grow up into Him who is the head, that is, Christ. Ephesians 4:14-15

I believe *"speaking the truth in love,"* is the most important thing in this verse and in our lives. And I believe the truth is what God puts in our hearts when we love Him. Without His love in us, working through us, I don't think we can discern what is true and what is not.

I look around at the thousands of different churches, and it amazes me how many different sets of beliefs there are. So many churches today came into existence simply because one person, or a group of people, did not interpret the Bible the same way the church they were attending interpreted it. So they left that church and started a church of their own, so they could interpret the Bible *their* way. In other cases, a new church was formed because the people who formed it didn't agree with how the Sunday service was being delivered or how the Sunday school was being run. I wonder where God's love was on the list of things that caused folks to leave one church and start another church.

People allow themselves to be tossed back and forth and blown here and there. They are deceived by the whims and fancies of other men who convince them their way is the right way.

I believe you should begin with God. Love God; accept Jesus as your Lord and Savior, then God will open your ears to the truth He wants you to hear. Be careful that you do not allow a man and his opinions, interpretations and beliefs to become your truth. Jesus said, *"I am the way, the truth, and the life."* I say, "Any questions?"

July 28

From Him the whole body, joined and held together by every supporting ligament, grows and builds itself up in love, as each part does its work.
Ephesians 4:16

That is beautiful!

Each part does its work.

The human body is complex, and to most of us who have not studied it, it is simply amazing how it works. But if you remove one part of it, it can cease to operate properly or even completely stop working.

In this day and time of scientific invention and increased understanding of the body and how it works, we have devised artificial parts that are astounding in their own right. But nonetheless, whether they be the original part or a manmade replacement, all the parts must function properly, or we will not be able to do all the things our bodies are meant to do.

Are the scientists, doctors and surgeons who invent these parts and diagnose and perform these operations playing God? I don't think this is the case. I believe these things are discovered, invented and allowed by God. These bodies we inhabit are miraculous, but they are still just vessels and will be useless when we leave them and this earth.

But the point here is not about the physical body, it is about the body of Christ, which each and every believer becomes a part of. I believe each and every part of our body is essential to God's plan. You and I are part of the body of Christ. We are held together by Christ; built up by and filled with God's love; used by Him to complete His work.

Ain't it cool?

July 29

Be imitators of God, therefore, as dearly loved children and live a life of love, just as Christ loved us and gave Himself up for us as a fragrant offering and sacrifice to God. Ephesians 5:1-2

We are God's children, created in His image.

Does this mean we look like God? No, I think what it means is if we love God, and His Spirit dwells within us, we are like Him in spirit; our hearts become as one with the heart of God. In order to be an imitator of God, our Heavenly Father, we must sincerely love Him.

This seems so simple. How can we *not* love God?

Has anyone ever loved you too much? I have seen such situations; situations where one person in a relationship required every moment of their partner's thought, and all the attention and time that could possibly be given. The giving partner began to feel there was no time for anything else. The receiving partner was too needy.

A friend asked me one time if, with regard to a relationship, I would prefer to be wanted or needed. I thought it through for a few minutes and replied I would definitely rather be wanted. We agreed that when another person *needs* you, the relationship tends to get one-sided.

Recently, I thought about the need/want question with regard to God and came to the conclusion that God definitely does not *need* for us to love Him, but He certainly *wants* us to. And as far as the other way around, I believe we may think we *need* to love God, and I guess He won't mind if that's the case, but I think He would rather we love Him because we *want* to.

I don't know about you, but I *want* to love God.

July 30

Husbands, love your wives, just as Christ loved the church and gave Himself up for her. Ephesians 5:25

The church Paul refers to is the body of all believers in Christ. Paul teaches a marriage between a man and a woman should be treated the same as the relationship between Christ and His church—the body of believers.

Would you give yourself up for your spouse? I would. I have no doubt in my mind that if the choice was mine, and I could take on her pain, suffering and even death, I would do it. It is possible I might do it for any of you as well, but as to my wife, it is a certainty.

I don't know what else to say to this subject. It seems pretty cut-and-dried to me.

I will say to you I encourage each of you to love your spouse sincerely and completely. My philosophy—it hasn't always been so—is to try to out-love my wife. I want to love her so much, that it will be impossible for her to love me as much as I love her, no matter how hard she tries.

How can that fail?

July 31

This same way, husbands ought to love their wives as their own bodies. He who loves his wife loves himself. Ephesians 5:33

I guess I must love myself because there is no doubt I love my wife. I'm sure you must be wondering what it is about my wife that makes me love her so much.

I think she's one of the prettiest, smartest, most loving people I have ever met; she's a great mother to her children; she is a wonderful wife to me; she is a superb employee to those she works for; a terrific partner to those she works with; a fantastic supervisor to those who work for her; the most patient editor and proofreader a writer could want; and I could go on and on. Oh, and she doesn't play golf.

I'm just kidding about the golf thing. After a few frustrating trips to the driving range, she gave up the game. But, seriously, I think a guy needs his "me" time just like a gal needs her "me" time. We all need those times away from our spouse. Don't we? (Why do I suddenly feel so alone?) Ha! I crack myself up sometimes.

But back to my wonderful wife; do you know why I love her so much—the number one reason? Because she loves me more than I could possibly ever love her, no matter how hard I try. And her love is unconditional. (Lord knows I've tested it!)

But she just keeps on loving me. Yesterday, I said, "I want to love her so much, it will be impossible for her to love me as much as I love her, no matter how hard she tries." But did you notice the word "want" in that sentence? The truth of the matter is she is so far ahead of me, I will never catch up. But by golly, I'm going to try. God loves you and me so much we will never catch up, but I'm going to give that a try, too!

August 1

However, each one of you also must love his wife as he loves himself, and the wife must respect her husband. Ephesians 5:33

When I came to this verse on my list of those about love, ol' Archie Bunker piped up in my mind again: "Ah, jeez, Lord, can't we just skip dis one right here?"

Then I realized the words "submit to" and "head of" were not in this verse. Whew! Dodged that bullet!

But you know what? I'm just kidding with you again. I think most of the arguments regarding these verses are due to people trying to interpret them literally so they can use them in a way to gain power over their wife. And I have no desire to have any power or control over my wife. She's my partner and my best friend! Why would I want to control her? Why would I want her to submit to my authority?

When people try to conveniently arrange these verses for their benefit, I am always curious why Ephesians 5:21 isn't brought up. *"Submit to one another out of reverence to Christ."* Are we to submit to one another—except for our wives? That wouldn't make much sense.

I think you can see where I stand on this issue. I won't belabor it.

I love my wife *more* than I love myself!

End of.... no.... *beginning* of story!

August 2

And this is my prayer: that your love may abound more and more in knowledge and depth of insight. Philippians 1:9

God's love, and your love toward Him, will combine to open doors of knowledge and insight. I have found since I began writing these encouragements, my love for God has increased profoundly. And it seems as my love increases, I gain a better understanding and insight to what God desires from me.

In a nutshell—this will come as no surprise to any of you that have been reading these devotionals—what God appears to want from me, is for me to love Him. And as my love for Him increases, my knowledge and understanding increases as well. What I am experiencing is a sort of whirlwind effect where love leads to understanding, and understanding then leads to more love, and the cycle continues for what I hope will be an eternity. What started out as a small circle seems to grow wider as it spirals upward toward God.

I say I hope the cycle of love and learning will continue forever, and I have faith it will. I will never completely understand God or know all He knows, but with an eternity to love Him and learn of Him, who knows what the limits are?

I hope the things I am writing are encouraging and help those who read them to better understand and love God. The writing of them has been a most incredible blessing to me.

August 3

> *If you have any encouragement from being united with Christ, if any comfort from His love, if any fellowship with the spirit, if any tenderness and compassion, then make my joy complete by being like-minded, having the same love, being one in spirit and purpose.*
> Philippians 2:1-2

Paul knew the power God's people could have if they worked as one. I have always known God loved me, but I had no idea He wanted *me* to love *Him*. I have always believed God's love is the key to everything—I believe God *is* love. But I did not realize my love for God is as important to Him as His love is for me. When I realized that truth, lights began to come on.

As I was writing this, I suddenly envisioned myself walking around a lake. God slides up to the shore in a boat more awesome than anything I've ever seen. The ground vibrates beneath my feet as the boat idles in the shallow water. God says, "Want a ride?" I want to, but I'm thinking the boat is too big to be on such a small lake. God revs the motor and says, "I love you, you know?" I grin and say, "I love you, too, Lord," and decide a short spin won't hurt anything. Besides, it's God, and He loves me; how can I turn down a ride with God? Well, once I'm in, God spins the boat around, and all I can hear is the roar of the engine. Then suddenly, I realize it's not the engine I'm hearing, but God's voice. He's talking at a speed I shouldn't be able to understand, and yet I do. He's telling me all this wonderful stuff—things I've heard before, but never understood—and I understand! It's all so simple. And as we speed across the lake at a speed I didn't know existed, my mind filling with the things God is telling me, I look out at the lake and realize it's no longer small; in fact, it goes on as far as I can see.

The experience of knowing how unlimited God's love is, combined with our returning that love to Him, can open doors to insight and knowledge we didn't even know were there.

God's love is a two way street. Return His love and open the door, my friends. You won't regret it.

August 4

Brothers, I do not consider myself yet to have taken hold of it. But one thing I do: forgetting what is behind and straining toward what is ahead. Philippians 3:13

I *had* to write an encouragement to you (but more to me) using this verse. This has been "my" verse for about twenty-five years or so. I claimed it as mine back then due to a mix-up with some church-league softball shirts. The pastor of the church and I had both chosen the number three, and I told Him to keep the number for his shirt, and I would change mine. I came up with the idea to find a verse that said something about me and change the 3 to 3: whatever. After much searching through all of the chapter threes in the Bible, I came to this one, and on the back of the shirt I placed Philippians above the 3, and :13 beside it. A lot of the guys followed suit—no pun intended.

The verse fit me well back then, and it still fits today. I may know more about God, I may understand God better, but I do not consider myself as having even put a dent in what there is to know and understand about Him. But one thing I do: forget what is behind and strain forward to what is ahead.

I've made lots of mistakes in my life—some big, some small and everything in between—but I've learned to let them go and move on. Some of them still linger in my mind and maybe always will, but I don't let them get me down like I used to. I've found loving God is a full time job, and the pay is great. Some of those mistakes hurt me, and some hurt others; some were costly. But I learned something from most of them—I seemed to always have to learn the hard way. And as for the costly ones, Jesus paid for those. Yes, sir, He paid them all.

Thank you, Jesus.

August 5

You learned it from Epaphras, our dear fellow servant, who is a faithful minister of Christ on our behalf, and who also told us of your love in the spirit. Colossians 1:7-8

Love in the Spirit is the love of God flowing from within us, out to those around us. When we love God, and His Spirit fills our hearts, we cannot prevent His love from spreading to others.

There are many people in this world I do not agree with. Some of them make me angry with their devious and wicked schemes. I know my anger toward them will do nothing to stop them in what they are planning and hoping for. They may even profess to know God, but if you listen closely to what they are saying, you will hear what they really mean. God will open your mind and allow you to hear the false lines a wicked man slips into his eloquent speech. God will give you insight when His love and Spirit live within you.

It is not our duty to judge those who do wrong. It is, however, our responsibility to pray for them. We must lift them up to God and pray He will open their hearts to His love, knowledge and wisdom and cause them to turn from their evil scheming and do what is right.

I hope I don't sound pious in my thinking by saying these things. I certainly am not one who can point fingers at another. My house is indeed constructed of glass, and to throw stones would invite trouble I don't need.

I merely want to point out there is evil in this world, and we shouldn't ignore it. We should, by praying for them, turn it over to God. After all, God may have a part in His plan for that evil man or situation. God may not appoint evil, but I believe He often, if not always, uses it and turns it to His advantage.

Love God so His Spirit within you will recognize evil and keep you from its path. Trust God to use everything to His advantage and to the advantage of those who love Him.

August 6

For He has rescued us from the dominion of darkness and brought us into the kingdom of the son He loves, in whom we have redemption, the forgiveness of sins. Colossians 1:13

We have been *redeemed* and *forgiven* our sins by God, who sent Jesus to die for us and rescue us from the dominion of darkness. As I read those words, then write those words, the love of God overwhelms me.

I have been in the dominion of darkness. I have gone in, come out, gone in, come out, over and over throughout my life. Each time I was drawn back into the light, I vowed never again would I go back to that world where darkness hides the evil gleam in men's eyes. Sadly, I am only a man, and I sometimes—too many times—do not succeed in keeping my promises to God. The good news is, God's love does not waiver when mine does. His love is always the same—enormous and beyond our comprehension.

I will never be perfect, but I *will* love God. My love will probably never be as awesome toward God as His is toward me. I won't say that is definitely the case, because maybe with God's spirit within me, I can love Him as much as He loves me.

I know it's worth a shot, so I'm definitely going to believe it *can* happen.

August 7

> *My purpose is that they may be encouraged in heart and united in love, so that they may have the full riches of complete understanding, in order that they may know the full mystery of God, namely, Christ, in whom are hidden all the treasures of wisdom and knowledge.*
> Colossians 2:2-3

Wow! Sometimes these verses seem to blast off the page and slam into my mind!

I've talked before of how each of us wants our life to have purpose and meaning. We want to know we made a difference. We also want to understand God and experience the fullness of His love for us. We want to understand the mysteries of God and be full of His wisdom and knowledge. And here, in this verse, the mystery is revealed: to have all these things—full riches, complete understanding, wisdom and knowledge—we must be united in love. But what does that mean? Is it another mystery?

No! It is a mystery solved! I believe it means just what I have begun to understand more and more as I write and learn about God's love; what *we* have to *do* is love God. Then He—His love—will fill our hearts and minds, and we will love ourselves and others with His agape love. When we are enabled by Him to love in this manner, we will be united in spirit with others that love Him. And as it is written in Matthew 6:33, *"But seek first His kingdom and His righteousness, and all these things will be given to you as well."*

Love God, thereby seeking His kingdom and His righteousness; allow Him to unveil the mysteries and release all the wonders He has for you.

August 8

> *Therefore, as God's chosen people, holy and dearly loved, clothe yourselves with compassion, kindness, humility, gentleness and patience. Bear with each other and forgive whatever grievances you may have against one another. Forgive as the Lord forgave you.*
> Colossians 3:12-13

As I read these verses, the list of what Paul was saying believers must do seemed to be a bit of a challenge. When I came to verse thirteen, the challenge of all those things slipped silently away.

Almost every time I feel like someone has done me so wrong I will never be able to forgive them, I think of how God forgave me. There is no comparing God's forgiveness of us with anything we might have to forgive another person for.

I have found, in most cases, the things we are contentious with others about are, in the grand scheme of things, usually not that important. A question I think we need to ponder when we find ourselves in contention with another person is, does it really matter? I find in many instances, it does not matter. That's not to say there are not battles we need to fight.

Some of you who know me are well aware that if I perceive something to be unfair, I am quick to jump in and offer my opinion. I can be a formidable foe if I believe someone is treating others unfairly—especially if the unfairness stems from selfishness and/or greed.

After the fray, I sometimes have a hard time forgiving the opposition. But all I have to do is remind myself how God forgave me, even after all I've done, and I realize I have no choice but to forgive those on the other side of the aisle. I know it's hard sometimes, but we must learn to forgive others and move on. If the battle has been fought, won or lost, let it go.

August 9

And over all these virtues put on love, which binds them all together in perfect unity. Colossians 3:14

Perfect? There are sixteen words in that sentence; why did that one word jump out at me?

Because my first thought was, "That's not possible!"

Then, just as quickly, a voice inside me said, "Sure it is." And not being one to argue with voices from within me, I said, "Oh, really? Explain it to me!" (I was just kidding about not arguing with myself. I do it all the time.)

The explanation I got came in the form of two questions: "Who do you think you are?" and "Do you think you are the only one that God loves?"

"Oh," I said. "Right."

Sometimes we forget God's love is the same for everyone. I think each person's relationship with God is personal and unique, but in the end it all comes out the same. I love God, and He lives within and through me to accomplish His will—His plan. You, and others, love God—each in your own unique way—and He then lives through you to accomplish His will—His plan.

We all love God, and by that fact alone, we are in perfect unity. The differences in us and the way we love God are of no consequence.

We're all on the same team, but we don't all play the same position.

August 10

Husbands, love your wives and do not be harsh with them.
Colossians 3:19

Why would I be harsh with my wife?

Oh, let me see… I had a bad day at work; the Cowboys got beat by the worst team in the league; it's cold and windy, and I can't play golf today; my computer went to be with all the other broken computers.

How many times do we let our circumstances upset us and then take out our frustrations on the people we love most? Too many!

We let things bother us or upset us, and then we become grouchy, unhappy or both. We snap and snarl and cause those around us to become nervous or even fearful of us. I hate it when I do that!

I especially hate it when I do it to my wife. She doesn't deserve that!

And the sad thing is, when it happens it's not because I'm unhappy with her, and I don't intend to hurt her. Yet I allow my frustrations and disappointments to control my mood, and she has to deal with them along with me. Sometimes, that is exactly what we want—someone to share our misery. And that ain't right!

This subject is getting away from me, so to keep it brief, I will just encourage you by saying, "Love God." I believe when we love God our circumstances will no longer hold sway over our emotions and actions, but rather, our emotions—our joy—will sway our circumstances as God's love overpowers all.

August 11

We continually remember before our God and Father your work produced by faith, prompted by love, and your endurance inspired by hope in our Lord Jesus Christ. 1 Thessalonians 1:3

Many times in our lives, we reach a point where we are worn down by the trials that have come against us, and we begin to lose hope. Our endurance wanes, and we start to wonder if the enemy has won the battle.

It's important at those times we remember where our hopes lay—with Jesus.

At those times, no matter what our task might be, and no matter what challenges have come against us to try and prevent us from accomplishing the task, we must remember to love God. If that is our first reaction to trouble, I believe we will be inspired by hope, and trouble will have no power over us.

When our first reaction to the challenges that come against us is to turn our attention to God, love Him, then have faith that He is beside us and will assist us, our obstacles will not be able to stand in our way. *"If God is for us, who then can be against us?"* Romans 8:31

I believe everything hinges on loving God, and we can do nothing if we do not first love Him.

Boldly meet the trials you face, knowing your love for God has equipped you with His power, and no foe can stand against you and God.

August 12

We loved you so much that we were delighted to share with you not only the gospel of God but our lives as well, because you had become so dear to us. 1 Thessalonians 2:8

When, in this verse, Paul says they shared their lives as well, he is bestowing on the people of the church of Thessalonians a tremendous compliment; he is telling them because he loved them so much, he was able to bare his soul to them and tell them of his innermost thoughts and feelings.

I have found very few people in my life I have felt so strongly about that I could open up to them. I am fairly sure most of you will agree those kinds of friends are few and far between.

I have some now—my wife, Sherry, of course, is at the top of the list.

A couple of others come to mind when this subject arises, and I spoke to one of them recently on the phone. Our conversations are almost always jovial, many times irreverent, and always open. Neither of us has any fear of what the other might think of what we say regarding our feelings and beliefs, hopes and fears, concerns and sorrows, or anything that might be on our mind. He is a true friend, and sadly, we do not see one another or talk to one another as often as either would like. He said so as we concluded our recent conversation, I agreed and told him I missed talking to him.

We need people in our lives we can bare our souls to. For even though we can always take our troubles and trials to God, a sympathetic and understanding friend here in this topsy-turvy world can be a great comfort. If you have friends like that, cherish them and keep in touch with them. They are truly a gift from God.

August 13

But Timothy has just now come to us from you and has brought good news about your faith and love. He has told us that you always have pleasant memories of us and that you long to see us, just as we also long to see you. 1Thessalonians 3:6

Some of my fondest memories of my childhood are of times spent with relatives. My maternal grandparents, my mom's two sisters and their families, all lived in and around the same area in the Texas panhandle, and we spent many holidays, and other times as well, together. But then my family moved to Arizona, and looking back, it seems that was the beginning of the end of our close-knit larger family.

Many of those family members are receiving these encouragements via email, which I am thankful for. I'm thankful for the Internet because it allows us to stay in touch so easily, and I am also thankful my larger family stills keeps in touch.

As I moved into adulthood (kicking and screaming, and vowing it would never happen) I hoped for the closeness of the larger family we'd had when I was a child. Unfortunately, that is not only not how things worked out, but far from it. We are scattered to the four winds, especially my immediate family, but we stay in touch and get together when we can.

Life takes us where it takes us, and things don't always turn out the way we'd hoped, but family is important to me, even though they are far away. Most all of my memories of family are pleasant—I still smile broadly when I recall the airport incident with my brother, Ken, in Albuquerque—and I long to see all of my family. I know they feel the same way—except maybe Ken—and I love them all very much.

(Come on, Ken, It was April Fool's day!)

If you live near your family, enjoy them. If you don't live near them, stay in touch. It's important!

August 14

May the Lord make your love increase and overflow for each other and for everyone else, just as ours does for you. 1 Thessalonians 3:12

When Paul says, "May the Lord make your love increase," I don't think it is a casual use of the word "make." I believe Paul knew, that by first loving God, their love would automatically increase and overflow, because that is how God's love works.

For us, it may seem difficult to love someone who isn't doing things exactly the way we want them to or the way we think they should be doing them. God overlooks a lot of the things we do because He knows we are who we are and will make mistakes and will do things he wishes we wouldn't do. But that does not change His love for us. He constantly loves us to the fullest extent we can be loved. His love surpasses even our greatest understanding of love.

As human beings, our love is capable of increasing or decreasing. We give love or deny it, increase it or decrease it, in relation to what those we love do or say. That ain't right, folks!

But! I think the only way we can change the way we love others is by not trying to change it.

What did he say?

He said, "By not *trying* to change it." *Let God change it.* Our greatest command is to love God. When we do that, He will live within our hearts, and our love will be as His when it overflows toward others.

Hey. That's my story, and I'm sticking to it.

August 15

Now about brotherly love we do not need to write to you, for you yourselves have been taught by God to love each other. 1 Thessalonians 4:9

I almost think Paul was saying this tongue-in-cheek. In the verse that follows, he goes on to encourage the people to love more and more. But I won't try to read between the lines or interpret what Paul is saying.

What really gets my attention in this verse is when Paul says, "For you yourselves have been taught by God to love each other." For me, this is the key. God teaches us—puts it within us—to love each other.

Over and over we see instruction in the Bible about love, and what I keep seeing and hearing is God is love. God is the professor of love; the ultimate authority of love; He invented love; without Him there would not be love.

It seems as though I could go on and on with the list that ties God to love. But even if I did—if I filled pages and pages with God equated to love—I could never even touch the surface of what God's love is. The awesomeness of it, the extent of it, the feel of it, is beyond our limits of comprehension and understanding.

We will know it, and we will experience its enormity and excellence someday. And I am convinced we will know it if we do but one thing; love Him.

August 16

But since we belong to the day, let us be self-controlled, putting on faith and love as a breastplate, and the hope of salvation as a helmet.
1 Thessalonians 5:8

In Chapter five of his letter to the people of the church in Thessalonica, Paul is instructing them as to the second coming of Christ. In the second verse of Chapter five, he tells them *"for you know very well that the day of the Lord will come like a thief in the night."*

Since my youth, I have heard many proclaim the second coming of Christ is near. I have scoffed at most and even found amusement in some. There have been those who were so sure, they predicted the very date and prepared for it in various ways. People today are pointing to things and situations around the world that are the "signs" of the Lord's return. They are convinced the day is upon us!

I do not believe we are capable of interpreting or discerning the signs that will signal the second coming of Christ. That is not to say it is impossible. In Revelations 3:3, Jesus said, *"Remember, therefore, what you have received and heard; obey it, and repent. But if you do not wake up, I will come like a thief, and you will not know at what time I will come to you."*

I'm not sure what He meant by, *"If you don't wake up,"* but His statement, *"I will come like a thief, and you will not know at what time I come,"* is pretty plain and simple, don't you think?

My take on all this is it doesn't matter. As long as we are busy loving God and letting Him complete His plan through us, we're ready—we're awake.

Hey! Maybe I did understand that first part of what Jesus said!

August 17

Hold them in the highest regard in love because of their work. Live in peace with them. 1 Thessalonians 5:13

At first reading of this verse, I wondered if it was saying we should hold those the writers speak of in high regard for what they do. After reading more of the verses surrounding it, I began to think what they were saying was we should hold them in high regard because of what they do, not because they do it.

What I'm trying to say is the people of that age were the same as we are today. They had the same greatest command as we do; love God first. The teachers and pastors of the day were not doing what they did of their own accord. They were doing what they did after first loving God, continuing to love Him and allowing Him to lead them and teach the people what He wanted them to know.

Yes, it's simple. Our job is to love God. But as our love for Him develops and He is able to draw us nearer to Him, He imparts wisdom and understanding, so we might in turn impart the same to others. Some of us will do so by writing, some from behind a pulpit, some with song and some by other varied means.

We are chosen by God to assist Him in His plan. We don't know in what manner He might use us, and some of us may not know until we stand before Him. We might think we know, but in the grand scheme of things, that is all we will do: *think* we know.

One thing we *can* know for certain is we love Him, and He loves us.

August 18

We ought always to thank God for you, brothers, and rightly so, because your faith is growing more and more, and the love every one of you has for each other is increasing. 2 Thessalonians 1:3

I don't think it was an accident that, as their faith grew, their love for each other increased. Their faith was faith of something unseen and faith in an eternal life with God. I believe their faith increased because their love for God increased. They were caught up in the whirlwind of faith, hope and love; love leading the other two, and all three spinning until the head and tail could not be distinguished.

I believe the more we turn our love toward God, the more the world will slow, and we will begin to understand more of what goes on in it. The things that bother us will fall away like a scab from a wound. A wound that took too long to heal, and then one morning you woke up, and it was gone.

God's love heals all wounds.

Sometimes I sense I have said all that needs to be said.

This is one of those times.

August 19

The coming of the lawless one will be in accordance with the work of Satan displayed in all kinds of counterfeit miracles, signs and wonders, and in every sort of evil that deceives those who are perishing. They perish because they refused to love the truth and so be saved. 2 Thessalonians 2:10

Not all will spend eternity with God. There are those who will never "*love the truth and so be saved.*"

What does that mean? "*Love the truth and so be saved.*"

I believe the "truth" is Jesus. In John 14:16, Jesus says, *"I am the way and the truth and the life. No one comes to the Father except through me."*

This is, quite simply, how we obtain forgiveness and eternal life with the Father—by loving Him. God came to earth in the form of a man—Jesus—was crucified on the cross and raised on the third day so those two things—forgiveness and eternal life with Him—could be ours.

The sad truth is some will choose not to love God. They will, instead, be fooled by counterfeit miracles, signs and wonders. They will perish because they do not love God. I can't imagine their fate. Because as wondrous and indescribable as the love of God for eternity will be for those who love the Truth, so much the opposite will it be for those who refuse to love the Truth. I don't even want to think what the horrors of Hell might be.

I choose to love God, not for fear of Hell, mind you, but simply because He asked me to.

August 20

> *But we ought always to thank God for you, brothers loved by the Lord, because from the beginning God chose you to be saved through the sanctifying work of the Spirit and through the belief in the truth.*
> 2 Thessalonians 2:13

This is one of those verses that contain so much good stuff, I don't know where to start or which to talk about. There's *"loved by the Lord"*, *"God chose you"*, *"sanctifying work of the Spirit"*, and *"belief in the truth."* Wow! Lots of good stuff!

I'm going to go with *"sanctifying work of the Spirit"*.

It's the things God does when we love Him, and by loving Him, we allow His Spirit to live in us and work through us. Those things He does through us are things that if we tried to do them without Him, we would fail miserably.

A big "for instance" is me writing these encouragements. I might be able to write them without loving God, but the words would probably mean nothing to those that do love Him. And they probably wouldn't mean anything to me!

I'm not going to test that theory.

I'll just continue to love Him.

August 21

> *May our Lord Jesus Christ himself and God our Father, who loved us and by His grace gave us eternal encouragement and good hope, encourage your hearts and strengthen you in every good deed and word.* 2 Thessalonians 2:16

Good golly now, I like the sound of that! How good can it get? Encouragement from God! It makes me want to jump for joy!

I mean seriously, what if every morning you turned on your computer, signed on to the Internet, and there in your mailbox was a daily encouragement—not from me, but from GOD. Wow!

But that encouragement is there—not in your email—but right there in your heart. If you wake up in the morning, and before you even roll out of bed, just lay there for a few seconds—be still—and say, "Good morning, God. I love you." When you do, you just signed up for God's encouragement! And there's no monthly fee!

God sent Jesus to die for our sins so we can spend eternity with Him. By His grace we are saved, and if we love Him, we become one with Him, and because He loves us, we have eternal encouragement!

I might have gotten excited and said some of that kind of funny, but I think you get the picture.

God loves us! He encourages us every day!

Awesome!

August 22

> *May the Lord direct your hearts into God's love and Christ's perseverance.* 2 Thessalonians 3:5

This verse is short, but sort of complicated. But you know me, I like to keep things simple—especially when it comes to God.

What I see in this verse is an affirmation that when we love God, we are filled with His love and His Spirit. We are then able to persevere as Christ persevered for our salvation so we could spend eternity with our Heavenly Father.

The verse was short, so I think the encouragement will be short, too.

Love God, be filled with His love and persevere.

Oh, and have a great day!

August 23

The goal of this command is love, which comes from a pure heart and a good conscience and a sincere faith. 1 Timothy 1:5

Love comes from a pure heart and a good conscience and a sincere faith.

"Okay! I'd like a pure heart, a good conscience and sincere faith! How can I get them? How much do they cost?"

You can get them simply by loving God, and they're free. Jesus paid for them.

When you love God, and are filled with His Spirit and love, your conscience will be good, and your faith will be sincere. It appears to me there is no other way to obtain either of those things.

When our goal is love, there is only one place we can get the real thing—from God.

Order yours today! The supply is endless!

August 24

Even though I was once a blasphemer and a persecutor and a violent man, I was shown mercy because I acted in ignorance and unbelief. The grace of our Lord was poured out on me abundantly, along with the faith and love that are in Christ Jesus. 1 Timothy 1:14

Timothy, the writer of this book in the Holy Bible, was not always a good man. By his own confession, he admits to his shortcomings and admits also to the fact that God, by His grace, instilled love in him. I don't know the history of it, but at some point, I'll bet you Timothy began to love God. God obviously had a place for Timothy in His plan. He called Timothy to Him, and Timothy heeded the call.

It is my belief when God calls, we come. If we are among His chosen, our free will is null and void. We still have free will in choosing to love God, and in some cases—mine, for sure—we may take our sweet time in doing that. I must confess, much as Timothy did, it was my ignorance of the importance of loving God that kept me from making the decision sooner. But let me tell you, once I realized the importance and value of loving God, I got right on it!

I am comforted by stories like Timothy's. I am one who, in my own mind, does not deserve the love of God. I spent so many years not loving Him, turning my back on Him and living life *my* way. And yet, He waited patiently on the other side of the river, sitting on that big rock and watching my every move, letting me learn things the hard way. I think He might have shed some tears and probably even laughed at some of the things I got myself into. But He waited…. and watched.

And when at last I yelled across that river and said, "I love you, God!" He jumped up off that rock and yelled, "I know you do, son! Now, get on over here! I've got a plan, and you're part of it!"

August 25

Don't let anyone look down on you because you are young, but set an example for the believers in speech, in life, in love, in faith and in purity. 1 Timothy 4:12

When Paul wrote this letter to Timothy, Timothy was a young man. It's very possible some of the older believers were not sure what to think of this youngster preaching and teaching to them. What could this young whippersnapper know about God they didn't already know? Paul encouraged Timothy to show the people his worthiness by the way he conducted himself—to let his light shine.

I believe this was probably an easy thing for Timothy to do, because he loved God, and of all the things Paul instructed Timothy to set an example in, the most important was love. I think Paul and Timothy knew that to leave love out of the list was akin to having no list at all. Without love, which is God, none of Timothy's actions would demonstrate to the people he was sincere in his beliefs. The good news—and I think Timothy knew it well—was as long as Timothy loved God, God would send His Holy Spirit to live within him and help him take care of the other things on the list.

All this applies to you and me, and in order to be an example to those around us, regardless of our age or stature, we must love God. He will take care of the rest. I imagine some of you—maybe many of you—disagree with my simplistic theory, and that's okay. I'm not trying to convince you of anything, but merely trying to give you encouragement. If there are things God puts in your heart for you to do, then by all means I encourage you to do them.

I have found that by focusing on God and loving Him, rather than focusing on a to-do list, I am more able to *do* the things God wants me to do. So I will continue to make loving God the first priority.

August 26

> *But you, man of God, flee from all this, and pursue righteousness, godliness, faith, love, endurance and gentleness.* 1 Timothy 6:11

There seems to be a separation between those who teach and preach, and those who follow. It seems to me there is something in between as well. I feel I fall into the in between area. A while back, a friend and I were talking about these encouragements I was writing. He was complimenting me on them and said, "There's a preacher in there somewhere, bro." I scoffed at the statement, telling him I surely was no preacher—not in the conventional sense, at any rate.

I am a few steps beyond follower, I guess. I've never been one to follow too much and have always considered myself a leader. For whatever reasons, I always seem to take charge and people seem to follow, or they fall in alongside me.

I think in this passage, Paul is instructing Timothy—a man of God and a teacher—to flee from what is ungodly and pursue what is Godly. It seems as though Paul is instructing Timothy what to do, rather than what to be, and I still believe it doesn't matter if you are a teacher, a preacher or a member of the congregation, if you love God sincerely, all the other things will come naturally. (Or should I say, supernaturally?)

I am convinced our first and greatest command is to love God. When we truly and completely do that, I believe He will fill us so full of His *righteousness, godliness, faith, love, endurance and gentleness*, we will not be able to remember what it was we used to do that disappointed Him.

August 27

For God did not give us a spirit of timidity, but a spirit of power, of love and self discipline. 2 Timothy 1:7

That's what I was talking about yesterday—being filled with God's love. To be filled with God's love is to be filled with God's Holy Spirit—His power, His love, His self discipline.

God is all those things and every other thing that can be considered good. When we love Him and allow His Spirit to come into us, we have all those things, too. They become second nature—maybe I should say first nature? They become things we do without giving a thought to them. They become natural to us.

When we love God, He walks with us and talks with us all day long and even whispers to us as we sleep. And everything He says is about how much He loves us.

A beautiful hymn popped into my mind the other day as I was driving ("popped into" is a way of saying God put it there). It was the chorus to "In The Garden," written by Charles Austin Miles in 1913.

"He walks with me, and He talks with me, and He tells me I am His own, and the love we share, as we tarry there, none other has ever known."

God's love for us is unique because each of us is unique. The love we share with Him is between each of us and Him, and no one else will ever know that love the way we know it.

These daily words of encourage are no more and no less than that—encouragement. I profess to know nothing except that God loves me, and I love Him. I encourage you to love Him, too.

August 28

What you heard from me, keep as the pattern of sound teaching, with faith and love in Christ Jesus. 2 Timothy 1:13

I believe you will hear what God chooses for you to hear whenever He chooses that you should hear it, and nothing but your love for Him will cause Him to speak. What I mean by that is I have heard about God for all my days, but until I realized the only thing He wanted me to do was love Him, the words and lessons fell on deaf ears. Only when I looked up and said, "God, I love you," did I begin to hear what He was saying to me.

I always believed in God, always had faith in Him and lived full of hope that I would spend eternity with Him, but I never said, "I love you, God." I didn't say it because I was ignorant of the fact that was what He wanted. I didn't get it.

I get it now, and this verse pounds it home. Paul is again instructing Timothy—and possibly all teachers—as to what he should do, but I see in the verse some of what I was saying the other day; some are teachers; some are students.

I certainly do not consider myself a teacher. I am God's student, and I am quick to admit I was a poor student for many years. I didn't pay attention and cut class all the time. I figured I could just slide by and still get a diploma on graduation day. Then I heard I could pass with flying colors and graduate with honors by acing just one class—Loving God 101.

The funny thing was, when I began studying and learning in the classroom of loving God, all the other lessons seemed to get easier. It was as though I had already learned them and was merely taking refresher courses. Huh. Go figure.

August 29

Flee the evil desires of youth, and pursue righteousness, faith, love and peace, along with those who call on the Lord with a pure heart.
2 Timothy 2:22

How old do we have to be before we stop fleeing the evil desires of youth? In my mind I still think I'm young, but my body sometimes proves otherwise. I get emails all the time—most of them from Cousin Salley—about what happens when we get old, and I always wonder why she sends them to *me*. But on the other hand, I sometimes look in the mirror and wonder what my grandpa is doing there.

The thing is, it doesn't matter how old or young we are, the evil desires of youth are in us. I might not be able to do anything with them at my age, but they are still there. We are not perfect and never will be. Even though we love God with every fiber of our being, we are sinful in nature, and we will sin. It may be a small sin, it may be a large sin, but still, we will sin.

I saw a movie about an old man that was ornery as anyone can be—he cussed, drank, hated his neighbors and on and on—and when he went to confession, he told the priest three little things he'd regretted in his entire life. The priest asked, "That's it?" The old man replied, "That's it."

But to that man, that *was* it. The other things he did, he considered were okay. I wondered if he considered them okay, because he knew he was a sinner, but God had sent Jesus to die for those sins, and he no longer had to concern himself with the little things. In a way that makes sense.

My point is, we aren't perfect and should not spend our energy trying to *be* perfect. If we put our efforts toward loving God, He will fill us with His righteousness, faith, love and peace, and He will take care of the small stuff.

August 30

You, however, know all about my teaching, my way of life, my purpose, faith, patience, love, endurance. 2 Timothy 3:10

Paul gave his all for Jesus. In this statement he makes to Timothy, he is not boasting, but stating facts and admonishing Timothy to follow in his example. The message is for us too. And we should look to Paul as an example of what a life dedicated to Christ can be.

A life dedicated to loving God will not be all roses and sunshine. There will be times we are tested by man and times when we are tested by God. I believe we can pass every test and endure things that come against us if we keep our eyes on God and love him ceaselessly.

Patience is a quality of love. Faith is a quality of love. If we love God, He will give us patience and faith, and our love for Him and all others will endure whatever challenges are thrown at it.

I believe once it gets into your heart and mind that God is love and the single most important command is to love Him, you will not be able to get it out of your heart and mind. It will stick there like a song that won't stop playing in your head.

Like this one: *Then sings my soul, my savior, God, to thee; How great thou art, how great thou art.*

I hope that song stays in your mind all day!

August 31

Teach the older men to be temperate, worthy of respect, self-controlled, and sound in faith, in love and endurance. Titus 2:2

As I grow older, I am becoming more temperate, self-controlled, sound in faith, in love and endurance. I left out worthy of respect, because I don't think that is something I can claim. I hope I have gained the respect of some I have come across, although I can guarantee I haven't gained it with all those I've known.

Sometimes I wish I could go back and undo some of the wrongs I've done. But then maybe that's why God lets us make those kinds of mistakes, so the pain of them will change our hearts and cause us not to repeat them. There are still some wrongs I've done that I hope to make right, but we will see where God takes us with that.

All I can do is the best I can do each day to treat everyone with love, respect and kindness, and hope those I have wronged in the past will forgive me.

Growing older is good in a lot of ways. All the temperance and self-control helps me to be a better person. I'm not fast enough to run away from trouble anymore, so I just keep my distance from it. I've heard it said nothing good happens after ten o'clock at night. I can certainly vouch for that from past experience, but I'm on daylight savings time senior-style nowadays, and I couldn't tell you what goes on after ten o'clock. I'm an hour or two into my eight hours by then.

It's all good though; saves me a lot of money on pickup body repairs.

September 1

Your love has given me great joy and encouragement, because you, brother, have refreshed the hearts of the saints. Philemon 1:7

When I first began to write these encouragements, I had no idea how they would be received. I literally just thought they would be something to write that might be beneficial to some who read them. It was just kind of a whim. I quickly realized it was more than that, because the more I wrote, the more excited I got and the more I seemed to understand what I was writing. God seemed to open my ears and eyes as I went along.

The real catalyst that set me sailing along this course was when I thought it would be a neat idea to print the first several days—forty or so, if I recall—put them in a binder and give them to my mom for Christmas. The look on her face, the tears, the sheer joy and excitement caused by that simple, unedited bit of writing was all the confirmation I needed to know this was something worth doing.

Since then, I have been constantly encouraged not only by the things I write—I think they encourage *me* as much as anyone who reads them—but by the comments and feedback from some of those who read them.

To those who have taken the time to respond and made this so worthwhile, I will paraphrase Paul's words, "You have given me great joy and encouragement, because you have refreshed my heart."

Thank you.

September 2

God is not unjust; He will not forget your work and the love you have shown Him as you have helped His people and continue to help them.
Hebrews 1:9

I like that. What I hear in this verse is when we show our love to God by helping His people and continuing to help them, He will remember our efforts. This seems like another one of those dog-chasing-its-tail or whirlwind situations, because it kind of goes in a circle that never ends.

God loves you; you love God; God fills you with love, and that causes you to want to help His people. And it just seems to grow and grow from there.

I feel so blessed to know that in this small way—just a little note of encouragement to whoever might want to read it each day—I am able to help God's people.

I need nothing in return. God's love is more than enough. This is the least I can do, and if He has more for me to do, I'm ready.

I encourage each of you to love God and see what He has for you to do to help His people. It is extremely rewarding!

September 3

God heard the boy crying, and the angel of God called to Hagar from heaven and said to her, "What is the matter, Hagar? Do not be afraid; God has heard the boy crying as he lies there." Genesis 21:17

In our darkest hour there should be no fear. God knows our every hurt and pain and is always there to comfort us. Whether we are old or young, standing in the wide-open or hidden beneath a bush, God sees us and hears our cry. His first words, should we listen for them, are, *do not be afraid*.

Those four words are God's promise to us when we love Him and have faith in Him. As I've said before, where there is love there is no fear. If we truly and completely trust God, we will fear nothing.

That is not to say we will not have pains and challenges, for life itself is those things. What I think it means is we can face and endure all things—all pains and challenges—knowing God will see us through them. I would add it is not wrong for us to cry out to God in our time of need. When we are faced with a hurt or challenge that overwhelms us, we should cry to the Lord in simple prayer, thanking Him for hearing us, being with us and delivering us from the things that come against us.

God is with us today.

Do not be afraid.

September 4

Because the Lord disciplines those He loves, and he punishes everyone He accepts as a son. Hebrews 12:6

These words are quoted from the book of Proverbs, and at first reading, they might cause one to pause. We tend to think of God as a good and loving God and not as one who punishes us. But if our earthly fathers had not disciplined and punished us when it was necessary, where would we be?

I know even that gives a few of us pause, because in some cases the discipline of our fathers went beyond instruction. But even that, I believe, God used to bring us to where He ultimately needed us to be.

God's discipline and punishment is necessary, too. As an earthly father teaches us the right way to live, so God teaches us. If He were to allow us to go through life doing whatever we pleased, suffering no consequences, where would we wind up? Would we say, "Hey, I like God. I can do anything I want, and He lets me get away with it." If there was no wrong and no consequences because of it, would we know what good is?

God forgives us of our sins, but he allows us to suffer the consequences as well.

But I encourage you to not dwell on doing things so as not to be disciplined, but rather, dwell on God's love for you, and love Him increasingly and sincerely. When you do that, I'm thinking there won't be near as much to be disciplined for.

September 5

> *Blessed is the man who perseveres under trial, because when he has stood the test, he will receive the crown of life that God has promised to those who love Him.* James 1:12

The King James and other translations use the word "temptation" rather than trial. In any case, I do not believe the words temptation or persevere are the important words in this verse. I believe the important words are the last five: "to those who love Him."

God has promised the crown of life—everlasting life with Him—to those who love Him. When we love Him, we will stand the test, because He will stand with us. Even when He allows us to be tempted or disciplined, He is still right there with us. He will allow neither beyond what we can endure.

He will not allow it, that is, if we love Him.

God has blessed me abundantly, but I believe the greatest blessing yet to come, is when at last I feel His breath on my face as He welcomes me and places His cheek upon mine. I cannot imagine the way that will feel.

The crown God promises us if we love Him is not a crown of gold and jewels, but a crown of joy and love.

For you rednecks (guys like me) who are reading this, the crown of life will be sort of like a gimme cap, but it won't have the name of your favorite sports team or beer across the front. It will have printed in bold letters: GOD.

September 6

Listen, my dear brothers: Has not God chosen those who are poor in the eyes of the world to be rich in faith and to inherit the kingdom He promised those who love Him? James 2:5

So is this verse telling us only the poor of this world will be rich in faith and inherit the kingdom God promised those who loved Him? Don't be silly!

God has chosen rich and poor and everything in between, and our inheritance is not based on what we do or what we have; it is based on loving God. He doesn't care if we are rich or poor—money means nothing to God—He only cares if we love Him richly.

I struggle with the concept of money. I work at a job I don't really enjoy a lot of the time, but I am reluctant to leave it because the pay is good. Oh, there are other good things about it, but the pay is what holds me there.

What I really would like to do is be able to write for a living. I love to write!

But I think I'm getting close to being able to do just that, and I'm looking excitedly to God for His word that I can pull the plug on this "job thing" and put my full attention to writing.

What is it you really want to do? What's holding you back? Money? Fear?

Ouch! I think I just punched myself!

September 7

If you really keep the royal law found in the scripture, "Love your neighbor as yourself," you are doing right. James 2:8

There is no need to try and read anything into this simple verse. It says what it means, and it means what it says. To love everyone is the "royal law."

We've been over this in days past, and it will come up again, I'm sure, but sometimes loving others—certain others, for sure—is very difficult to do. But I have to ask you, are *you* always easy to love?

I know there have been many times in my life where even God must have had a hard time loving me. I'm thankful He never gave up on me and always loved me, no matter what I did. To realize how much He really does love me is a true wonder to me. The thought that He loved me just as much back when I wouldn't give Him the time of day.... Wow! What a wonderful God!

But what about us? What about our ability to love those who are difficult to love? How do we do that? I've said it before, and I haven't changed my mind; we do it by first loving God. When we love God, He lives within us, and since God is love, love lives within us. The more we love God, the more love lives within us and the more love emanates from us toward others. Got it?

Well, gitcha some! (That's redneck for "get you some")

God loves you. Love Him, and let His love work from within you.

September 8

Though you have not seen him, you love him; and even though you do not see him now, you believe in him and are filled with an inexpressible and glorious joy. 1 Peter 1:8

Can we truly say we have not seen God? Can we look around at the wonders that are His creation and say we do not see Him? Can we look at our hands as they fly across the keyboard or piano and say we have not seen God? The human body is a miraculous thing. The air, the seas, the mountains and valleys are all connected much the same as the limbs and organs and skin of our bodies. A flower, a bee, an ant, a butterfly; the list is endless, and always, each piece is a wonder in its own right.

God created us in His image. I don't believe that means in His physical image—though I don't know that for sure—but rather in His image as relates to love. God is love, and I believe He created us to be love—an image of Him.

I have not seen the face of God, though I have imagined it. I have imagined a smile and love-filled eyes; a brow unlined and long hair, gray and shining. I have heard His voice as well as His silence.

And yes, I believe in Him.

And yes, I am filled with an inexpressible and glorious joy.

September 9

Now that you have purified yourselves by obeying the truth so that you have sincere love for your brothers, love one another deeply, from the heart. 1 Peter 1:22

To obey the truth is to obey the word of the Lord, which to me translates: love God. I believe loving God is the only thing that will truly purify us. If we do not love Him, we are unable to separate ourselves from the world and all that would keep us from God's love.

I also believe the only way we can have a sincere love for others is by first having a sincere love for God. God is love, so how can we be love or share love if we do not love Him and allow His love to become a part of us—literally allow ourselves to become love.

Love comes from the heart—the soul—of us, and that is where God should be—in our hearts.

A song was in my mind when I woke up this morning. Songs often come into my mind unbidden, and sometimes they are obscure songs from my past. Some of them I don't even remember hearing. But this one is an old country song by Waylon Jennings, and the verse that was in my head was, "And the door is always open, and the light's on in the hall."

The song is obviously not about God or Godly things, but it made me think of how God always leaves the door open for us, and His light is always on so we can easily find Him. God speaks to us in many different ways as we go through our day, but He always speaks the truth, and in that truth, there is always love.

God is so good! How can we not love Him?

September 10

Above all, love each other deeply, because love covers over a multitude of sins. 1 Peter 4:8

I don't think this means if we love others, it will cover *our* sins. I think what it is saying is if we love others, we will overlook their sins and shortcomings. We will have the same kind of love for others God has for us. He loves us unconditionally and forgave our sins by grace, with the death of Jesus on the cross.

When we love God, we will know His love for us more deeply, and as God envelopes us in His love, and His love lives within us, we will love others more deeply. It will come as naturally to us as it does to God.

Too often, we tend to be unforgiving. When others are doing things the way we think they should, we love them. But when they do something we don't approve of, or something that isn't in tune with what we expect of them, we are quick to toss them to the side and stop loving them.

What if that was the way God treated us? Man! I'd be bruised from head to toe from getting tossed off to the side!

Love God, and let His love and forgiveness become the way you love and forgive others.

God does it for you and me every day.

September 11

Show proper respect to everyone: Love the brotherhood of believers, fear God, honor the king. 1 Peter 2:17

Fearing God, in my opinion, is not to shy away from Him, but rather to love and revere Him. I don't believe God wants us to cower at His feet, trembling in fear of His wrath. I believe He wants us gathered around Him, praising His goodness and mercy. He wants us to admire Him and speak of Him affectionately.

Honoring the king, or in our country's case, the president, is an entirely different thing. Our political system has become so corrupt and out of control it is difficult to look upon our leaders with the respect we should. Unfortunately, it has almost always been this way. There have been good leaders and bad leaders throughout the history of our country, and the same can be said of leaders of other nations. To honor a bad man is a very difficult thing to do. In some cases, I cannot do it. I pray if it is His will, God will put it within my heart to do so.

On the other hand, there are many who deserve to be honored. Among them is a group that consists of neither kings, nor presidents; they did not ask for power, fame, fortune, or for that matter, honor. They simply went to work on a Tuesday morning, September 11, 2001, and set about their tasks as they had many times before. Approximately 3000 of them did not return home that day. They died a senseless and horrible death at the hands of Godless men.

Today, I honor those who died in the attacks on our country on that day, especially those whose job it was to try and save lives. Many brave men and women gave their own life to save the lives of others, and in my mind *they* are *truly* worthy of honor.

September 12

For, whoever would love life and see good days must keep his tongue from evil and his lips from deceitful speech. 1 Peter 3:10

This is another tough one. The tongue—at least in my case—is truly an unruly member and has caused me tremendous pain and embarrassment over the years. I have a well developed sarcastic sense of humor that is the biggest culprit. Running a close second to it is that I have a bad habit of speaking before I think.

But I plead Philippians 3:13 on this one; *Brothers, I do not regard myself yet to have taken hold of it. But one thing I do: Forgetting what is behind and straining toward what is ahead.*

In other words, I'm working on it.

I also fall back on what I've been saying for months; God's love is the key. I believe when we love God, He will fill us so full of His love that somewhere down the line that evil old tongue will no longer embarrass us. It's a growing thing, I think. As our love for God grows and overflows from us to others, it drowns out the old things—the bad things. Without noticing—without even trying to—we change. We think on good things and when we think on good things, we speak good things.

I assure you, I haven't taken hold of it yet, but I'm reaching for it. And I *will* take hold of it.

Bear with me, please.

September 13

And to Godliness, brotherly kindness; and to brotherly kindness, love.
2 Peter 1:7

In the first chapter of 2 Peter, Simon Peter tells how God has equipped each of us for life and lists the things He has given us so we can live a good and Godly life.

All the things Peter lists lead up to love, and I believe the list is useless without love. In fact, I don't think we can maintain any of the other attributes without first being filled with the love of God. We certainly cannot be Godly if we don't love God.

It's kind of like if you are a carpenter, and you have all the necessary tools, but don't have a tool belt to put them in. You can still do your job, but it will take longer because your tools are always disorganized, and every time you want to do something, you have to dig through your pile of tools to find the tool you need.

We can try to be good and love others, but if we first put on the tool belt—the love of God— we will be better able to carry all the tools God will provide us to help us to love others and do His work.

Put your tool belt on. Let's go love some folks.

September 14

But if anyone obeys his word, God's love is truly made complete in him. This is how we know we are in him. Whoever claims to live in him must walk as Jesus did. 1 John 2:5-6

Say what? How am I going to walk as Jesus did? Nobody's perfect!
That verse six can jump out and give a guy a scare. I mean, come on. How am I, Sinner-Max, going to walk as Jesus did?
Well, how did Jesus walk? In love.
Oh…. Okay…. I get it.
Lots of verses and stories in the Bible can appear to say something they don't. Some people will probably say I got this verse all wrong. That's okay. That's how I understand it, and that's how I'm going to live it.
I believe God's love is made complete in us because we love God. So if God lives in us, we live in Him, and we walk as Jesus did—in love.
That's my story, and I'm sticking to it, folks.

September 15

Whoever loves his brother lives in the light, and there is nothing in him to make him stumble. 1 John 2:10

I believe this verse is rather simple, because God is light, and God is love. If we love our brothers, it is because we love God, and God's love and light live within us. But you know that, right? And if we love our brothers, we will do nothing to make them stumble. We will set a good example for them.

When I was young, I wanted to grow up to be a professional baseball player. I remember telling my mom—I was only eleven or twelve at the time—if I got to be a professional ball player, then kids would look up to me, and I could tell them about God. I think my mom kind of smiled at that and asked why I just didn't grow up and be a preacher.

I remember answering with something like, "*Mom*, preachers aren't famous. Who's going to look up to them?"

I think mom still prays that I will be a preacher, but I'm inclined to think I will do my preaching from the printed page.

But the fact is, a person doesn't have to be famous or have talent. God has a use for each of us. Maybe all he wants me to do is encourage the handful of people who are reading these daily encouragements. Maybe the poem I wrote in 1998, "*Pennies From Heaven*", is my life's work.

If God is okay with it, I'm okay with it. He calls the shots, I just shoot them.

September 16

Do not love the world or anything in the world. If anyone loves the world, the love of the Father is not in him. 1 John 2:15

That's not as hard to do as it might sound. In fact, when you get right down to it, there's not much in this world that can compare with love—especially when we're talking about God's love.

I don't love the things of this world, and I certainly have no love for the world as it is today. It's one giant mess, if you ask me. All most people care about is themselves, their money and their right to say and do anything they please—that's the definition of freedom these days. Our priorities are so far out of whack, we're going to the wrong game, and we won't know it until we see the players come out in the wrong color uniforms. And speaking of games, the Super Bowl has become more important to most people than Easter or Christmas.

I've lost interest in watching sports. Along with so many other things, sports have transitioned to the point where it isn't about winning any more—it's *all* about money. Every part of every sport is designed and promoted so it will gain maximum revenue. Players make millions, owners make millions, sponsors make millions, and the fans are willing to fork out a week's pay to see the millionaires strut around on the field and act like criminals off it.

I got carried away there. I know there are good men involved in sports, and I admire some of them. Kurt Warner, Drew Brees and Tim Tebow are some of my favorites. They are the kind of example to young and old alike that I had hoped (still hope) to be. (Please see Philippians 3:13)

Love God.

He loves you.

The world doesn't even know you exist.

September 17

How great is the love the Father has lavished on us, that we should be called children of God! And that is what we are! The reason the world does not know us is that it did not know Him. 1 John 3:1

The world denied that Jesus was the Son of God sent by God to save the world from sin. They denied He was God, and they persecuted, then killed Him because of who He claimed to be and the message he so boldly brought to the world. They did not know Him.

And the world—those who do not and will not know God—do not know us. We are invisible to them because they consider us fools to be pitied. Wicked, Godless men will not look into the light that is the love of God. They are afraid of it and shield their eyes and hearts from it by denying it.

How sad is that?

We are loved so much by God that He calls us His children. He gathers us 'round Him, and He tells us stories that demonstrate His love. He tells us we are His children, and though He admits we are adopted, we are heirs to His kingdom and all within it.

It's a miracle! God had our names in His book of those he wanted to live with Him and love Him, and He had them there before we even knew who and what He is.

Awesome! We're some lucky kids, you and me!

September 18

Dear friends, now we are children of God, and what we will be has not yet been made known. But we know that when He appears, we shall be like Him, for we shall see Him as He is. 1 John 3:2

 This verse does not have the word love in it, but it was in my list, and it interests me, so I will use it. It speaks of the second coming of Christ, what we will be like when we see Him, and what He will be like. It causes me to wonder; what does love look like? For if God *is* love then He will *be* the very picture of love when we see Him. Love will no longer be an unseen feeling; it will have a face and a presence. I can't even imagine what a sight that will be, to see Jesus and know we will spend eternity loving Him and being loved by Him.

 I wonder sometimes if the people who love me the most—my wife and my mom—are not the same as Jesus. Perhaps theirs is the very face and embodiment of love. I feel so loved by them and yet I know what I feel from them and what I feel for them—a tremendous love—cannot even begin to compare with the love Jesus and our heavenly Father have for us. Even the love of God we can perceive right now is but a glimpse of what awaits us.

 When God is finally before us and the beauty of Him and His love emanates and fills the air around us and caresses every fiber of us, it will be like nothing we have ever known or can imagine.

 Smile! You are a child of God!

September 19

This is the message you heard from the beginning: We should love one another. John 3:11

Have you heard enough about love? I haven't. I know some of these verses are repetitive, and I suppose many days these encouragements seem repetitive, too. I hear this commercial on the radio a lot—I'm not sure what they are advertising—where the guy says something to the effect of, "You won't become successful by doing four thousand things, you will become successful by doing twelve things four thousand times." (I probably didn't get that right, but I think it's close) In any case, I think their point is that doing what works, repetitively, gets results.

My point is, we might hear the same thing over and over, day after day, but until God opens our ears and heart to it, we won't get it. I'm just saying the same thing—love God—over and over, so you won't miss the day when God opens your heart to hear and understand His message about love.

I guess you could say this is kind of like our little classroom for "Love 101". So you folks, in the desks up front that already got it, just keep listening. I'm sure God has more for you. If you haven't got it yet, don't fret; God won't give up if you won't. As a matter of fact, I don't think He'll give up even if you do!

So love one another! That's the theme of this course! If you don't get it, I have to wonder if you're paying attention. And if you're not paying attention; go to the blackboard and write, "I love God," four thousand times!

September 20

We know that we have passed from death to life, because we love our brothers. Anyone who does not love remains in death. 1 John 3:14

The death John speaks of is a moral death. When we love God, and through His love in us as we become one with Him, begin to love others, we move out of the darkness of death and step into the light of life with God. Those around us will know we are of God by the light and love we project.

I must be part cat, because I think I've gone into the dark again about nine times now. But thankfully, Jesus knows GCPR, and He keeps reviving me and sending me back to the light. In case you're wondering, GCPR is, God's Cardiopulmonary Resuscitation. It's a little different than regular CPR, in that He still breathes life into you, but instead of pushing on your heart, He pulls on it until He gets your attention and then lifts you onto your feet and walks alongside you in case you need assistance.

I've been through it so many times, He can usually revive me and get me going again by just whispering in my ear, "Do you love me?"

But there it is, the key—loving God. It always comes around to that.

If you're hurting real bad, dial G-O-D, and help will be there in a flash, but if you're just slightly injured, be still, listen… God is whispering, "I love you."

September 21

This is how we know what love is: Jesus Christ laid down his life for us. And we ought to lay down our lives for our brothers. 1 John 3:16

Surely y'all have seen that poster someone always has at football games that has "John 3:16"—probably the most famous verse in the Bible—written on it. Did anyone else notice that 1 John 3:16 says pretty much the same thing as John 3:16? I wonder if John knew he was doing that. Interesting!

Anyway, as for laying down our lives for our brothers, I don't think John is suggesting we should die for others as Jesus died for us. We can't be Jesus, though it doesn't hurt to want to be like Him. I think what John is saying is we should love God and be an example to our brothers. When we love God and die to sin, we are in essence dying for others, as we show them God's love and encourage them to love Him, too.

What does love look like? I've asked the question before, and I've imagined God's love when we see Him will be like nothing we can even fathom. But what does love look like right now? Does it have a physical presence we can see? Can we reach out and touch it, or get a handful of it? I think we can, and I think I know what it looks like.

It looks like my grandpa when I look in the mirror.

Go look in your mirror. Tell the person you see there you love God. I think the person in the mirror will smile.

September 22

If anyone has material possessions and sees his brother in need but has no pity on him, how can the love of God be in Him? 1 John 3:17

How do we deal with this? I surely do not have the answer.

I can't—and you can't—help every person we see who is in need. These days if you drive down the city streets, you will see a person in need on almost every corner. How can we possibly help all of them? In my own mind, I have a hard time wanting to help any of them. I tend to think many of them beg because it is easier than finding a job and maintaining a house and vehicle. They take the easy way—at least it seems easiest to them. In any case, I feel that many of them—the homeless-- choose to live the way they do, not out of necessity, but simply as a matter of choice.

I think we need to defer to God for guidance on this subject, especially with regard to the homeless. As for a brother in need, I believe in helping those around me. I help where I can and as much as I'm able. I admit I'm choosey about who I help, but hey, I'm doing the best I can.

I love God, and I believe the love of God is in me. If God puts it in me to help others—even those I'm not sure I want to help, I'll do it and do it gladly.

If we know of someone truly in need, we should ask God how He wants us to help that person. I think God will answer and lead us in the way we should go. I also believe helping someone doesn't just bless the one we help; it allows God to bless us, too. I know we can't out-love God, and I don't think we can out-give Him either.

September 23

Dear friends, let us not love with words or tongue but with actions and in truth. 1 John 3:18

We say things all the time we don't really mean. One of my favorites is when someone asks me, "How are you?" Without a second's pause, I invariably answer, "I'm good, and you?" And the fact of the matter might be I'm not good at all. I might be feeling poorly, have a problem on my mind or some other such thing.

But when I say "I love you," you can take that to the bank, as they say. It took me a long time to gain what bit of understanding of love I have, and I do not approach the subject lightly.

The subject of love is too important to regard lightly. It is, in my opinion, everything and *all* things in one tidy—and quite large—package. It is God. God is love, and how can we take God and love lightly.

If you love God, by all means, tell Him you love Him. If you love others, tell them as well. But if you don't love God and others, don't think for one minute you can just say it and not mean it. God will know, and so will they.

September 24

Dear friends, if our hearts do not condemn us, we have confidence before God. 1 John 3:21

The last three days, we talked about laying down our lives for our brothers, about helping our brothers in need, and we talked about loving with actions, not just words. This verse, though it does not contain the word "love," tells us God knows our attitudes about all three of those things by what He sees in our hearts. Others will know as God knows, because what is in our hearts manifests in how we live our lives.

You've heard the saying, "He wears his heart on his sleeve," haven't you? I'm not sure where the saying comes from, but what it means to me is a person shows their inner feelings by their outward actions. You can *see* they care about the lives and needs of others and they love others. It's obvious in how they live.

If we love God and allow Him to be in us and guide us, our hearts will be pure and free from condemnation.

And it will show.

Love God.

Wear Him on your sleeve.

September 25

And this is his command: to believe in the name of his Son, Jesus Christ, and to love one another as he commanded us. 1 John 3:23

Believe and love. Not too much to ask, is it? It's all God asks—commands. Just believe He loves us so much He would die on the cross for us. Just love Him. That's all, two little things.

Suppose you were applying for a job—a job you were in no way qualified for. In fact, all your life you had shown you were not only unqualified for the job, but instead, you had actually done everything you could do to show how unqualified you are.

The supervisor looks at your resume, tosses it aside, and says, "You're in."

Your eyes get as wide as dinner plates and you say, "Seriously? How much does the position pay?"

He says, "How much do you want?"

You: "All I can get!"

Him: "It's a deal."

That's the deal God gives us. We're in no way qualified or worthy, but He gives us everything He has—a full measure of faith, hope and love.

He's looking for good people right now. The only qualifications are that you believe in His Son and love Him.

Is anyone interested?

September 26

Who believes that Jesus is the Christ is born of God, and everyone who loves the father, loves his child as well. 1 John 5:1

It's a no-brainer if you ask me. How could we not love Jesus? I guess the only way would be if we didn't believe in Him, and that is not an option as far as I'm concerned.

I have close friends who have close friends outside our friendship that I don't know. It's always been my attitude though, that a friend of my friend was a friend of mine. I figure if someone I care about, admire and trust feels the same about another person, then I can assume the other person is worthy of my admiration and trust as well. Man! That can get you going around in a circle!

But that, too, is a good way to describe it—a circle of friendship. One passes it to one, and that one passes it to another until eventually it comes back to the one who started it all.

I believe that can be said of God's love, too. But it's more of a circle around God than one that comes back to Him. We pass His love to one another as it emanates from Him to us, and He is the center and focus of the love we all have for Him. We are kind of like the planets rotating around the Son, but, in this situation, we are all the same distance from Him.

Love the Father, love the Son. No problem!

September 27

This is how we know that we love the children of God: by loving God and carrying out His commands. 1 John 5:2

There it is again, as simple as it can be, God's recipe for love.
Ingredients:
1. As much Love for God as you can round up
2. Book of God's commands
3. Generous sprinkling of Love for Yourself
4. Large amount of Love for others

Put Love for God in your heart and allow to rest there until thoroughly ready to add remainder of ingredients. (Do not rush this step) Then as Love for God begins to rise, open Book of Commands and allow Love of God and Commands to blend in your heart. Do not be alarmed if your heart begins to swell. Ingredients 3—Love for Yourself and 4—Love for Others will be added by God. Serves: Anyone that wants some. Serving size: Huge

Enjoy!

September 28

This is love for God: to obey His commands are not burdensome.
1 John 5:3

You might look at the Ten Commandments and read all the instructions in the Bible and think there is no way you can do all it says to do. If you look at it that way, and think you have to obey God's commands before you truly love God, you are going about it backwards. Folks who try to do things this way quickly become discouraged, and many give up.

I believe the key is to love God first. He will then come into your heart and cause you to obey His commands. He will also fill you with His love—He is love—and you will love yourself and others.

God does not demand we love Him, and He does not demand we follow His commandments. Following His commandments is a result of us choosing to love Him.

There is a catch though.

If God chooses you to be on His team, he will keep calling until you love Him. He's the world's most persistent telemarketer. He calls night and day, and you can't put Him on the do-not-call list. You can erase His messages, but they will continue to play in your head, so don't waste your time.

Save yourself some time; take the call. You will find that loving God is the best offer out there, and His commands are not burdensome. In fact, they will actually remove burdens from your life.

Answer that call!

September 29

And this is love: that we walk in obedience to his commands. As you have heard from the beginning, his command is that you walk in love. 2 John 1:6

I believe to walk in love is to walk hand in hand with God, and as we do it, we will become like Him. We are created in His image, and His desire is to love us and be loved by us. God is all about love. He's not about rules and regulations. He tried that when we started messing up in the beginning, and from what I can tell from all the stories in the Bible, the rules thing didn't pan out.

After the fall of man in the Garden of Eden, God tried to get man back in line. He gave us all the rules and regulations, swatted our behinds and sent us on our way. He still loved us, though, so He kept giving us chances to do things His way and come back to the good life He had for us. I think He finally realized we just couldn't do it on our own, so He sent Jesus to fix things for us.

What Jesus did, was return things to the way God originally intended them to be. He made love the number one priority. Loving God became the greatest command, and Jesus takes care of the rest.

So there it is! Our job is to love God. That is *the* command. If we do that one thing, God will live within us, and all the other things will come naturally.

Hold your hand out, let God take it in His, and let your love flow to Him. Hang on though, because the love that comes back from Him will knock you off your feet!

September 30

Keep yourselves in God's love as you wait for the mercy of our Lord Jesus Christ to bring you to eternal life. Jude 1:21

Mercy is defined as compassion or forbearance shown to an offender. That is what God, by sending Jesus to die on the cross, shows us—mercy. God has mercy toward us, and if we do the one thing He commands us to do—love Him—He will reward us with eternal life.

What do we do while we wait, looking eagerly toward the day when we will at last be with God and begin a life of all-consuming love with Him? After all, waiting is never much fun.

Some friends and I play in an annual golf tournament, and it is always a blast. One of my best buddies says the same thing every year as we are waiting for the start of the tournament; "Okay, let's go! I'm tired of *almost* golfing!" He's joking, but he's serious, too. He knows how much fun we're going to have, and he doesn't like the time we spend waiting for things to get started.

Since we were children, we have experienced this kind of excited waiting. Christmas, birthdays, the big game, all seemed to take forever to arrive. I wait anxiously and impatiently each year for spring to arrive. Winter—even though it isn't that bad in Central Texas—is not my favorite time of year, and I can't wait for it to be over.

All these things are situations where we are allowing time to pass swiftly—even though it appears to drag on forever—while we stare off into the future, not enjoying the now we are in.

I am trying to learn to enjoy the times that seem irrelevant. As I look back, I wonder how much I let pass by me while I was waiting for the "good stuff" to get here.

I've found the more I love God, the more I enjoy *all* the things that are happening while we await His return.

October 1

And from Jesus Christ, who is the faithful witness, the firstborn of the dead, and the ruler of the kings of the earth. To him who loves us and has freed us from our sins by his blood. Revelation 1:5

The book of Revelations is a fascinating book. There are only a few verses in it that mention love or use the word love. I looked at them and thought maybe I would not even attempt to make sense of them or try to write about them. But this one seemed to make sense to me, so I thought, why not?

The first thing that struck me is the statement that Jesus *is the faithful witness*, for *that* He certainly is. Who better to testify on our behalf? He has taken all our guilt upon Himself and rendered us innocent of all charges.

Then Jesus is described as *the firstborn of the dead*. He has defeated death and is the first to do so, but we will follow when we cast off our sinful nature and follow Him to everlasting life.

And the next one—my favorite—*the ruler of the kings of the earth*. Yes, this one makes me smile. I am disturbed by the evil men and women of this world who are elected to, inherit, or in some instances, take by force a high office; so many of them ignorantly believing they arrived in their position of their own accord and ability. Some of them use God's name to obtain votes and favor, then sneer at His name in private. Many of them know but one God, and that is money. My prayer for these men and women is they realize the error of their ways and ask God's forgiveness.

We should pray for our leaders; pray they will do what is right; but we should also remember God is ultimately in charge.

October 2

May the God of hope fill you with all joy and peace as you trust in him, so that you may overflow with hope by the power of the Holy Spirit. Romans 15:13

Today I will switch topics again. I've probably bored you long enough with the verses regarding love, so I am moving on to verses in the Bible that deal with "peace" and "joy." These are two of my favorite topics, and I hope you enjoy the encouragement they offer.

I will say it right now (and more than likely repeat it during the next few months): I believe no person or circumstance can *take* your peace or your joy from you. You have to make the decision to *give* them away. If you have hope in God and are at rest in your faith in Him, you will be filled with love for Him, and He will empower you by His Holy Spirit. With that kind of power working in you and for you, nothing or no one can touch your peace or your joy.

We have been encouraged to obey the greatest command, which is to love God. I believe in the days to come, we will understand that when we love God, we will find peace within ourselves, and our joy will grow.

Fear nothing, love God, trust God, put your hope in God, and He will give you peace and joy beyond your wildest imaginings.

They are yours to keep.

Don't give them away.

October 3

And the peace of God, which transcends all understanding, will guard your hearts and your minds in Christ Jesus. Philippians 4:7

The peace of God. I can think of nothing quite so desirable to me than to know the peace of God. I come close to it sometimes, I think, but I don't know if I have ever quite achieved it. Or if I have, it hasn't been to the degree it is available. Not even close.

I have felt closer to God as I write these encouragements, and I've even commented how I seem to be writing more to myself than to others. But the closeness and the understanding I seem to come so close to at times, seems to avoid my grasp. Sometimes I feel as though I've stumbled into a vast storehouse of knowledge and understanding for a few days or weeks, and then as if a switch has been thrown, I feel disoriented and confused. I've let my peace be taken, which as I've already said, I don't believe is possible. I think, more likely, I gave it away.

And so, I repeat what I told you months ago: *I do not consider myself yet to have taken hold of it. But one thing I do: Forgetting what is behind and straining toward what is ahead.* Philippians 3:13

One day I will know God's perfect peace and joy because I will not stop until I take hold of it.

But I refuse to look back, because in the past is not where the answer lies.

I encourage each of you to join me as I press forward toward what is ahead.

October 4

Though you have not seen him, you love him; and even though you do not see him now, you believe in him and are filled with an inexpressible and glorious joy. 1 Peter 1:8

We have never seen Jesus, and yet we love Him, and the more we love Him, the more real He becomes to us. This is mysterious and yet so real. I know the more I write about God and the more I learn about Him, the more I love Him, and the more real and close He becomes.

The inexpressible and glorious joy seems to grow with each day, and yet I don't think I have come close to the feelings God has for us. I have experienced small amounts of joy in my life, but I know there is so much more. I hope by the time I finish writing these encouragements, I can say I know that joy. I hope, too, some of you can say it as well.

But I do believe in God, and I do love God. Even though I have not seen Him and do not see Him now, I have faith that I *will* see Him. If it is only then I know His complete and overwhelming joy, I can wait.

I don't think we have to wait, though. I think we can have it now if we just keep loving God and reaching out for it.

I'm sure going to give it a try!

October 5

If the home is deserving, let your peace rest on it; if it is not, let your peace return to you. Matthew 10:13

Jesus was instructing His disciples before sending them out to do His work. In this passage He tells them if the people don't treat them well, they should not let it trouble them. He tells them to go in peace, and if the people are courteous, friendly and hospitable, then they should treat them likewise and accept their kindness. If the people are not gracefully receiving of them, Jesus tells them to stay at peace—not to let the rudeness of the inhospitable rob them of their peace.

I may have stumbled through that, but I think Matthew 10:13 contains valuable instruction Jesus gave to His disciples that is still applicable for us today. I know too often, I let someone who treats me discourteously or badly make me angry or unhappy. I let it ruin my day, thereby *giving* them my peace.

I used to say they stole my peace, but I have come to believe they cannot take it from me unless I allow them to. When someone treats me badly, I can choose to remain happy, positive and at peace, and go on about my business, or I can choose to dwell on it and be angry or unhappy. When I allow the latter, I have given them my peace.

I'm not very good at this yet, but what I want to learn to do, is to be able to smile and walk away from those who want to see me angry or unhappy. I want to be able to say, "God, that's one of those tough ones, but if you love them, I will, too. But I'll need your help."

Maybe someday I won't need His help so much, but while I do, I'm going to take advantage of it.

October 6

But the angel said to them, "Do not be afraid. I bring you good news of great joy that will be for all the people. Luke 2:10

Can you be still for a few minutes and try to imagine being in the town where Jesus was born on that day? Can you imagine the joy you would feel, knowing God had sent His Son to live among us so we could have eternal life with Him? And yet many were not joyful; they were afraid. Others were not joyful; they wanted to kill Him.

Nothing much has changed. Some are still frightened; some still want us to believe He was not the Messiah; some say He is dead.

And the saddest thing is, many who do believe in Him and worship Him have no joy. They live in a state of "woe-is-me" and condemnation and do not experience God's love and forgiveness. Some are convinced they are so bad God can't possibly forgive them, and their only hope is to grovel at His feet and hope He lets them into heaven. I believe He will let them in, but what kind of life is it they live in the meantime? How will that type of image bring others to God? Not very well, I should think.

We need to observe the joy the birth of Jesus was meant to bring us. We need to react to each day as if we'd just scored the winning touchdown; smiling and pointing to the heavens and shouting, "Thank you, Jesus!" (Y'all know I wanted to say, "You da man, Jesus!" I just didn't know if it would be proper.)

October 7

Do not suppose that I came to bring peace to the earth. I did not come to bring peace, but a sword. Matthew 10:34

God knew, and His Son knew, that Jesus—the Prince of Peace—would bring discord and strife into the world, because not all would accept Him as the Savior. To those God has chosen as His people, Jesus brings a peace that is theirs if they choose to follow Him and love the Father. For the wicked, evil ones who choose other gods and turn away from the one, true God, there is no peace, but a sword that severs them from the blessings that accompany God's love.

That's my take on this verse, which at first reading set me back on my heels. I was stunned. I had probably read it before, and it was just a big question mark I let slip into the "what-did-He-mean" column. I've had a lot of those over the years.

But I feel as though I must've been reading in the dark a lot of those times, and now the lights are on. Maybe the lights are just candles, but everyday more candles are being brought into the room, and as the room gets brighter, the words of God become clearer. I don't pretend to have suddenly grasped the totality of God, but I *have* come to believe I must do one thing to unlock the door to understanding God and His plan for my life.

Love Him.

Peace and joy are ours if we but lift our hands to the Lord and praise Him. And there is no greater praise than love.

October 8

Blessed are you when men hate you, when they exclude you and insult you and reject your name as evil, because of the Son of Man. Rejoice in that day and leap for joy, because great is your reward in heaven. For that is how their fathers treated the prophets. Luke 6:22-23

In these instructions to the disciples, Jesus encouraged them to not be concerned when men rejected the message they brought to them. Jesus knew not everyone would believe and not everyone would receive. The same is true—maybe more so—today. There are many who openly scoff at the idea that God exists, much less that He is in control.

When we see things going on in the world, such as the ungodly demanding their rights and trying to force believers to the side, we should not be afraid or angry, we should feel blessed; blessed because we are saved by Christ and will spend eternity with Him. Our reward is great in Heaven. What happens here is only meaningful in that we can do our part in God's plan for His people. I believe some of those who appear to be on the wrong side are also helping God, they just don't know it. Some of them might even be a member of God's family and don't know *that*!

But God knows, and He is running the show. Our job is to love Him and allow Him to use us—our gifts, abilities and talents, whatever they might be—in His plan.

Rejoice and leap for joy! High five the sky and know God's hand is slapping yours. We are His children, and He loves us.

October 9

Salt is good, but if it loses its saltiness, how can you make it salty again? Have salt in yourselves, and be at peace with each other. Mark 9:50

Jesus compares the salt used to preserve meat to the gospel. Salt preserves the meat, and without salt, the meat will rot and fall apart. So it is with those who follow God; if they do not preserve the peace with each other by applying the gospel—God's salt—they will deteriorate and fall apart.

God's people are a group bound together by their love for Him. Whether they congregate or live separately from one another, they are still a part of the larger family of God. When we love God, we are brought into His family and bound together as one as we all share the bloodline and the redeeming shed blood of Christ. The word of God is the salt that keeps the body of Christ—the church—whole.

When our objective is to love God, we will seek Him, and His word is the place we will find Him. When we love Him and seek Him, He will supply us with peace, joy, understanding, and more, so we can do the things He requires of us.

To be at peace with each other, we must first be at peace with God. When we love God, He will fill us with His peace and being at peace with others will be effortless. Peace, by the salt of God, will be preserved.

October 10

The kingdom of heaven is like treasure hidden in a field. When a man found it, he hid it again, and then in his joy went and sold all he had and bought that field. Matthew 13:44

Jesus often spoke in parables to explain the mysteries of God the Father and of His own mission on earth. I am often puzzled by the examples He uses to illustrate a point, but as my love for God increases and He gives me understanding, they begin to come clear.

This parable compares the treasure found in the field to finding the truth hidden in the gospel; the truth that we have been cleansed of our sins by the death of Christ on the cross. This discovery brings us great joy when, after we find it, we store it in a safe place—our hearts—then let go of the things that were once important to us and put all our attention to loving our Lord.

The treasure is our salvation; the hiding of it again is placing the love we have found in our hearts; selling all we have is merely letting go of the importance of those things and finding our joy in our salvation and the one who bought it for us.

If you really think about what is important, you will understand this parable of the Hidden Treasure. What is important is not what we *do* or *have*, but what has been *done* for us and what *awaits* us when our jobs on earth are done.

Knowing we have eternal life with our God should fill us with joy beyond our imaginations.

October 11

And you, my child, will be called a prophet of the Most High; for you will go on before the Lord to prepare the way for him, to give his people the knowledge of salvation through the forgiveness of their sins, because of the tender mercy of our God, by which the rising sun will come to us from heaven, to shine on those living in darkness and in the shadow of death, to guide our feet into the path of peace. Luke 1: 76-79

Zechariah spoke these words of prophesy over his son, John, foretelling the part he—John the Baptist—would play in God's plan of salvation. Zechariah's prophesy quite neatly laid out the plan God had for His people. John was to give the people knowledge of salvation through the forgiveness of their sins, explaining to them that this was being done because of the tender and loving mercy of God. John would also tell of the rising sun—the Son of God—that would come to them from heaven to shine on those living in the darkness of sin and idolatry; a Savior to lead them from the shadows of death into the light of God's love and peace.

John played a key role in God's plan for us. We play a role as well. Perhaps we do not carry the load John the Baptist carried, but our responsibility is just as important. God's plan is like an intricate watch, in which each tiny mechanism contributes to cause the time displayed to be correct. If one piece of the mechanical workings of the watch is left out or does not function the way it should, the time will be either behind or ahead of where it should be, or the watch might stop completely.

God's watch is accurate to a degree we cannot even measure. His timing is always perfect. Every tick of the watch is planned to perfection. Even when we stumble, another piece of the puzzle falls into place.

Be at peace, knowing God' plan is perfect, and He is in control.

October 12

Those on the rock are the ones who receive the word with joy when they hear it, but they have no root. They believe for a while, but in the time of testing they fall away. Luke 8:13

Are you talking to me?

That is the question that comes to my mind when I read this verse. I know many times when I am tested, I fall away and forget where my strength and courage come from. It saddens me deeply when I do it.

Sometimes I will fall into a deep hole of self-pity or condemnation, reeling in the throes of woe-is-me. And the sad thing is, what I've done or allowed to happen is usually not that bad or that important in the overall scheme of things. I tend to beat myself up over small things, if you know what I mean.

Oh sure, I've pulled off some whoppers in my time. But it's funny; I can usually get over the whoppers sooner and more completely than I can some of the little ones. I guess maybe the big ones are so terrifying, we have to literally shove them from our thoughts or we won't be able to tolerate ourselves.

I continue to strain forward. I don't want God's word—His love—to fall on rock. I want to be fertile ground where His love can take root and grow and bear fruit. That fruit being more love for Him which will spread to others, creating a garden where God can sit with us and tell us about the wonders He has in store for us.

October 13

Glory to God in the highest, and on earth peace to men on whom his favor rests. Luke 2:14

This is a verse that seems to have been misinterpreted by many over the years. I have always thought it spoke of peace among men, but reading it today, I believe it is speaking of the peace, as in peace of mind, God gave to us when He sent Jesus to live among us and die for our sins.

I am starting to believe peace on earth among men is not attainable. There have always been wars, and there will probably always be wars. Nations will always disagree, and many of those disagreements will center on religion.

But peace of mind is available to anyone who will turn from the disagreements and possessions wars are fought over and look instead at God and His love for us. These things, these ideas, these properties are of little importance in the overall scheme of things.

Our time on this earth is short, and what we do with it is important. By loving God and allowing His peace to envelope us, we allow our lives to be used for His purpose.

Maybe the hippies from the sixties had it right. They did, after all, promote peace and love—perhaps in a misguided way—but I think they had the right idea.

Peace, y'all.

October 14

A wife of noble character who can find? She is worth far more than rubies. Her husband has full confidence in her and lacks nothing of value. She brings him good, not harm, all the days of her life. Proverbs 31: 10-12

I want to break from the forum today. I won't write about not being afraid, love, peace or joy, but will write about someone special who helps me to face life without fear; loves me more than I deserve; brings peace into my life, and fills my days with joy.

My precious wife celebrates her birthday today—I believe she said she was 39—and I just want to thank God for her. I can't imagine where I might be without her, and I cannot plan a future where she is not by my side.

She loves me, as I said, more than I deserve, and I do what I can to return that kind of love back to her. I believe the secret to a successful marriage is for both parties to try and out-love the other. If the love is from the heart—a heart God has entered and resides in—love cannot fail.

There are no jewels that compare, nor are there words to describe this beautiful and talented lady who walks beside me. I have endeavored to honor her with poem and song, but my efforts seem to not do justice to the friend she is and what she has done for me.

No matter my need, she meets it. No matter my whim, she indulges it. She loves unceasingly and completely. Her heart is surely full of God and His love.

God is love, and she was created in His image.

I am blessed.

October 15

If a man of peace is there, your peace will rest on him; if not, it will return to you. Luke 10:6

When the disciples went out to preach the gospel to the people, they knew some would welcome them, and some would not. Jesus instructed them to be aware of both and to discern the good from the bad and not to waste time with those who did not receive them well. Jesus knew the time was short, and they had much work to do. The plan must go forward, and the workers must not tarry.

I sometimes feel the same about those around me. Some folks I feel comfortable with even though we might not see eye to eye, others seem to be on a different wave length, and I feel as though we can't even carry on a conversation.

Then there are those who are negative. It seems they can counter every good thing you say with something bad. Nothing is ever right in their world, and they see nothing in the future that will improve it. These are the types of folks who can have your joy and peace and be gone with it before you know you gave it to them.

If someone you are around or encounter brings you down, or just doesn't seem right to you, walk away.

Seek out men and women of peace. Seek those that emanate God's love as if they breathe it in and exhale it. Around them you will find peace.

October 16

At that time Jesus, full of joy through the Holy Spirit, said, "I praise you, Father, Lord of heaven and earth, because you have hidden these things from the wise and learned, and revealed them to little children, Yes, Father, for it was your good pleasure. Luke 10:21

I think this verse tells of the joy Jesus felt as He spoke to the Father about the people He had called to them. He praised God for the ones He had called, and He praised Him for the hiding of the truth from those who did not believe. The verse says very clearly to me that not all are called to God.

But even the learned and wise who chose not to believe and sought to kill the Son, are a part of His plan and are used for His good pleasure. Everything, and every person, on this earth is under the control of God, whether they know it or not, even if they deny He exists.

To know we are loved by God, to be filled with His Spirit and love, and know we are a part of His plan should fill us with a joy the world cannot imagine or explain. And to top it off, we will spend eternity with Him when our work here is done.

To praise God is to love God. Praise Him for the joy He has given you.

October 17

As he approached Jerusalem and saw the city, he wept over it and said, "If you, even you, had only known on this day what would bring you peace—but now it is hidden from your eyes. Luke 19:41-42

Jesus was saddened by the knowledge the people of Jerusalem had not accepted Him and the peace He could have brought to them. In this case the peace was not only the peace He brought in the sense of the love sent by God for His people, but the earthly peace among men that could save the great city from destruction. Because of their unbelief, they would perish.

We may not see it—some believe we will—but great cities will once again perish. Man in his arrogance builds houses and skyscrapers and thinks by his ingenuity they will stand. Perhaps they will… perhaps they won't. Maybe they will be laid to waste and stand empty when all is said and done.

Our hope—the hope of God's children—rests not in making buildings stand, but in building our inheritance, which lies in eternity at the foot of the throne of our Father. We are His children, and He chose us and loves us. We should not let our hearts be swayed by the lies and promises of a world that worships structures and money.

Don't be blinded by the things of this world. If you must be blinded, let it be by the light of Christ as you set your eyes on Him and love Him with all the strength you have. You will be amazed that when you give your all, your strength is constantly renewed and replenished.

October 18

> *The bride belongs to the bridegroom. The friend who attends the bridegroom waits and listens for him, and is full of joy when he hears the bridegroom's voice. That joy is mine, and it is now complete.* John 3:29

John speaks of Jesus as the bridegroom, those who follow Him as the bride, and of himself as the friend of the bridegroom—the best man, perhaps. John tells of the joy he feels as the bridegroom finally enters the church and is joined to His bride. John's work is finished; his part of the plan is completed. His *joy* is complete.

Our joy should be complete as well, knowing Christ has gathered us to Him and will never leave us or forsake us and will stay with us in sickness and in health. And even when death shall take our earthly bodies, He will provide us a new and unblemished body so we will be able to live in eternity with Him in a heaven where there is no sickness or pain.

Our marriage to Christ is the greatest of all blessings. There can be no bridegroom as faithful or devoted as He. Our only duty to Him is to love Him unconditionally as He loves us. He does not demand it, but He chose us, and how can we not love Him? What has He done that would cause us not to love Him? What has He not done that we could not want to love Him?

I have no answers for those questions. I have no reason not to love Him.

October 19

> *"I have told you these things, so that in me you may have peace. In this world you will have trouble. But take heart! I have overcome the world.* John 16:33

Much of Jesus' teaching was done with parables, but as the end of His time on earth neared, He spoke plainly to His disciples, telling them what was to come and what they must do. He wanted them to be at peace even though He knew the world would do all it could to take their peace from them. He told them they could have peace *in Him.*

In Him. *So that in me you may have peace.* May have.

Jesus does not say because of Him we will have peace. He says *in* Him we *may* have peace. Jesus did not remove the things of the world that can attempt to take our peace from us, but He did conquer those things with His death on the cross. He bound Satan by His actions and allowed us the choice to believe in Him and thereby have peace within our souls, knowing that while we are in Him, evil cannot take our peace from us. But we had to choose to love Him—to follow Him and be one with Him.

We can choose to face the world on our own and deal with troubles and trials without help from God, or we can choose to love Him and rest easy, knowing He has a plan for our lives, and the plan will serve His greater plan for His family.

I have rested in God's arms—His peace—and I have fought the enemy alone. Those times when I have ignorantly and sometimes stubbornly waded into the fray alone, I have been beaten and bruised severely, and my spirit has been wounded. But even at those times—after utter defeat—God remained watchful, His offer still open.

I want to rest now, in the loving arms of my Father. I want His peace.

October 20

"As the Father has loved me, so have I loved you. If you obey my commands, you will remain in my love, just as I have obeyed my Father's commands and remain in his love. I have told you this so that my joy may be in you and that your joy may be complete. My command is this: Love each other as I have loved you." John 15:9-12

I believe it is possible to have joy without Christ, but I do not believe it can be a complete joy without Him. We may have victories and times of success without Him, but they will fade and become distant memories. To experience the love of God is to me the ultimate joy.

To know that He—the creator of all things—made us in His image so we might share a profound and indescribable love with Him is awesome and wonderful. And to love God is the greatest command.

Jesus tells the disciples—and us—He has loved us as God has loved Him, and if we love God, we will love each other, and our joy will be complete.

The word love—in some form—appears six times in the four short verses above. If you consider that God—and Jesus—is love, it appears twelve more times in the form of me, my, his, and I. If you consider that we are created in God's image and can therefore be said to be love as well, it appears another eight times in the form of you, your, and each other. That is twenty-four words out of sixty seven. I would say the overriding theme is love.

No matter how you dissect it, the point is God loves us, and if we choose to love Him, He will live within our hearts and fill us with His Spirit and His love.

Our joy will then be complete.

October 21

You know the message God sent to the people of Israel, telling the good news of peace through Jesus Christ, who is Lord of all. Acts 10:36

In the beginning, man had perfect peace with God, but fell from it by sinning. It has been like a snowball rolling down a mountain ever since. Sin led to sin, which led to more sin. God saw only one way to stop the mountain from being swept away by the avalanche of sin: Jesus.

Jesus stood before the mountain of sin and destruction and pointed to the valley of love and peace. He offered us an escort off the slippery slopes. In Luke 18:12, He said, *"Come, follow me."* That was His message.

God told the people of Israel about the coming of Christ and the peace he could bring to them, but they were too wrapped up in the snowstorm of their own ideas and theories on how to control sin—rules and works—and they would not believe Jesus was the Son of God. They could not see the valley for the snow.

We have the benefit of knowing Christ has taken our sins upon Him. We have the added benefit of knowing His peace is ours if we chose to accept it. All we have to do to accept it is love Him and believe in Him.

And then… there will be peace in the valley.

Remember that old song? Sing it today.

October 22

I tell you the truth, you will weep and mourn while the world rejoices. You will grieve but your grief will turn to joy. John 16:20

Jesus was in the last of His days on earth and was attempting to comfort and ready His disciples for His death. He explained to them the world would rejoice at His death, while they—the disciples—mourned and grieved. But then He tells the disciples their grief would turn to joy.

How heart wrenching it must have been for the men who had lived and walked the earth with Jesus. I can't image the empty feeling they had in the pit of their stomach knowing the Lord Jesus was going to leave them. Not only leave them, but be killed!

Then Jesus tells them their grief will soon turn to joy. *Say what?*

I can imagine the confused and horrified looks on the disciple's faces as they looked to one another, then back to Jesus.

But they didn't know the whole story. Even though Jesus had told them many times the story of what was to come—His death and resurrection—they still didn't get it. It just wouldn't sink in that the time was here.

There have been so many times in my life I have looked at the things of God as explained to me by men, and I didn't get it. It just seemed to avoid my understanding. But the more I turn to God and rest in Him and love Him, the more I seem to understand. I sometimes sit and wonder what is going on, but it's different now. Instead of not understanding God, I'm wondering how all of a sudden I seem to understand Him.

It just dawned on me; that's how love is. The more you love someone, the more their needs and desires matter to you, and suddenly you begin to see who they really are.

October 23

A woman giving birth to a child has pain because her time has come; but when her baby is born she forgets the anguish because of her joy that a child is born into the world. John 16:21

Jesus uses childbirth to explain His resurrection and the joy it will bring to God's people. He compares their grief and suffering at His death to the pain and anguish a mother feels when in labor and during childbirth. He is trying to explain to the disciples that His death is not the end, but the final step leading to the new beginning—the new life He has brought to the world. Their joy when He arises from the tomb will be like that of a mother when she gives birth to a son. Their joy will be when Jesus rises, and their sins are washed clean.

I have a friend who should understand this concept quite well. Her story is one of a difficult life filled with struggles and pain. But much of her pain was forgotten when at the age of forty-one she gave birth to her first child, a beautiful little girl. That little girl changed my friend's life and filled her with joy. Suddenly, life seemed worth living. That child could virtually have saved my friend's life, as she has since given her life to God and is learning to love Him more each day.

Jesus, rising on the third day after he was placed in the tomb, is like that child coming into my friend's life. When He rose, it was a new beginning for mankind. We are forgiven, and life can begin fresh and new when we accept Jesus as our Savior and begin to love God.

Picture this: a baby—Baby Jesus—is placed in your arms. He looks up at you, and you see in His eyes a love like you have never seen before. A love so pure and complete, it washes over you, and you feel like a new person. Your love for the Child is so deep, you cannot contain it. Your joy overwhelms you as the baby's arms open wide, and He smiles up at you.

Get the picture?

October 24

So with you: Now is your time of grief, but I will see you again and you will rejoice, and no one will take away your joy. John 16:22

See! I told you no one can take away your joy! Jesus said so in this verse! Ha! I love it when a plan comes together!

When Jesus walked out of the tomb, our lives were changed. By walking out of the tomb, He was saying to the world, "I am the way, the life and the truth. Follow me, and your joy will be complete."

I can imagine Jesus pointing to the sky and thinking, "All for the Father!" Maybe He did the world's first victory dance as He celebrated the most famous victory of all. (Probably not, but *we* should!)

We should dance and point to the sky and wear a smile that can't be wiped off our face. Our joy is complete. Jesus has conquered death and sin. We are free! We have won. We should be full of joy that cannot be taken from us.

So why aren't you smiling? Why aren't you standing up right now, shaking your booty and raising a we're-number-one finger to the sky?

Oh. I see. You gave away your joy.

Here's the thing, folks. I'll say it nice and slow: You-can't-<u>give</u>-it-away-either.

Nope. You might set it to the side while you moan and whine about something or somebody that wants to take it from you, but it is yours. It will always be yours. It's like that favorite old T-shirt; you can wear it forever, and you will fight anyone who tries to take it from you. Your joy is the same. You always have it; you just have to decide you're going to wear it.

Jeesh! That's simpler than I thought.

October 25

Until now you have not asked for anything in my name. Ask and you will receive, and your joy will be complete. John 16:24

It is my belief that what Jesus is telling the disciples in this verse is; when He walks out of the tomb, His prophesied birth, death and resurrection will be complete. At that time, the disciples and the world will know He was sent by God and is God. Therefore, they may now pray in His name.

What an awesome thing that must have been.... to stand face to face with Christ and hear Him say those words. I can see the disciples, elbowing each other and whispering excitedly, "Can you dig this, man? We taught the gospel with God!"

"Yes!" One of the others might answer, "And He says we can ask *anything* in His name, and we will have it!"

You can bet your bottom dollar those guys were filled with joy. They had just been handed a lottery ticket with the winning numbers on it. The prize was all the love and life they could ever want—forever-style!

The things Jesus told the disciples—the things He promised them—were not just for them, they were for you and me, too. We can ask anything in His name, and we will receive it. Our joy will be complete.

Here's a question for you: If you could ask Jesus for just one thing, what would it be?

October 26

I am coming to you now, but I say these things while I am still in the world, so that they may have the full measure of my joy within them.
John 17:13

In this passage, Jesus is praying to the Father. He asks that God allow His disciples—and I believe He makes the same request for us, too—to have the full measure of His joy.

The full measure…. how much joy is that? Surely, it is more than you or I have ever experienced.

I was thinking this morning about joy and trying to remember my happiest, most joyful moment or period of time. I can't think what it might have been. Life seems to have been a series of mostly disappointing moments and times, interspersed with times that were "satisfactory". I mean I've been content, and at some times happy, but I can't remember a time or event when I was filled with the full measure of joy.

That is pretty sad.

The fact is, there were many times in my life when I *should* have been filled with the full measure of joy, but the world and its trials overshadowed or lessened those times of happiness. The good times seemed to just come and go amidst the work and struggle of making a living and trying to "get ahead in life". I'm not even going to try and identify the good times, because I'd probably use the wrong ones for examples, and somebody would say, "But what about…?"

I plead, Philippians 3:13. I am happy now. My joy is not complete, but God is filling me with more of it each day. I will continue to press forward, leaving the door to my heart open wide to God, so one day I will have the full measure of joy He has for me.

October 27

You have made known to me the paths of life; you will fill me with joy in your presence. Acts 2:28

The path of life was made known to us by Jesus, and when we remain in His presence, He fills us with joy. Why then do we not remain in His presence?

I'm sure all of you know what it's like to feel alone, and I imagine most of you have had the experience of feeling like you are alone, even when there are people around you. I wonder if that is how Jesus feels sometimes as he wanders among us.

I can picture Him at a party thrown during the Christmas season, sitting alone on a sofa, watching people as they smile and laugh and raise their drinks to "the season." He sits there, wanting so much to be a part of the festivities, and yet knowing most of the people don't even know He's in the room. Someone notices Him and comes over, sits down, and strikes up a conversation. That person soon discovers this lonely figure is actually the most interesting and special person he's ever known. Just being around this quiet man and getting to know Him fills the person with an indescribable joy. The person wonders why he hasn't noticed Him before.

That's how life is. We run around doing all the things we think we need to do, hustling here and there with so much on our minds. But Jesus is seldom included, and yet He's right there, following along with you to work, school, shopping, playing, and partying. And the whole time, He's wondering why you're so stressed out and unhappy. He's wanting you to take His hand and let Him be a part of your day so He can show you that all those things you are so stressed over are a piece of cake if you let Him help you.

I've gotten carried away. But I love the thought of Jesus following me around! Don't you?

October 28

And the disciples were filled with joy and the Holy Spirit. Acts 13:52

I wonder sometimes if joy and the Holy Spirit are the same things. God is so many things—all things good—and He is the Holy Spirit, and He is love. Joy is a result of God being in us, so God is joy, and therefore, I think the Holy Spirit must be joy.

I almost start laughing when I think stuff like that. It always brings to mind the thought of a dog chasing its tail; chasing it for the sheer joy of chasing it, knowing it will never catch it.

God's love is such an endless, whirling circle of all that is good!

God, love, the Spirit, love, God, joy, love, the Spirit, love, God, peace, love, God, hope, the Spirit, love, joy, peace, God!

See what I mean!

I believe the key to it all is choosing to love God. If we don't love God, we are chasing after things that don't matter. And even when we catch the tail we are so desperately chasing, we suddenly realize we don't know what to do with it... and most times, we don't even remember why we were chasing it! Without God, there is no joy in the chase, and there is certainly no joy in the catch.

God is joy. Love Him and be filled with it. If you're going to chase your tail, chase it with joy.

October 29

"Yet he has not left himself without testimony: He has shown kindness by giving you rain from heaven and crops in their seasons; he provides you with plenty of food and fills your hearts with joy." Acts 14:17

Here in Central Texas, we have been experiencing a severe drought. Until October, we hadn't had any substantial rainfall for several months, and it is a problem. People, livestock, crops, industry, recreation, and so many things depend on rain to replenish our water supply so our lives can continue in the fashion we would like for them to.

I don't worry a lot about the lack of rain. I figure God will supply all our needs, and rain is certainly one of them. Rain will come when it will come, and there is no sense getting all in a tizzy about it. If we need to change some of the things we do until it rains, then we change them. Worrying won't bring rain.

I have heard it said there is a spiritual drought in this country. That sounds to me like God has not sent His rain—His love—for some time. I disagree! God rains His love down on us constantly! The problem is we have our umbrella above us. We want God's love—His rain—but we don't want it to interfere with the way we live. Can we still do the things we want to do if God's love is pouring down on us? Well, it is… and we do.

God is raining His love down on us every minute of every day. Our umbrellas—our desire for worldly things—might deflect it, but even if it does, it will form a puddle at our feet, and we will be standing in it. We cannot deflect or avoid God's love.

I believe if we just throw our umbrellas away and turn our faces up into God's rain of love, it will wash away the things of the world we think are important.

Let it rain! Let love reign!

October 30

The jailer brought them into his house and set a meal before them; he was filled with joy because he had come to believe in God—he and his whole family. Acts 16:34

An earthquake opened the cell doors, and the jailer, thinking he would be punished, and probably killed because the prisoners had escaped, was about to take his own life. Paul stopped him, telling him they were still in the cells. This incident and Paul's words led the jailer to believe in Jesus, and he and his whole house were saved that night.

What led the jailer to Christ? An earthquake? No, I think what got to him was the fact that even though they could have walked away, Paul and the others stayed put, knowing they would imperil the jailer if they fled. Their love—the love God had filled them with—kept them from letting harm come to an innocent man. I believe the jailer saw their love and knew he wanted to know a God who could love him that much.

How many times have we stood at a door God has opened for us and not gone through it? I know I have many times. I wish I could say I stood outside that open door for noble reasons, but in most cases, it was simply because I did not recognize God had opened the door and was allowing me to go through it. I was too busy *doing* what I wanted to do, unaware that God loved me and was taking care of me. I thought I had to *do* it myself. I was smart, strong and capable; why did I need God?

Then one day—the day that little bell went off—I realized how much God loved me, and I realized all He wanted was for *me* to love *Him*. Looking back I could see all the doors that had been left open for me, but I knew God didn't want me to go back to those doors. He has many more He will open in the days to come. On the other side of those doors is joy beyond my wildest dreams.

He has a plan, and I'm part of it!

October 31

But glory, honor and peace for everyone who does good: First for the Jew, then for the Gentile. For God does not show favoritism.
Romans 2:10-11

Before I began writing this, I added verse eleven, because when I read verse twelve, the first thought I had was, "How come the Jews are first?" I figured many of you would wonder the same thing, and I didn't want that to be the point of focus. God doesn't show favoritism, so we won't concern ourselves with who is first.

The main thing is we will all be glorified, honored and at peace if we do good.

Wait a minute…. We only get to experience those things if we *do* good?

I'd say, "yep."

You might ask, "But I thought it wasn't what we *do* that matters?"

I don't think what we do matters. I think the only thing we *have* to *do* is love God. When we do that, He will fill us with His love and Holy Spirit, and we *will* do good. If we just *do* good and don't love God, then I believe it is just works. And I believe works on our own, without the love of God driving them, are kind of like building castles in the sand. As soon as the tide comes roaring in, they will be washed away.

If we love God, we won't have to think about doing good; it will be our nature to do good, just as it is His nature. God is love, and if we love Him and are filled with His love, then we will love others as He loves us.

Love God. The peace it will bring you is like a nap in your favorite chair on a Saturday afternoon.

November 1

And the way of peace they do not know. Romans 3:17

Chapter three of Romans speaks of the fact that man is sinful by nature and does not know the way of peace. The only way to obtain peace of mind is by loving God and accepting Jesus Christ as your savior. When we do those two things, the Holy Spirit and God's love will fill us with love and peace like we have never known. I don't think it will come upon you in a flash of glory and knock you off your feet, but rather, it will come upon you in direct measure to your love for God.

It's like the snowball going downhill I've mentioned before. You might start out tentatively loving God, then He puts His Spirit and love into you, and it feels so good, you love Him more, and it just keeps gaining momentum until your very existence centers around loving God.

Some of you might say, "Whoa, I don't know if I'm ready for all that!"

What? You don't want peace of mind? You don't want to walk around all day smiling and feeling good inside? What is it you have going right now that you think you will have to give up or stop doing?

You see, it's not like I'm not just like you, because I am. I'm still hanging on to some things; still hedging on a full commitment to loving God. But I already started the snowball rolling, so I don't think I'll be able to keep the brakes on for too much longer.

The thing is, I haven't noticed I'm missing anything. I still seem to be the same guy I was last December when I read Rick Warren's book, *The Purpose of Christmas*. I admit, I spend a whole lot more time thinking about God and loving Him now. I'm happier and more at peace than I was then. I feel like God loves me and I'm a part of His plan.

Yep…. I'm the same guy…. only different.

November 2

Do everything without complaining or arguing, so that you may become blameless and pure, children of God without fault in a crooked and depraved generation, in which you shine like stars in the universe.
Philippians 2:14-15

I want to take another break from the theme today to honor my mother on her birthday. I searched for a verse I thought would do her tribute, and this one jumped out and said, "Pick me!" I could not argue the choice because I was immediately reminded of things my mother did when I was growing up.

I did not fail to notice the many times she sacrificed her own needs and wants for her children. She worked hard at menial jobs so we could have the things we needed. And I know many of those things we could have easily done without, but we were just kids and thought the things of the world were necessary. Mom went the extra mile to see we had them, and she did so without complaining.

I saw all she did and tried in some ways—lame though they were—to repay her devotion to us, but, like I said, I was a kid, and I mostly did what kids do. Mom also kept a rein on my foolish ways—as much as she could, anyway—and did her best to keep me from trouble. She didn't have to say too much, because my concern that I would disappoint her kept me from a lot of trouble. (I didn't say it kept me from all of it!)

I can't say my mom is, without fault—no one is—but I can say she shines as bright as any star in the universe. Her light and her love for her children never dim, and it has kept us within walking distance of God's path our entire lives. Even when we strayed into the darkness, we could always look to her light and know we could go there.

Thanks, Mom.

November 3

Therefore, since we have been justified through faith, we have peace with God through our Lord Jesus Christ. Romans 5:1

I noticed right away this verse does not say we are justified by anything we did or do. It says we have been justified through our faith; and therefore, we have peace with God through Jesus.

I like that!

I like it because it demonstrates we cannot earn our way into God's heart by what we do, but simply by believing God gave His only Son so we could spend eternity with Him. By having faith, we can be at peace while we wait for the day we will join Him.

Peace is a wonderful thing. I can't tell you how much time I've wasted over the years being worried and distraught—usually over things I could not change and sometimes over things that never even happened. Such a waste of time!

Not that I don't still do it, mind you, but I don't do it near as much anymore. When troubles or challenges come at me these days, I tend to face them with the certainty that either I will overcome them, or at the very least, get past them. I believe all things work to the good according to God's perfect plan, and anything I have to defeat or get past is all part of His larger plan. I figure if He wants me to defeat it, he will show me how, and if He wants me to simply endure it, He will get me through it.

By facing life's problems and challenges this way, we can be at peace. Knowing God loves us, and is with us always, should allow us to stand up to any situation confidently and calmly, knowing our God is bigger than anything that can come against us. Like a little girl watching tigers and bears and other wild animals at the zoo. She stands calmly, fearlessly, peacefully, her hand in her father's hand, confident her dad won't allow any harm to come to her.

This is how we should face the world—our hand in His hand.

November 4

The mind of sinful man is death, but the mind controlled by the Spirit is life and peace. Romans 8:6

Man, left to his own devices, is sinful. Our carnal nature rules; we do not have faith; and therefore, no hope. We may contain hope for earthly things, but there is no hope we will spend eternity with our heavenly Father. We have nothing to look forward to except the things of the world and death. On the other hand, when we choose to love God and make Him the center of our lives, we are filled with His love and His Spirit. Our faith is then in the hope of eternal life with Him. We are at peace because we are at rest in His love for us.

I am the first to admit that none of this comes easy. As I said, we are by nature sinful, and at every turn we are confronted with sinful opportunities. I can tell you over and over that the key is to love God and be filled with His Spirit, but let me assure you, it's a lot harder to do than it is to say. The world distracts us at every turn, and our minds are so easily diverted from God to the things the world offers us.

I believe one way to combat this is to talk to God constantly—pray without ceasing. You don't have to talk to Him in any special prayer-like way, just talk to Him like he was walking alongside you. Tell Him you love Him, and you can't wait to see Him. Tell Him thanks for the beautiful day or the rain. Tell Him your foot hurts, and you sure will be glad when He takes the pain away. Tell Him what you're thinking! He knows anyway, but He still wants you to tell Him how you feel.

God is always right there with you, wherever you are. Talk to Him, he will fill your life with love, peace and joy.

November 5

Be joyful in hope, patient in affliction, faithful in prayer.
Romans 12:12

This verse follows the same recipe as the verse from yesterday, with a few added ingredients. All the things in both verses must be combined with God's main ingredient—love—to make them complete.

The added ingredients in today's verse are hope, affliction and prayer.

To me, hope is what we have when our faith is combined with love.

Afflictions are like yeast; they come and provide us opportunity to grow.

Prayer is the constant communication with God that mixes all the ingredients together to obtain the desired end product.

The end product is peace.

It's a "peace" of cake if you have all the right ingredients and follow the recipe.

November 6

If it is possible, as far as it depends on you, live at peace with everyone.
Romans 12:18

Why can't everyone just get along?

I'm sure most of us have heard that before, and it's a good question. In his letter to the Romans, Paul seems to indicate it might not always be possible. Sometimes, there will be people who just flat don't want to get along with others. I've known some who seem to enjoy the exact opposite. The more discord there is, the happier they seem to be. I tend to find somewhere else to be when those folks are around.

Because as Paul said, sometimes it depends on me, and if I've done what I can to get along, and there is still strife, then I feel it best to not be involved in the situation. I *"shake the dust off my feet,"* and go on about my business.

Here's an illustration: An electric golf cart has six twelve-volt batteries. As the batteries begin to age and lose their power, they do not necessarily do so equally. One may deteriorate faster than the others, and the six of them may weaken at different levels. I am told that as the batteries weaken over time, the cart will perform to the level of the worst of the six batteries.

I think this same thing often happens when we allow ourselves to be around negative people. The negative person will begin to drain the strength of the more positive people in the group, and before you know it, everyone's attitude has come down to the level of the most negative person in the bunch. That is when we need to find ourselves some better company.

Sometimes, though we may have tried our hardest to encourage them, the bad just want to stay bad, and the sad just want to stay sad, and we have to move on.

There's nothing wrong with moving on.

November 7

For the kingdom of God is not a matter of eating and drinking, but of righteousness, peace and joy in the Holy Spirit. Romans 14:17

Some might translate this verse to mean it does not matter what we eat or drink, and, as pertains to being Godly or righteous, I agree with that assessment. But I would also say it does not matter as long as the eating or drinking of any given thing is done in moderation. If we eat or drink anything in excess, it will not be good for us.

I believe the matter of eating and drinking with regard to this verse was more about being under the law as opposed to being under grace. Before Jesus took our sins upon Himself on the cross, we were under the law exclusively. When we disobeyed, we were punished. Then God sent Jesus to wash us clean of our sins and give us a chance at redemption by grace—believing in Christ and loving Him.

Lest you misunderstand the second part of the verse—*but of righteousness, peace and joy in the Holy Spirit*--I would add that righteousness is not something we gain by *doing* anything, other than believing in Jesus Christ and loving God. When we believe in Jesus and love the Father, the Holy Spirit then dwells in us, and we are made righteous and filled with peace and joy.

Don't get hung up on what you think you need to *do*, or what others say you need to do. God's greatest command is to love Him. Do that!

Believe in the Lord Jesus Christ and love Him.

I am convinced it all starts right there.

November 8

Let us therefore make every effort to do what leads to peace and to mutual edification. Romans 14:19

What is the *effort* we should make that will lead to peace and to mutual edification?

I would say the effort we should make is to love God.

You should have known that was what I'd say!

But seriously, what else is there to say? We love God; He fills us with love and His Spirit; TA-DA! We have peace and mutual edification!

Notice I said *we* in that last sentence. This formula works best when all concerned parties love God. Otherwise, things are too one-sided, and the mutual edification becomes more like a force-feeding. There is nothing mutual about that, and it usually doesn't work.

We can have mutual edification with God, too. Think about it. God loves you, you love God. If you talk constantly with God, telling Him what you've learned about Him and how much you love Him, it will edify Him. And He will definitely edify you, by teaching you more about Him. There you go!

Let me warn you though, if you're going to take up this talking-with-God-constantly thing, don't do it out loud unless you're alone. People tend to give you some really strange looks and move away from you.

November 9

May the God of hope fill you with all joy and peace as you trust in him, so that you may overflow with hope by the power of the Holy Spirit. Romans 15:13

Hope is defined as: *"confident desire," a feeling that something desirable is likely to happen.* It can be the same as, or a part of, faith. Our faith and our hope is we will spend eternity with God.

Without God, what would we hope for? What would we put our faith toward? Better yet, if God had not sent Jesus to atone for our sins, what would we hope for then? Where would the world be now?

God did send Jesus, and by His grace we are saved, and as we love Him and trust Him, our hope, supplied by the power of the Holy Spirit, will overflow. God will fill us with His love, Spirit, peace, and joy. God is all those things, and he wants us to share them with Him throughout eternity.

He commands that we do one thing in order to unleash all those things, and that one thing is to love Him.

Love God—the God of hope—and be filled with His love.

November 10

So that by God's will I may come to you with joy and together with you be refreshed. Romans 15:32

In the days before most roads were paved and most streams had bridges over them, people were fond of saying they would be somewhere if, "the Lord be willing and the creek don't rise." There are many places in Central Texas—and I'm sure other places as well—where the creek is still apt to rise during heavy rains. A normally dry stream will run full and become impassable, and so a person might not be able to get where they intended to go.

Getting to the other side of a swollen stream can characterize many things in life, and when we get right down to it, the Lord's will guides everything we do. Even when we choose to do wrong, He sometimes must allow us to do it. I believe He very often allows us to take the wrong path and go off where we shouldn't, just so we will learn the error of our ways.

I heard on the radio the other day they have begun installing barriers similar to those at railroad crossings at the most dangerous of such streams in the San Antonio area. A sensor tells an arm when the water has risen to an unsafe level, and the arm comes down and blocks the road leading into the normally dry stream bed. It seems a shame people have to be physically restrained from entering a dangerous situation, but that is the way it is. We want to cross the raging stream, and by golly, no one can stop us.

God tries to stop us from going where we shouldn't in much the same way. He places a sensor in us—our conscience—that warns us when we veer from the path toward dangerous waters. But so many times, we don't heed that little voice telling us to stop. We plow on into the raging stream and get washed into a sea of troubles. Then God comes to our rescue, and we feel like such a fool.

I have to confess I've spent a lot of time in cold, raging streams, hollering for God to rescue me. (Speaking figuratively, of course)

November 11

Everyone has heard about your obedience, so I am full of joy over you; but I want you to be wise about what is good, and innocent about what is evil. Romans 16:19

I believe Paul knew full well the believers in Rome were good and faithful followers of the Gospel. He had heard good things about them and was proud of them. Their actions brought him joy. But at the same time, he reminded them they must seek wisdom about what was good and what was evil.

Too many times, we are living a life that makes God joyful, but we get sidetracked by the evil that abounds in this world. A person has to stay on his toes these days to stay out of trouble. There is a snare on every corner.

I believe the way we stay on our toes is to be aware of what is going on around us and stay close to God. If our attention is on God and our efforts are directed toward loving Him, we will be less likely to get caught in one of those snares. God will give us wisdom, and we will know what is right and what is wrong.

Love God and allow His guidance to give you wisdom.

Not only will this fill God with joy, but it will fill you with joy as well.

November 12

The God of peace will soon crush Satan under your feet. The grace of our Lord Jesus be with you. Romans 16:20

When Jesus returns he will finally and forever defeat Satan, and as His followers, we will share the victory. Together with God we will crush Satan under our feet.

Satan is alive and running amok in the world. You know that, don't you?

Be self-controlled and alert. Your enemy the devil prowls around like a roaring lion looking for someone to devour. 1 Peter 5:8

Satan doesn't want us to love God, and he will do anything and everything to keep us from doing it, or stop us when we start doing it. Satan will lie and deceive us any way he can.

When I start wondering if what I write is helping anyone, that's Satan whispering in my ear as I type, "You really don't think anyone is going to read this, do you?" He laughs and says, "See! I told you this wouldn't work! Who told you you're a writer?"

But I stand on the promises of God and have faith that God is using me and I am His pencil; I am part of God's plan. I know I'm helping people. I refuse to listen to the lying roar of the king of liars. To me and my God, he sounds like a sickly kitten.

When he whispers his lies in my ear…. I say, "Get thee behind me, Satan!" And when I say that, I'm fairly certain God smiles.

November 13

Not that we lord it over your faith, but we work with you for your joy, because it is by faith you stand firm. 2 Corinthians 1:24

No one can control your faith. It can't be preached up or down, and no one can take credit for how much or how little faith you have. Or for that matter, whether you have faith or don't. Faith is a matter between you and God. No one else is involved. Every part of your relationship with God is the same in that respect; just you and Him.

It is good to have brothers in Christ, though. The encouragement we receive from each other is invaluable. Sherry and I encourage each other constantly. I'd venture to say we do it almost daily, and sometimes several times a day. We have an understanding that when one of us is down, or upset, the other's job is to encourage and get them back into a faith-filled mode. We help each other to stand firm.

If you don't have someone to help you like I do, I hope these little encouragements I send you each day help. That's one of the main reasons I send them. And if you need more, I'm just an email away, and I'll even give you my phone number if you want it. I just want to work with you for your joy, so by *your* faith you will stand firm, knowing God is in control and everything is going to be okay. I just want to help.

November 14

I have great confidence in you; I take pride in you. I am greatly encouraged; in all our troubles my joy knows no bounds. 2 Corinthians 7:4

We all need to hear words of encouragement. In fact, I think we need to hear something encouraging every day.

I told you the story about my young buddy, Cooper—the "You da man," story. Not long after that, my wife and I read in one of our devotionals that we—all believers—are anointed. Every believer that loves God is anointed by Him to do certain things to accomplish His plan. Some have talent, some have gifts of the Spirit, others may have the ability to influence others by the way they live their lives. But one way or the other, each of us is anointed by God to achieve His perfect will.

One day as I was pulling away from the house in my pickup, Sherry was standing at the garage door waving goodbye. We always do this, no matter which of us is leaving, and the wave is accompanied by a shouted, "I love you," which is returned by the one leaving. On this day, she pointed at me and yelled, "You anointed!" I caught on immediately, pointed back at her, and yelled, "*You* anointed!" We've been doing it ever since.

When Sherry shouts, "I love you," and "You anointed," it causes my spirits to soar. I know she means it when she says she loves me, and I know she believes it when she says I'm anointed. Those words encourage me and fill me with joy. I *need* to hear them, and when I'm gone—I work out of town every week—I miss those words terribly.

Take advantage of every opportunity to tell people you love and appreciate them. Point out something they do that is good and compliment them.

Because you know what?

You Anointed!

November 15

Out of the most severe trial, their overflowing joy and their extreme poverty welled up in rich generosity. 2 Corinthians 8:2

Most of us have never been persecuted for our belief in God, nor have we had to suffer at the hands of men who hated us for what we believed. We live in a country where most of us have never been hungry, and even more so, have never been denied much of anything we desired. We are truly blessed to live in a land of liberty and plenty.

The people of Corinth did not have it so good. They had been ravaged, pillaged and plundered. They lived in poverty, and yet they overflowed with joy. They welled up with generosity, which is to say they were proud to give to others from the meager supplies they had.

When I read about these people, shame washes over me. I have so much—too much—and still sometimes I grumble about one thing or another.

It's too windy; it's too cold; my boss doesn't appreciate me; there's too much traffic, I wish I had this or that, somebody's been eating my porridge.

Good grief!

I need to stop complaining and start thanking God for all I have!

We need to stop listening to the grumbling lion and start realizing we've got it made.

We've got God! He's got us! He picked us! (Is anybody else dancing?)

Where's a cheerleader when you need one?

November 16

> *Finally, brothers, good-by. Aim for perfection, listen to my appeal, be of one mind, live in peace. And the God of love and peace will be with you.* 2 Corinthians 13:11

I'm not sure what Paul wanted from the people of Corinth. Surely he didn't expect them to gain perfection, and so he tells them to merely aim for it. That reminds me of an old saying from my school days: Shoot for the moon. If you miss, you'll land pretty high anyway.

To be of one mind was equally unattainable in my opinion, and even more so today. In Paul's day, there was only one doctrine regarding Jesus, but surely there were already those who thought they knew a better way to interpret what Jesus had meant and what God's intent was. Today there are literally tens of thousands.

Live in peace. Now there's another toughie. In Biblical days there was just as much war and disagreement as there is now, and there weren't near as many people.

But hey, he finished on a strong note: *And the God of love and peace will be with you.*

I don't mean to poke fun, but sometimes I think Paul was just like the rest of us. He was tired and in signing off his letter, rattled off some exhortations that sounded good, but weren't necessarily attainable. (That ought to bring the scholars running and hollering)

But the way I see it, Paul was just trying to lift the spirits of the Corinthians and let them know if they did their best and continued to love God, God would take care of them, and His love and peace would be with them.

No need to get all complicated about it.

November 17

But the fruit of the spirit is love, joy, peace, patience, kindness, goodness, faithfulness, gentleness and self-control. Against such things there is no law. Galatians 5:22-23

When we choose to love God, His Spirit moves into our heart and brings all the good things God has to offer with it. We are no longer under the law, and the more we love God, the less it will matter. We will be so filled with His Spirit we will no longer care about things that are sinful.

I am a long way from being there, but, by golly, I'm headed that way! (That's kind of like what it says in Philippians 3:13, only different)

I know it sounds simple when I put it this way, but I think it is simple. I think men and religion way over-complicate God. I really think if we just love Him, He will provide all the good things listed in verses 22 and 23, and we will continue to understand Him more and more.

It certainly won't hurt anything if we spend a lot of our time and energy loving God. Will it?

I know as I write these encouragements, I learn more and more about God and understand more of the Bible. And the more I learn and understand about God, the more I love Him.

I think you should try it—loving God.

It works for me!

November 18

For he himself is our peace, who has made the two one and has destroyed the barrier, the dividing wall of hostility. Ephesians 2:14

As I write this, the phrase, "*dividing wall of hostility*" rings loud. I have never been too interested in politics, but I have become more interested in the past few years due to some alarming situations which threaten the core beliefs of our nation. During this time of interest, I have been stunned at the anger that seems to be increasing almost daily between the two major political parties. And I'm not talking about the anger of one group of politicians against the other group; I'm talking about the common citizens. People are angry at the people on the other side!

I won't hedge on you; I get angry about what is going on, too. I get especially angry when politicians attempt to take away our freedom, which they seem determined to do. And I am confused when people who support the politicians trying to take our freedoms disagree with me and say that what they are doing is fair and right.

I pray that God can take down the barrier of hostility that is growing in our country. I believe our nation was founded on Godly principles and can be saved by them as well.

I think our part, as believers, is to continue to pray for our leaders and not let ourselves get caught up in the emotion—the hate and anger—that is brewing. We must be the sweetener and cream—the love and light—in the dark and bitter drink being brewed that makes it palatable. No artificial sweetener or powdered cream either; we need the real thing!

As the stir stick of political power and greed is lowered and begins to stir up the drink that is the people of this country, don't allow yourself to be drawn into the swirling anger and darkness. Be the love—the sweetener—and the cream—the light—that makes the drink one we can all continue to savor.

November 19

> *By abolishing in his flesh the law with its commandments and regulations. His purpose was to create in himself one new man out of two, thus making peace.* Ephesians 2:15

"Lord, what fools these mortals be."
This famous line from Shakespeare's "A Midsummer Night Dream," must be something the angels say quite often to God. It is amazing how we continue to make a mess out of things when we can so easily turn things around by simply loving God and believing in His Son.

Adam and Eve got things rolling the wrong way, then the Jews and the Gentiles got things all messed up and confused, and it has been going downhill ever since. God must be watching in utter amazement as we scurry around like ants on a mound, making a mess out of things.

I believe our problem lies in the fact that we continually overcomplicate God. God tried to make it easy on us when He took us from under all the laws and rituals. We couldn't seem to keep things straight; the Jews wanted to do it their way, and the Gentiles wanted to do it their way. So God sent Jesus to simplify things, and now we've so complicated and distorted what Jesus is about we're all confused again. Instead of just Jews and Gentiles arguing who's got it right, there are thousands and thousands of different religions and groups arguing about who's got it right.

Suggestion: Love God. Get things right between you and Him. He'll take it from there.

November 20

He came and preached peace to you who were far away and peace to those who were near. Ephesians 2:17

When we love God, we will receive His words, His instruction and His peace. We will receive it no matter where we are. Somehow He will get it to us.

I've mentioned the thousands of different groups—churches and otherwise—that exist in the world today, and I may have made it sound like a bad thing. In some cases, when false doctrines are being taught and preached, it *is* a bad thing. But I believe in a way—a good way—these many varied teachers and preachers are needed in today's world. As long as the message of Christ is being preached, the details will work themselves out. (Hold on, the phone's ringing. I think every religious leader in the world is calling me to complain about what I just said.)

I believe we need different strokes for different folks. Some will read these encouragements and say, "Whew! That guy's a nut!" Others will read it and say, "I like this. It says things in a way I can understand." The same is true of many preachers (I *do not* propose that I am a preacher). I know many times I can turn on a radio or TV show where a preacher will be giving his message, and I will not agree with what he is saying or maybe not understand what he is saying. Then I may find one on another channel that makes perfect sense to me. In many cases, the message might be the same, but the way it is presented is different.

I believe if you love God and put your faith in Him, He will lead you to the channel you understand. I've noticed the more I love God, the more channels I seem to understand.

I'm thinking about subscribing to the deluxe package. God says I can bring as many friends as I want. Are you interested?

November 21

Make every effort to keep the unity of the Spirit through the bond of peace. Ephesians 4:3

A perfect world would be a world where everyone loves God. Unfortunately, everyone does not love God. I believe what Paul says to the Ephesians, and to all believers, is we must do our best to be in unity with all believers. We must be at peace with our brothers.

As I've said before, I don't think this means we have to agree with everything other believers say and do, but we must remain as one group, unified by the common denominator—our love for God.

I've taken some classes over the years on leadership and how to motivate employees. One of the key principles in almost all those classes was that as a supervisor, you should recognize that each employee is unique. Though you might be expecting the same job and performance from a group of people, each would most likely need different instruction. One employee might react well to definitive, detailed instruction, where another might better understand a condensed version—the details confuse that person. I found this principle of teaching and training to be invaluable throughout my career.

I believe it applies to God as well. Even though I believe the first step to a relationship with God is to love Him, I may not be the one who explains it to you in a way that makes sense. But then you might read a book written by someone else that says the same thing I say, only in a different way, and it makes perfect sense to you.

Love God first. In His perfect timing, He will lead you to the details.

November 22

Stand firm then, with the belt of truth buckled around your waist, with the breastplate of righteousness in place, and with your feet fitted with the readiness that comes from the gospel of peace. Ephesians 6:14-15

I've always liked this verse, especially the first two words: *"Stand firm."* The rest of the verse is great, too, as it paints a picture of a believer dressed to go into the world and represent Christ.

I've told you I've failed miserably many times in my life, and I hope I have also relayed that I have stood firm many times as well. I am human and have failed, and will fall again no doubt, but in my faith, I will stand. Not always as firmly as I would want to, but I *will* stand.

My stance has become more firm as I write these encouragements. My love for God grows constantly, and I am learning and understanding Him more each day as He reveals His truth and supplies me the uniform so that I may play my part in His plan.

My peace is more and more established and firm as well, so I guess the shoes are starting to fit.

Sometimes I wonder where all this is heading, but then I remember I'm following God, and He will take me where He needs me.

This suit—this uniform—He's fitting me for still needs some work, but it's starting to fit a little better. I'm starting to like the way it feels, too.

I've got a peaceful, easy feelin', 'cause I know God won't let me down. And I'm standing firmly on His word.

November 23

In all my prayers for all of you, I always pray with joy. Philippians 1:4

I like that: *I always pray with joy.*

If there's something that rubs me wrong, it's people who pray these long drawn out, rehearsed "prayers", that are nothing but boring tributes to their own religiousness. Most of the time you would think they were at a funeral, when they're blessing a meal! For crying out loud, folks.

I can just see God up there, grinning and elbowing Jesus in the ribs. "Check it out, Son. Joe Bob Down-in-the-mouth is saying grace again. I've never seen anybody choke up over his chow like this guy does."

But seriously, praying shouldn't be a ritual or something with a bunch of thee's, thou's and all that mumbo-jumbo. I think we should just talk to God. If you want Him to bless your meal, say, "Lord, this is one fine bunch of grub mama fixed us. Bless it real good because we're going to dig in now."

You know what I mean? I don't mean we should be flippant or disrespectful, but say stuff like you mean it, and not like you're talking to the judge at traffic court. Well, I've seen how some people talk to the judge at traffic court, so that might not be a good example.

Learn to talk to God—pray without ceasing. I think you'll like it. I'm pretty sure he does.

November 24

> *If you have any encouragement from being united with Christ, if any comfort from his love, if any fellowship with the Spirit, if any tenderness and compassion, then make my joy complete by being like-minded, having the same love, being one in spirit and purpose.*
> Philippians 2:1-2

Being like-minded may seem impossible, but I believe it is easier than we might suspect. I'm sure it won't come as a surprise to you when I say I believe the key to being like-minded with fellow believers in Christ is to love God.

When we love God and believe in Christ, we will be filled with the Spirit of the Lord, encouraged by our uniting with Christ, find comfort in God's love, show tenderness and compassion, and by all those things, be united as brothers in Christ.

We will be one in spirit because God's Spirit in each of us will be the same Spirit, and as God by His Spirit instills in us the will and desire to do His work, we will then be one in purpose. We may each be given different tasks to do for the Lord, but all the tasks will lead to the end result that He desires. In my opinion, there is no greater purpose than to love God, and it may be the only purpose.

When we love God, our joy can be complete.

November 25

Finally, brothers, whatever is true, whatever is noble, whatever is right, whatever is pure, whatever is lovely, whatever is admirable—if anything is excellent or praiseworthy—think about such things. Whatever you have learned or received or heard from me, or seen in me—put it into practice. And the God of peace will be with you.
Philippians 4:8-9

I love Philippians 4:8! It is such a beautiful verse to recall when things aren't going the way you want them to. I don't know how many times I've been in the midst of trouble of some sort and called up that verse. Of course, being the Biblical scholar I'm not, I usually got it all mixed up, but it still does the job. Sometimes all I can think of is to think about something good. That's not in the verse, but it is the right idea.

The main thing is to get your mind off the things that are dragging you down and think about good things. True things, noble things, right things, pure things—even things that aren't in the verse. Get your mind off the problem and start thinking about all you have going for you. Then look for a solution to the problem.

Too many times, we let our circumstances pull us down to the level of the situation. Bad times will come, but we have to learn how to rise above them. I've heard it said: we mustn't let our circumstances control us, we must control our circumstances.

There is nothing this world can throw at you that God can't help you overcome.

When troubles surround you, don't try to stare them into submission. Look away—to God—and He will help you through any situation.

November 26

For God was pleased to have all his fullness dwell in him, and through him to reconcile to himself all things, whether things on earth or things in heaven, by making peace through his blood, shed on the cross.
Colossians 1:19-20

God used Jesus and His death on the cross to reconcile Himself to all things; *all* things, including our sins, no matter what they might be.

When Jesus died on the cross, then rose on the third day, He took all our sins with Him to the Father. He did not, however, take our sinful nature with Him.

We have to make the choice to believe in Jesus and to love God. That is when the burden of our sins will be lifted up to God, and He will wipe the slate clean. I am convinced that, then, we will be filled with the Holy Spirit, which brings with it love and all the things God is.

I'm not saying we will at some point become perfect and God-like. I *am* saying we have the opportunity to be as close to God and as much like Him as we can, in proportion to our love for Him.

It seems reasonable to me, that the more we love God, the more we will allow Him to work in us and through us, and the more we will become like Him.

It's like the old "practice-makes-perfect" theory. If we do something enough, it will become second nature to us, and we will get very good at it. If, for instance, we loved God as many hours as a professional golfer practices golf, just imagine how much we would love Go.

Can you imagine if you were the most God-loving person in the world?

We're already on the team! We're number one!

November 27

Let the peace of Christ rule in your hearts, since as members of one body you were called to peace. And be thankful. Colossians 3:15

It seems there are two things in this verse that have double meaning. The first is *"Let the peace of Christ rule in your hearts."* It can be saying we should be at peace, our hearts being filled with the love God fills us with when we accept Jesus as our savior and love Him. It can also be saying we should, as a result of that same belief, love fellow believers, and be at peace with them.

The second place where it can mean two things is, *"And be thankful."* I believe it means to be thankful to God for the love and peace He gives us, but it could also mean we should be thankful to our brothers for their peace toward us.

Regardless of how you perceive the verse, the theme is peace, and for me, peace is often an elusive thing. I don't know about you, but I am constantly misplacing mine, and sometimes I have a difficult time finding it. Usually, the best way to find your peace is to retrace your steps to the time when it slipped away from you. Sometimes that's easy, and sometimes it's not. In my case, I've found the loss of peace often stems from anger; I've let someone or something make me angry.

The funny thing is, when I trace back to the place in time where I left my peace, I find out that what I was angry about really didn't matter. I allowed myself to be unhappy, angry and even sad over something that was, for all intents and purposes, trivial.

Don't sweat the small stuff. Keep your mind on Jesus. When something comes along and tries to tell you it is so big God can't handle it, put a big smile on your face and walk right past it, because you *know* that ain't so! Then thank God for filling you with His love and peace.

November 28

You became imitators of us and of the Lord; in spite of severe suffering, you welcomed the message with the joy given by the Holy Spirit.
1 Thessalonians 1:6

In another message, I told you a story about how the batteries in a golf cart operated only to the level of the worst battery in the group, and how that compares to us when we allow one negative person to bring the rest of the group to their level.

Another thing about those six golf cart batteries that can be paralleled to us is the recharging of them. The batteries on the golf cart need to be recharged almost every time after the cart is used. If the cart hasn't been driven very long, it doesn't take long to charge the batteries. But if it's been driven a lot, they need a good long dose of electricity to get them back to full power.

We need the same kind of treatment as those batteries, but our recharging comes from God, and the source of our power comes from reading His word and receiving instruction from other believers. We need to plug in to the power of God and recharge ourselves with His good thoughts, His love and His joy.

Here's a key point about those batteries and charging them that I think applies to us as well: When we plug the charger into the cart's batteries, it doesn't send all the power back into them instantly. It takes several hours, the power trickling into the batteries a little at a time, to bring the batteries back to their full power. I think the same method works well for us; we react better to small doses of God's instruction continually, rather than large shots of it all at once. Now this may not be true of everyone, but it certainly works for me. I'm able to understand God better if I take it nice and slow, whereas when I try to take in too much at once, I trip the circuit breaker in my little ol' brain.

Plug in and recharge whenever you feel God's power and joy waning. Read, watch or just think about something uplifting. Keep your joy running at full power!

November 29

For what is our hope, our joy, or the crown in which we will glory in the presence of our Lord Jesus when He comes? Is it not you? Indeed, you are our glory and joy. 1 Thessalonians 2:19

Paul, Silas, and Timothy—the writers of this letter to the Thessalonians—looked upon their fellow believers there and other places they had visited, as a part of the victory resulting from their teaching about Jesus Christ. I don't think they attributed the saving of souls to themselves, but rather celebrated the fact that God had called these people, and the fact that God used them—the apostles—to assist Him in His work.

I think the apostles were merely saying their hope was that when they stood at the feet of God, they would be filled with joy, knowing they had served God's purpose.

Paul knew he wasn't perfect—he said it many times—but he put his hope in the fact that he did the best he could and would one day stand before God with the rest of God's children, knowing he had been a good example to those standing with him.

Do the best you can every day and be at peace with yourself and life. Love God, be filled with His love and Spirit, and let the love and joy in you cause others to see God's light.

Jesus *will* come back. Leave a light on for Him—*your* light.

November 30

Hold them in the highest regard because of their work. Live in peace with each other. 1 Thessalonians 5:13

We should hold pastors and those who teach the word of God in high regard. Their task is not an easy one, and just like you and me, they are human and will make mistakes. But if their heart is good, and they love the Lord, we need to give them a little slack, just as they do us.

Too many times these days it only takes one small mistake to wipe out years of good work. The media is quick to pounce on Christian leaders and try to show them as hypocritical. The media also likes to point out anything a Christian leader says and/or believes that will stir up controversy. For some reason, the American public has become addicted to controversy. I don't understand why that is, but as a result of it, I tend to watch the news rarely.

We hold our leaders to a high standard, but let's not forget they are human just like us. We expect them to forgive us when we mess up, and so we should forgive them as well. This should also be true for all of our fellow believers. We all need to learn to be more forgiving and tolerant of one another's mistakes and failures.

Man! I hate it when I realize I'm talking to myself! I'm terrible about seeing the fault in someone and instantly forgetting all the good things about them.

I need to love God more, so He will put some more love and patience inside me.

December 1

Be joyful always; pray continually; give thanks in all circumstances, for this is God's will for you in Christ Jesus. 1 Thessalonians 5:16-18

This is a wonderful group of verses! Because of Jesus, we can be joyful always and talk to Him constantly, thanking Him for all things, no matter what our situation might be! All this is God's will for us!

I know sometimes it's hard to be thankful when times are hard or something isn't going the way we want it to, but those are actually the times when we should be most joyful and thankful. Say what?

Most of those times and situations would be a whole lot harder to deal with if we didn't have God to lean on, wouldn't they? See what I'm saying?

And at the risk of being labeled a fatalist, even if you are looking down the barrel of gun and know the person holding it is going to pull the trigger, what better time to yell out, "Praise God! I'll see you real soon, Jesus!" Either the crazed person holding the gun will pull the trigger and you'll go to be with Jesus, or maybe you'll scare the daylights out of him and he'll miss—divine intervention, you might say.

Hopefully, we won't ever run into such a drastic situation, but the same applies to all the daily battles and trials we face. We should learn to stay joyful no matter what and keep praising and thanking God. He's going to get us through anything we face. I believe that!

Stay joyful and keep talking to God—pray without ceasing!

December 2

May God himself, the God of peace, sanctify you through and through. May your whole spirit, soul and body be kept blameless at the coming of our Lord Jesus Christ. 1 Thessalonians 5:23

Can our whole spirit, soul and body be kept blameless? I would say yes, in the sense that Jesus purchased our forgiveness on the cross, but no in the sense that to be blameless might be compared to being perfect. Perfect is not something you or I will ever attain—on this earth.

I believe what we *can* do is love God persistently, and allow His Spirit to fill us with His love. If we do that, and do it from the depth of our soul, we will become more and more like God—in His image—the God of peace.

I sometimes read these verses, and it all seems so simple. We don't have to do anything but love God—that's what I keep hearing. And yet every day, even after I read these verses and write about them, I go out and get wrapped up in the things of the world. I do and say things I shouldn't and many times get discouraged because of it. And in the process, I forget to do the most important thing—love God.

One of my neighbors told me she thinks you have to sing praises to God, and there are times when that is great advice and therapy. I was mowing the greens on our little golf course one day, and in the solitude—out of the blue—I thought of a situation that made me angry. I immediately began to sing out loud, *On the Wings of a Dove*. (I have to go with a song I know, and I don't know the words to that many.) But the point is, I soon forgot what it was that had upset me.

Whenever strife comes at you, sing! Love God and be filled with His love and peace!

(Thanks for the advice, Iris.)

December 3

Now may the Lord of peace himself give you peace at all times and in every way. The Lord be with all of you. 2 Thessalonians 3:16

One of my most valued possessions is my peace. I've mentioned it before and may mention it again before the year is done; our peace cannot be stolen, we have to *let* it be taken. We do this when we start looking at the problem instead of looking to God and the solution. Our peace comes when we love God and put our hope and trust in Him.

Many times, I have allowed a situation or person to make me angry or sad over something that ultimately had very little meaning. I allowed myself to spend hours, sometimes days, in strife and unhappiness over something that turned out to be nothing. I allowed my peace to be taken from me.

I'll do it again, I'm sure. I'm a mere mortal and will make mistakes throughout the rest of my life. But more and more, I want to be able to recognize when trouble and strife knock at my door and be able to not answer.

When you realize something is there to take your peace, don't answer the knock on the door. Instead, turn to God and say, "Thank you Lord for getting me around or through this situation, or just plain making it go away."

When your focus is on how big God is, problems and trials seem small in comparison.

December 4

I urge, then, first of all, that requests, prayers, intercession and thanksgiving be made for everyone—for kings and all those in authority, that we may live peaceful and quiet lives in all godliness and holiness. 1 Timothy 2:1-2

In this world we live in, it is sometimes difficult to pray for everyone, and it is certainly difficult to give thanks for some of them. Some people want us dead! Some want us under their control so they can forbid us to do the things we believe we should do, such as worship God. I find it very hard to give thanks and pray for these people.

I guess the way to look at it is if we hate those who persecute us, we are allowing ourselves to operate on their level, instead of rising above the situation and allowing God to handle them.

I always like the example of the eagle—how it is able to soar effortlessly higher than any other bird. Smaller birds sometimes pester the eagle, and rather than engage them, the eagle simply allows the wind currents to lift it above its tormentors. The eagle also has the ability to use the force of a storm to its advantage.

God's love is the wind current that lifts us above any trouble we might encounter. By loving God, we can spread our wings and soar above the troublesome things of this world. No trouble or storm is too big for us when our power comes from the wind—the mighty breath of God.

December 5

Flee the evil desires of youth, and pursue righteousness, faith, love and peace, along with those who call on the Lord out of a pure heart.
2 Timothy 2:22

The second letter to Timothy could be said to be the last words of the apostle Paul. He wrote to Timothy from a prison cell he probably did not expect to leave alive. His time on earth—his part of God's plan—was nearly at an end. Paul wanted to impart all the knowledge he could to the young preacher, Timothy, before he went to his reward—eternal life with the Lord.

I cannot imagine the life Paul must have lived, traveling from city to city on foot or perhaps on the back of a donkey. He traveled dusty roads, had no place to call home and had to depend on others for food and shelter. That's not to mention the persecution, beatings and imprisonment. Yet he stayed faithful and did his work without complaining, knowing his reward was in heaven, not on earth.

And I complain because it's too cold (55 degrees) and windy to play golf.

I was actually stunned when I wrote that last sentence. I sat and looked at it for a minute or so, letting the hard slap of its reality sting.

We have so much to thank God for. We live in a land of more-than-enough. I contend that we throw away enough food every day in this country to feed all our homeless. And still, we complain.

Instead of focusing on the things of this world and our own "problems", we need to start praising God that we are able to be part of the solution. We need to put aside our selfish desires and pursue God's love, allowing Him to fill us with His righteousness, faith, love, and peace.

December 6

But blessed is the man who trusts in the Lord, whose confidence is in him. He will be like a tree planted by the water that sends out its roots by the stream. Jeremiah 17:7-8

I love this parallel, and it seems I see it a lot lately. It makes so much sense. When we are near to God and our trust is in Him, he supplies all our needs. Even when times are bad, we can draw courage from Him to get us through the tribulations we face.

I grew up in a small town in the desert south of Phoenix, Arizona. There weren't many trees in the surrounding deserts. When I was in my late teens, I had a friend who had a small plane he'd take me up in it once in a while. One thing I noticed while flying high above the desert, was all the trees that lined the banks of rivers. They even grew along dry washes that only had rain in them when the infrequent storm came through. Those trees could only live in the hot, dry desert if they were near a source of life giving water.

Our lives are much the same. If we separate ourselves from God and wander into the world without Him, we will perish. Without God there is no nourishing hope and our trials are more than we can handle alone. But when we plant ourselves near the constantly running stream of God's love, we can withstand any storm, because our roots are firmly established and our trust is in Him. And the more of God's love we have, the more our roots strain toward Him to gain even more of the life-giving love He has for us.

Have confidence in God; trust in Him. Plant yourself by the stream that runs full of His love.

December 7

Your love has given me great joy and encouragement, because, you, brother, have refreshed my heart. Philemon 1:7

As I have written these daily messages, I have learned so much and been encouraged by the things I've come to understand. But most of all, I have been encouraged by those who have responded to tell me the things I'd written for that day brought them joy and encouragement. (For those who may be reading this in book form, I wrote these encouragements during the first few months of 2009 and emailed them to friends and relatives each day of that year.)

Those responses were my "atta-boys", and they encouraged me tremendously. Knowing the simple message I'd sent out that day touched someone and helped them to not be afraid, to love God or to experience God's joy and peace, gave me great joy and encouraged me to continue. The comments and thank-you's refreshed my heart.

We can refresh someone's heart every day and bring them joy by simply encouraging them. By telling them they are special to us and that we love them.

Tell those around you how much they mean to you, and tell them often. Tell them all the things you love about them and how much you appreciate their love for you.

Refresh someone's heart today.

December 8

You have loved righteousness and hated wickedness; therefore God, your God, has set you above your companions by anointing you with the oil of joy. Hebrews 1:9

I believe the oil of joy spoken of in this verse is God's Spirit. The one who loved righteousness and hated wickedness was Jesus, who was filled completely with God's Spirit.

How full of God's Spirit can you and I be? I would think we will never be filled with it to the extent Jesus was, because then we would be perfect. But who knows? Maybe we *can* be that filled with God's love and Spirit.

In any case, I believe we are anointed with the oil of joy—God's Spirit—and as we love God and he fills us with His love and Spirit, our capacity for it enlarges. It's that snowball-rolling-downhill thing I've mentioned before. The more we love God, the more He fills us with His love and Spirit, and it just keeps expanding.

As our love for God increases and His Spirit fills us, we begin to put the wicked things of the world aside, and we are drawn closer to the love of righteousness. Our priorities change as our minds begin to focus on loving God.

I believe it is not in our acts of righteousness that God's Spirit is gained, but rather by the gaining of God's Spirit—which He *gives* us when we love Him—we begin to act righteously. We are righteous not of our own accord, but by His.

Love God. Be anointed with the oil of joy.

December 9

You sympathized with those in prison and joyfully accepted the confiscation of your property, because you knew that you yourselves had better and lasting properties. Hebrews 10:34

Sometimes life seems so unfair. Try as we may, we seem to constantly be taking one step forward, only to take two backward. It seems we are always battling against the forces that would keep us from enjoying life. It sometimes certainly feels this way in my life.

My dream for the past thirteen years or so has been to write full time. I do it only as a hobby right now, and the desire to do it on a full-time basis constantly tugs at me. But I am held to a job I feel no love for by the debts I have accumulated. My most fervent prayer is God will show me the way to my dream—that He will open the doors.

I sometimes feel my dream is my property, and because of poor choices I have made, the world has confiscated it. As I read today's verse, I wondered how I should react to the confiscation of my dream. Should I joyfully accept it? Should I consider myself imprisoned by my debt and job? Maybe so.

But then I think my joy should come from knowing I am doing something with the talent God blessed me with. I am writing these words of encouragement to you, and at the same time, encouraging myself. I should rejoice, knowing God has allowed me to be His instrument of encouragement to those who read these words.

I can think of no greater blessing than to know these words I write have blessed someone today. I am joyful for that and rejoice because my dream still lives within me, and my reward—eternal life with Jesus—can never be taken from me.

I am blessed! I joyfully accept where God has me today!

December 10

Let us fix our eyes on Jesus, the author and perfecter of our faith, who for the joy set before him endured the cross, scorning its shame, and sat down at the right hand of the throne of God. Hebrews 12:2

Jesus did it all—He authored the book for us and perfected our faith—and He did so with joy, knowing that by enduring the cross, we would then be able to join Him at the throne of God. How awesome is God that He would do this for us?

And all we have to do to gain a seat with Him in heaven, is fix our eyes on Jesus; no act, no thought, will gain us a place at God's table. Our RSVP is our belief in Jesus.

This world would have us think that gaining earthly possessions and power is the key to success and happiness. The world wants us to think that only by doing great things will we receive our reward. What the world does not understand is there is nothing on this earth of value. Nothing on earth can match what awaits us when our work here is done and we join Jesus and our Father.

Just look at the life of Jesus while on earth. He knew what His job was, and He focused on that and that alone. He did not allow the things of the world to distract Him.

We are not Jesus, but we can nonetheless keep our eyes upon Him and love Him. I believe when we do so, He will make us imitators of Him.

Keep your eyes on Jesus. Love Him. He will fill you with His love, peace and joy.

December 11

No discipline seems pleasant at the time, but painful. Later on, however, it produces a harvest of righteousness and peace for those who have been trained by it. Hebrews 12:11

I think sometimes we don't recognize we are being disciplined by God. We don't understand that the trials and hardships we endure—most of them self-induced—are meant to show us the error of our ways. God could easily direct us to make better decisions and protect us from the pitfalls we encounter—and I believe He often does so—but sometimes He knows we need to go through a bad situation. We need to see the result of our choice, so we will understand why it was not the right thing to do.

When we go through those tough times and get to the other side of them, we often look back and wonder why we made the decision that put us in the position we found ourselves in. I know many times when I look back at where I've been, I shake my head and wonder, "What was I thinking?" In many of those instances, the answer is, "I wasn't."

Thankfully, as I get older, I get a little wiser. I make better decisions, and my lessons are not as severe. Better choices lead to more peace, and, I guess, to righteousness as well. That is, if you define righteousness as making right decisions.

I think one way to look at it is to understand that trials and troubles are the sowing and watering which will produce a good crop. If you're going through trials right now, look closely at what God may be trying to teach you, and look ahead to the harvest He is preparing after the sowing and watering are done.

December 12

Make every effort to live in peace with all men and to be holy; without holiness no one will see the Lord. Hebrews 12:14

The instruction in this verse seems quite grave at first, but I believe it has to be taken in the context that we can only obtain a level of holiness that is attainable as mere humans. Jesus is completely holy, God is completely holy, but we are men and are holy only to the level our love of God lifts us to and allows us to be.

What this verse suggests we do is to make every effort to live in peace and be holy. I believe that effort consists solely of loving God with every breath we take. Peace and holiness will follow as God fills us with His Spirit and love.

God ordained that we would see Him, and I believe when we accept Jesus as our Lord and Savior, we are filled with God's love and Spirit. The more we return God's love, the more love, peace, joy, and holiness we will have.

I think I keep saying the same thing only in a slightly different way. But I don't know any other way to say it.

The answer is too plain and too simple.

Believe in Jesus, and love God.

That's all! It's *that* simple!

December 13

Obey your leaders and submit to their authority. They keep watch over you as men who must give account. Obey them so that their work will be a joy, not a burden, for that would be of no advantage to you.
Hebrews 13:17

The leaders spoken of here are the leaders of the church—the preachers and teachers. The suggestion is that we must obey their instruction, assuming they are more knowledgeable and are appointed by God to watch over us. We should attempt to make their efforts something they can enjoy and not treat them in such a way that it becomes a burden to them. Which I agree would be of no advantage to us.

If you belong to a church and attend regularly, I believe this is good advice. As I have stated before, I do not believe going to church is a prerequisite to eternal life with God, and I do not believe God will look unfavorably on us if we do not attend church. In my opinion, "The Church" is not a group of people who meet in a building every Sunday, it is the sum total of all those who believe Jesus died for their sins, and love God.

Too many of today's churches have wandered far from what I believe God's idea of a church is. Too much division and strife have caused believers to be scattered to so many diverse opinions and teachings that it's difficult to discern who is teaching what. I can only hope they are all teaching the two basics—we should believe in Jesus and we should love God.

If you attend church and are blessed and encouraged by doing so, I think that is wonderful, and I encourage you to continue. If you believe in Jesus and love God and are at peace not attending church, then I think that, too, is wonderful.

December 14

> *May the God of peace, who through the blood of the eternal covenant brought back from the dead our Lord Jesus, that great Shepherd of the sheep, equip you with everything good for doing his will, and may he work in us what is pleasing to him, through Jesus Christ, to whom be glory forever and ever. Amen.* Hebrews 13:20-21

When I read these two verses, I smiled. There is so much in this one sentence that can be, and no doubt has been, debated and argued about. But do you know where my attention goes immediately?

"Equip"

God will *equip* us "*with everything good for doing His will, and may he work in us what is pleasing to Him, through Jesus Christ*"

There it is in a nutshell. I believe God will equip us with everything good—love, joy, knowledge, understanding, compassion, etc.—to do His will. He will outfit us so we can go into the world and do what He needs us to do in order to accomplish His great plan.

We each have a part to play in God's plan. I'm not completely sure what mine is, but I do know I am going to do everything I can to find out. For now, I will assume I am in training. I may be accomplishing things—maybe already have accomplished some things—but I am learning as I go.

I learn something every day. I understand more every day.

Best of all, I love God more every day, and I realize more each day how very much He loves me.

December 15

Consider it pure joy, my brothers, whenever you face trials of many kinds, because you know that the testing of your faith develops perseverance. James 1:2-3

This concept should come easy to any of us who have played football on any level. Football is a game of intense conditioning, and when I was in school and we practiced in the hot Arizona sun, we faced many trials and tests.

When I was a freshman in high school, we started our summer practices with forty-some boys trying out for the team. The coach was hard on us, and the workouts were nothing short of brutal in the 100 plus degree heat. By the time we suited up for the first game of the season, there were less than twenty boys left on the team. If I remember right, we played some games that year with only thirteen suited up.

But we persevered. We faced all the trials and the humiliating, forty-something to nothing losses, and we developed faith—faith in ourselves and faith in each other. We went on to win quite a few games in the years that followed, and I look back at those days knowing they had a lot to do with the man I am today. We had a great coach the last two years of high school, and I owe him a lot for the things he taught me. One of the best of those things was to never quit; never give up, no matter what. He always told us when we felt like we couldn't go on, just reach down deep inside and grab hold of that extra effort; that last bit of strength and endurance. He told us to look at each play as if it were the last we'd ever play and give it all we could give.

Now I play for the best coach, on the best team. There is no test, no trial I cannot endure for God. And I will not quit or give up. I will persevere, and I consider it pure joy to confront the challenges that come my way to test the endurance of my faith.

December 16

But the wisdom that comes from heaven is first of all pure; then peace-loving, considerate, submissive, full of mercy and good fruit, impartial and sincere. James 3:17

And how do we obtain the heavenly wisdom packed with all those good things? You guessed it! By loving God. All the things listed in this verse are attributes of God. God is all things that are good, and all good things come from God.

We come from God! That means we are good, too! How 'bout that?

But it's true, and not only that, it is also true that God created us in His image. I don't take this to mean God looks like us or we look like Him, but rather He created us in His *spiritual* image. And that means we are all those things listed in today's verse. But most of all, it means we are love because God is love, and we are created in His image. Love is the main course, and all those other things are the side dishes.

When we believe in Jesus and love God, He fills us with the main course—His Spirit and love—and the more we love Him, the more wisdom and good things He adds to the menu, and the more we become like Him.

A friend of mine and I used to go to Chinese buffets a lot. One time, the place we went to had shrimp on the lunch buffet, and my buddy must've eaten three heaping plates of it. (The man can put away some chow.) When he was polishing off the third plate, the restaurant manager came to our table and said, "You go now! Shrimp all gone!" How funny is that?

But God's love—the shrimp on His buffet—will never be all gone, and He will never ask us to leave His table. We are His guests forever and can have all the love *and* side dishes we want!

December 17

Peacemakers who sow in peace raise a harvest of righteousness.
James 3:18

I don't know how many times I've gone off half-cocked in a situation and did nothing but make matters worse. I reacted to my emotions and went into the situation in anger or rebellion, solving nothing, and in most cases making things worse.

One of the byproducts of loving God is peace, and if we have God's peace inside us, we are more able to assess situations from a calm and rational point of view. Many times when we do that, we will see the situation is not what it first appeared, and even if it is, we might recognize it really isn't that big of a deal.

Another way to look at things is to decide if the particular instance is a battle worth fighting. One way to decide this is to ask what will be gained by winning the battle. Many times there is virtually nothing to be gained, and so, even if you win the argument or whatever the battle might be, you've wasted a lot of time and energy fighting for little or nothing.

You will gain more in situations like that by doing nothing. People around you will take note of how you handled the situation, and it may impact their way of handling things that come up in their own lives. Ta-Da! You harvested righteousness!

Love God and be filled with His love. Be at peace. Harvest righteousness.

December 18

You have made known to me the path of life; you will fill me with joy in your presence, with eternal pleasures at your right hand.
Psalm 16:11

I've slipped a little Old Testament in today—it just felt right.

As we enter into the Christmas season, I am filled with joy and feel the presence of the Lord. I imagine my hand in His as we gaze into the fireplace and think thoughts about Jesus and what He means to us. God's eyes are misty as His pride and love well up in Him; mine mist over at the thought of all the Father and Son have done for us.

I stare into the flickering flames, thinking about how God has chosen me, protected me, forgiven me, and tears flow down my cheeks. God takes my chin, turns my face to His, and smiles. He wipes the tears from my face with gentle hands and places a loving kiss on my forehead. "My faithful servant," He says in a soft voice, filled with love.

I place my head on His chest and weep tears of utter joy.

I do not deserve a God this awesome.

December 19

He must turn from evil and do good; he must seek peace and pursue it. 1 Peter 3:11

Sometimes a verse from the Bible seems confusing when we first read it, but I'm finding in most cases they aren't so confusing after all. This one for instance, where it says to seek peace and pursue it, seemed redundant at first. Then I realized it was not redundant at all, because seeking and pursuing are two very different things.

When we seek something, we look for it or try to find it; when we pursue something, we go after it or chase it. I'm sure a case could be made to show the two words have similarities, but I believe in this verse the meaning is clear. At least it seems so to me.

When we have lost something, we seek it and try to find out where it is. If someone tells us where it is, we go after it; we pursue it.

Just as when we lost our way and were seeking answers to life and its trials, we found out Jesus was the answer, and so we pursued Him. When we found Him and accepted Him as our savior, we found peace as well.

There is only one true peace, and that true peace is gained by loving God. When loving God is what you seek to do, He will fill you with the desire to pursue even more of the love, peace and joy He wants to share with you.

Seek God. Pursue God. Love God.

December 20

Grace and peace be yours in abundance through the knowledge of God and Jesus our Lord. 2 Peter 1:2

I am still lacking in knowledge of God, and it is noticeable. I just can't seem to stay at peace. I let too many things upset me, and most of the time they are things that aren't even important.

Too often we allow ourselves to become upset or angry over things that aren't important, and sometimes we imagine things that haven't even happened yet and get upset over them. We have enough knowledge of God to know better than to do this, but we still do it.

Example: The boss sends out a memo asking for your daily schedule—start time, lunch duration and quitting time—and you immediately begin to expect the worst. You decide he's heard you came in late one day, or took a long lunch, or left early a couple of days, and he's out to get you. You worry and fret about it, getting all worked up and thinking, "I'm a salaried employee! I work past quitting time a lot of days, I come in early. Sometimes I don't even take a lunch break!" The fact is, your supervisor has a new boss, and his new boss is trying to get up to speed on how things are done at the agency. You never hear another word about the situation. You got all in a tizzy about nothing.

I do things like this way too often. I let my circumstances control me. Instead of reacting negatively, we should react in peace, knowing we have nothing to fear. Stop expecting bad things, and know God loves you and is watching out for you. Love God, and He will fill you with His Spirit, love, knowledge, patience, and all good things.

I'm working on it!

December 21

So then, dear friends, since you are looking forward to this, make every effort to be found spotless, blameless and at peace with him.
2 Peter 3:14

It's hard to imagine myself spotless, blameless and at peace with God. It is so hard for me to not look back at all the wrong I've done. But God doesn't look back, so why do we?

I know many of you feel the same way. It's called self-condemnation, and we need to learn to not do it. God has an endless supply of erasers, and on the back of every one of them, it says, *Courtesy of Jesus.* God sent Jesus so He would not have to keep track of our sins and mistakes. He wipes them away and doesn't refer back to them—ever.

Give yourself a break; quit dredging up all those things you've done wrong. You're wasting all that time on *you* that you could be spending loving God.

Remember the scene I described a few days ago: sitting at the fire with God? Whenever you're tempted to get down on yourself, go to the hearth and sit with God. Go somewhere quiet and just imagine Him there with you. Lay your head on His chest and feel His mighty arm around your shoulders. He's not thinking about your past as He holds you; He's thinking about the great plans He has for your future. His lips are curled into a knowing smile, and His eyes sparkle as He pictures how excited you will be when you arrive at the wonderful days He has planned for you.

God loves you. He places you beneath a gentle waterfall of His forgiveness each and every day and washes you clean, and then sits with you at the hearth while the flames of His love dry you.

All He wants is for you to love Him.

December 22

We write this to make our joy complete. 1 John 1:4

Some translations read "your joy", instead of "our joy". I prefer the latter, because in the sense of writing these encouragements, it is my joy that is made complete. That's not to say I can't experience more and greater joy, but merely to say how much joy writing these daily encouragements has given me.

When I began, I thought writing devotionals would be an interesting thing to do—a good thing—but I never dreamed how much I would learn and how much closer to God it would bring me. This relationship with God is like getting that special car you dream about your whole life. One day—about this time last year—God handed me the key and said, "Here, take it for a spin," so I slid in for a test drive and found myself on the most wonderful, exciting ride of my life. It didn't take me long to realize that without a doubt, I want this!

The funny thing is, *this* has been sitting on the lot waiting for me all my life. I've always thought it would be nice to have one, I just didn't know there was one with my name on it, and Jesus had already paid for it. I thought I had to work and save up all my good deed dollars before I could have my very own special relationship with God.

Writing these encouragements for you has made my joy complete. I hope they have blessed you as well.

December 23

Grace, mercy and peace from God the Father and from Jesus Christ, the Father's son, will be with us in truth and love. 2 John 1:3

God has blessed us with so many good things, number one being His Son, Jesus. But in the days when the apostles walked the earth, many refused to believe Jesus was the Son of God. Sadly, many still refuse to believe it today. I find that hard to believe, especially this time of year when Jesus is so much on our minds. I sometimes wonder how folks can make it through the struggles of this life without Jesus to help them.

Most of you have probably gotten all of your shopping done, mailed the cards and decorated the house, so take some time this morning to just reflect on why we celebrate Christmas. And even if you have things yet to do, take a few minutes anyway.

Imagine Jesus sitting across from you at the kitchen table, sipping a cup of coffee. He has on His best white robe and is smiling at you over His cup. "It's your birthday, too," He says. "How so?" you ask. "Well," He says, "I gave my life on the cross for you, and when you accepted me as your savior, you were born again." He smiles and shrugs, takes a sip of coffee. You ask, "So wouldn't my "birthday" be on Easter?" Jesus chuckles, His eyes twinkle in amusement, and He shakes His head side to side. "Ah, yes," he says through a grin, "You folks are all about the technicalities."

However you imagine Jesus, take time to think about Him and talk to Him during this wonderful time of year when we celebrate Him. Take at least enough time to say, "I love you, Jesus."

December 24

Praise the Lord, all you nations; extol him, all you peoples. For great is his love toward us, and the faithfulness of the Lord endures forever. Praise the Lord. Psalm 117: 1-2

I'm almost finished with the verses about joy and peace, and so I thought I'd move from that format for the next three days. I chose three passages from Psalms to help us celebrate Christmas.

Psalm 117 consists of only the two verses above and is the shortest chapter in the Bible. I believe what it says illustrates what we should be feeling on the day before we celebrate the birth of our savior, Jesus Christ.

The Psalm begins and ends with, "praise the Lord," which is how we should begin and end every day, but especially the next three days. In fact, we should not only begin and end each day praising our Lord and Savior, but we should praise Him throughout the day, too.

The reason why we should pray for this is in verse two; His love is great toward us, and it endures forever. God showed this to us when He sent Jesus to walk among us, die on the cross and rise on the third day. God loved us so much He sent His Son to die for our sins, so we could spend eternity loving Him.

As you settle in this evening—hopefully surrounded by your loved ones—raise your eyes and your hands to the Lord, and for just a few minutes, love Him with every fiber of your being.

Praise the Lord.

December 25

Open for me the gates of righteousness; I will enter and give thanks to the Lord. This is the gate of the Lord through which the righteous may enter. I will give you thanks, for you answered me; you have become my salvation. Psalm 118: 19-21

I remember when I was eight, laying on the top bunk in our small mobile home, waiting anxiously for morning to come so I could see what Santa had brought us. The excitement I felt as I lay there waiting for the sun to come up was intense, and when it finally began to dawn outside my window, I dropped to the floor and rushed to see what lay beneath the tree. I had no idea what I would find, but I knew it would be good! All of that I remember vividly…. but I have no recollection of what I found under that tree.

I didn't know much, if anything, about Jesus then, but the fact that I don't remember what gifts I received that year, but remember waiting so anxiously to see them, is very close to what I feel now as Christmas morning is upon me, fifty years later. But rather than gifts, I am anxious to see what the Lord will bring me today. I pray that my love for Him will open the gates to His righteousness, so I may enter and give Him thanks, for He has become my salvation.

Sometimes I feel like that excited kid again when I think of what God has done for us and what He has in store for us when we finally meet Him face to face. I lay in my bed some mornings, re-living the same expectant excitement I felt on that Christmas morning fifty years ago. I don't know what God has in store for us, but I know it will be better than good!

Merry Christmas everyone!

December 26

The stone the builders rejected has become the capstone; the Lord has done this, and it is marvelous in our eyes. This is the day the Lord has made; let us rejoice and be glad in it. Psalm 118: 22-24

I remember other Christmases as I got older—twelve, thirteen or so—and I remember some of the things I received for gifts. Santa no longer existed, but Jesus did. Even then I had no real concept of what Christmas was about or what Jesus had done for us.

I do remember though—and it still seems very true today—that the day after Christmas was a letdown. We waited for weeks for the big day—Christmas day—and then after it had come and gone and the gifts had been given and received, there was this nothingness—this sense of what was the big deal, anyway. Even nowadays, the day after Christmas is a day where we all seem to breathe a sigh of relief that it's finally over, and we can get back to our lives. How sad is it that the very foundation of our lives, the most marvelous thing God has ever done for us—Jesus—so quickly moves from the forefront of our lives to the back of it?

This year, on this day after Christmas, do something special. I know it's a last minute thought, but sometimes a spontaneous celebration can be one of the best times you've ever had. Invite people over for leftovers, go caroling again, or take a gift you will return anyway, re-wrap it and give it to somebody down the street. Celebrate the birth of our Savior for an extra day this year. Maybe, instead of allowing the world to take Christmas from us, we'll make it even bigger!

This—the day after the day we celebrate Christ's birthday—is a day that truly the Lord has made. Rejoice and be glad in it! Merry "Day After Christmas"!

December 27

It has given me great joy to find some of your children walking in the truth, just as the Father commanded us. 2 John 1:4

My mother is God-like in a very special way—most mothers are—in that she forgives me and loves me in spite of all the bad things I've done in my life. She remembers the good things and keeps them on the shelf where she can see them and tosses all that other stuff into the box that holds the bad things—a box that will never be opened. Those bad things she puts into that box will never see light again and will wither and fade to nothingness. God does the same.

My mom often quotes the last line of Joshua 24:15: *As for me and my house, we will serve the Lord.* I know for many years this was Mom's prayer and greatest hope; that her children would serve the Lord. She has been a devout Christian for most all her life, even though I am sure she would admit to her own times of falling away. I can remember my brother and me agreeing more than once, that had it not been for the prayers of our mother, there was no telling where we might have wound up.

I know my writing these encouragements is a source of great joy to Mom. I know she takes great delight in the idea that in a way I am preaching the gospel. Knowing she feels that way is a source of tremendous inspiration and encouragement to me.

God created my mom in His image, and in her I can see and appreciate what an awesome God He is. In her, I can also see what love is. God is love. My mom is love.

December 28

I have no greater joy than to hear that my children are walking in the truth. 3 John 1:4

Sometimes life serves you lemons. When it does, make lemonade.

One of my cousins has lead a very successful life as a business man. He's worked hard and made a very good living for his family. Unfortunately, his family has suffered many troubles and trying times. I won't go into the details, but it has not been pretty.

This cousin is a determined Christian, and through all his troubles, has remained steadfast in his beliefs, even though like the rest of us, he too has fallen away from God at times and done many things he would rather not talk about.

My cousin and his family are all on the list that read these encouragements, and they all email me occasionally to tell me how much they appreciate them. It dawned on me one day that perhaps I had failed them. I should have been writing these things and setting a better example for them years ago. Perhaps I could have saved them some of the anguish and pain they have experienced.

But I know that's not how it works. They probably wouldn't have heard then what they hear now. God had lessons for them to learn and mistakes for them to make, so they could be trained for what He needed them to do for Him. The same was true for me.

If my cousin will listen closely, he will hear that his children are now walking in the truth. He will also see that even though he might have thought he received a box of lemons, God was giving him the opportunity to make lemonade. I have a feeling it's going to be a fine batch, too!

Praise God! He loves us so much!

December 29

Mercy, peace and love be yours in abundance. Jude 1:2

God's mercy is free and unlimited, ours for the taking.

Back in February of 2009, I saw a story on the news about how a national restaurant chain had offered free breakfast on a certain morning. I didn't pay real close attention to the details of the giveaway, but I did note that the participating restaurants were deluged with hungry patrons. We certainly can't blame them for that!

That story reminded me of how at Christmas time, folks will line up for hours, sometimes days, ahead of the time and date the most popular gift of the year is to be available or on sale. I've seen this when a new techno gadget becomes available, too. People will sit in lawn chairs and sleep in sleeping bags on the sidewalk in front of the store to make sure they don't miss out on the item or special price.

Wouldn't it be something if people started lining up at churches to get God's free gift of mercy and forgiveness? Can you imagine the beaming smile on God's face if that were to happen?

Unfortunately, they don't advertise the things of God too often. There's not enough profit in it for the advertisers, and the news programs and news organizations don't think people would be interested. Sadly, they're probably right. Most people are more interested in things that fall under the heading of instant gratification rather than those that have to do with eternity.

I encourage you (and me) to spend more time looking toward and loving God, and less time thinking about the "things" of this world. After all, one has a *forever* guarantee, the others don't.

December 30

To him who is able to keep you from falling and to present you before his glorious presence without fault and with great joy—to the only God our Savior be glory, majesty, power and authority, through Jesus Christ our Lord, before all ages, now and forever more. Amen. Jude 1:24-25

These two verses could be condensed to simply say, "Jesus is everything." He is all the things listed in these verses and so much more. He is all those things now and forever. And yet, we give Him so little of our time.

As this year nears an end, and we prepare to move into another one, let's make a resolution to give God more of our time and to love Him all day, every day. Let's make an effort to awake with God first in our thoughts, talk to God throughout our day, and thank Him when we lay down each night.

If we do this, I believe our lives will begin to take a turn, our love for God will continue to grow, we will be filled with God's Spirit and love, and His joy and peace will come upon us in a way we can't even imagine.

I believe it's that simple. Love God and keep Him first in your thoughts, and all the good things of God will be yours in abundance.

December 31

There is no fear in love… We love because he first loved us.
1 John: 18, 19

Tomorrow we begin another year. I pray it will be a year full of God's love and blessings for each of you. I pray you will be able to go into this New Year with boldness, knowing God is with you, and you have nothing to fear.

I truly and steadfastly believe there is no fear in love. True love is the absence of fear. It is complete trust in the one you love and the one who loves you. It is a confidence that you will never bring harm to them, nor will they bring harm to you. I could go on and on, but I think you get my point.

God's love for us is a perfect love, a love without fault or blemish, a love that endures all things, a love that never wanes, and a love that will never end. It is truly a forever love.

I believe if we love God with the fullness He loves us—as much as is within our human capabilities—we will be filled with His Spirit and become like Him in our ability to love others. We are created in God's image, which I believe to mean we become like Him when we accept Jesus as our Savior and allow God's Spirit and love to dwell in us.

God is love. He loves us. He wants nothing but for us to love Him.
Is that so much for Him to ask?
I think not.
A blessed New Year to all!